A HISTORY OF EDUCATION IN WALES

A History of Education in Wales

GARETH ELWYN JONES
and
GORDON WYNNE RODERICK

UNIVERSITY OF WALES PRESS
CARDIFF
2003

British Library Cataloguing-in-Publication Data.
A catalogue record for this book is available from the British Library.

ISBN 0–7083–1807–X paperback
    0–7083–1808–8 hardback

Published with the financial support of the University of Wales Guild of Graduates

Typeset by Bryan Turnbull
Printed in Great Britain by MPG Books, Bodmin, Cornwall

Contents

Foreword

Does Wales have a history of education? If printed record is a significant criterion the evidence is discouraging, since no extended narrative history exists. It must surely be time to attempt one – especially in the context of devolution and the unfolding of a distinctive education policy for Wales.

In subtler ways the time may be ripe. If we had posed the question in the 1950s, the parameters of any discussion would have been different. The unwritten assumption would have been that we were asking whether there was in Wales a history of formal education, even a history of state-sponsored or state-controlled formal education. Effectively, though not exclusively, in the United Kingdom the concentration was on the history of education after the Industrial Revolution. This makes some sense if our concern is with mass education. In Wales, as more generally, the nature of state involvement in education changed substantially with industrialization (whatever the controversies over the nature of the correlation) as government eventually took responsibility for the education of all its citizens. In the end it compelled them to go to school.

The history of education up until the 1950s or 1960s, then, tended to be about state involvement, Acts of Parliament relating to education, education in schools and other institutions. Such a restricted definition seemed to affect adversely the status of the history of education as a university discipline because it tended not to form part of the general social history which was then becoming so significant, particularly in the case of the history of Wales. The implications for any Welsh perspective were even more serious, because Wales was an addendum in the 'England and Wales' state.

In more recent decades fashions have changed, prompted originally by American initiatives. Most historians now root the study of formal education in the wider society. They take a much broader definition which involves all-embracing frames of reference, for example looking at educational experience from the point of view of children, and including more informal training and skills. If education is a much wider process than schools and schooling, or university studies, where does it end? For example, in no way should a medieval farmer be regarded as unskilled. The slate quarryman of north Wales was so gifted at reading the rock that he might have been encouraged to study for a doctorate in an earth-sciences department these days. Such skills were learned outside formal education, developed by assimilating crafts from the older generation, only occasionally through formal apprenticeships. Nowadays, the notion of education embraces vocational education and lifelong learning.

An anachronism which then arises is that while this wider definition of education/training might be in line with present ideas, it would have been derided in the not so distant past. The notion of formal education for most of what can be called the history of Wales, or 'England/Wales', and strongly resonant even in the present day, is that it is about passing on a cultural heritage from one generation to the next – the best that has been known and done, the received wisdom of previous generations, all amounting to a definition of high culture. It is no real solution to argue that this view of culture is now seen as unfashionably narrow, ignoring the vitality of popular culture, and even labelled an instrument of class oppression.

When any attempt is made to synchronize fashions in current history of education with the history of Wales, we encounter further complications over the question of whether there is a Welsh history of education. What was Wales, or 'When was Wales', in terms of its formal education, high culture, popular culture, language or religion? This leads to the over-arching question of degrees of continuity, which have resulted in very different emphases in histories of Wales.

So the historian of any aspect of Welsh history is confronted with issues of national identity which are central to the education narrative. The essential prerequisite surely must be that we have to accept elements of relativism in the story of Wales without embracing the extreme view that Wales and Welshness have no validity outside individual experience. Once we accept that there is something more than that, it poses the question of the experiences of which groups of individuals – those who live in Wales, those who call themselves Welsh, those who speak Welsh, those who subscribe to certain values? Whatever the eventual working definition, if it is the case that there is an agglomeration of such individuals who call themselves Welsh, then that constitutes a community with an identity – of which educational experience must, to greater or lesser extent, be a part.

Finally, how far back should we allow the shadow to be cast of a geographical divide which still roughly coincides with the eighth-century Offa's Dyke which divided Mercia from kingdoms across the border? In starting our history with the disappearance of the Romans in the fifth century (and there are some excellent precedents) we might be accused of being as significantly anachronistic in taking the later border and imposing it on an earlier period as by defining education in a different way from that of earlier societies. Again, the issues are complex in that, for example, formal education in the fifth and sixth centuries, as indeed for centuries afterwards, was essentially the preserve of the Church, and that Church remained essentially European up until the sixteenth century.

Centuries later, the United Kingdom state decreed that the people of Wales should be allowed to vote on whether to have more say in, among other things, their education system, a vote which resulted in the creation of the National Assembly for Wales in 1999. Very recently, the Welsh Assembly Government has produced blueprints for a different Welsh education system. If Wales is now increasingly defined by its institutions, then the chief of these, the Assembly, is increasingly identified by the distinctiveness of its education policies. This in turn could not have happened were Wales not a society with unique features. If historians of Welsh education are an endangered species, we hope that this book provides conclusive evidence that it is not for want of a subject to study.

Acknowledgements

In the course of writing this book we have incurred personal and academic debts far too numerous to list. However, we wish to make special mention of Professor Sir Glanmor Williams, who read the whole book in typescript, Professor Roy Lowe, who read much of it, and Lord Morgan of Aberdyfi, who read sections of early drafts. Their comments have been invaluable. Librarians at the Education Library, University of Wales Swansea, under the direction of Madeleine Rogerson, have been helpful far beyond the call of duty. The staff of the University of Wales Press, under director Susan Jenkins, and editorial manager Ceinwen Jones, have been invariably constructive and efficient. Janet Davies prepared the index immaculately. That the Press has been able to publish a paperback version of the book is due to a generous grant from the University of Wales Guild of Graduates, a body to which both authors are proud to belong.

CHAPTER ONE

⋊⋉

Monasticism to Puritanism, c.410–1670

Despite the withdrawal of Roman forces from present-day Wales and England early in the fifth century AD, the legacy of the Romans' language in these and other parts of western Europe was of the utmost significance. Not that Latin or Roman culture had made a massive impact on Wales in more than three centuries of occupation. The geographical area of Wales was subdued, but Roman settlement was limited in extent. Nevertheless, the impact of the Latin language in succeeding centuries, particularly mediated through the Church and all aspects of ecclesiastical life, was incalculable.

Of course, any definition of education, or the interplay of education and culture, in Roman Wales and in the subsequent centuries of the first millennium, needs to be considered in the context of the society of the time. Wales was a rural country in which the violence of warring factions and small kingdoms was endemic. For the vast majority, day-to-day existence allowed only for the hard labour required to survive in an unfriendly terrain (much of Wales is hilly or mountainous). Days were governed by the amount of natural light, and years by the rhythms of the seasons. This was a society in which the arts of war were crucial and highly regarded, and the skills of craftsmen such as metalworkers and black-smiths greatly valued. But there were high cultural arts, too, particularly in the households of the native aristocracy and rulers – for example, story-telling and poetry which preserved and praised the history and genealogy of families.

Literacy, in the form of reading or writing, was the preserve of very few and, in the post-Roman period, confined largely to clerics. Nevertheless, restricting the notion of education and the transmission of a cultural heritage to manuscript-based learning would be entirely inappropriate in a society in which books, at least in the sense associated with a post-print society, did not exist. For the mass of the population, education, culture and training were orally transmitted, particularly in the form of stories which glorified the achievements of tribes and attempted to make sense of success and failure in battle. The bards, the recounters of these traditions in their native Welsh language, held an honoured place in princely and noble society. Their training at the hands of the masters of their craft was lengthy. They were expected to have prodigious memories for traditional poetry and to create their own tributes to family exploits, particularly the military achievements of their patrons. But they might also eulogize the landscape and nature, as well as preserving historical traditions of the distinctiveness of Wales and the descent of its people from the ancient Britons.

The influence of the bards in Welsh society was long-lived, surviving conquests of Wales by Norman barons and by Edward I. Noble families, and later the gentry, continued to act as patrons, with the bards continuing their time-honoured role of praising benefactors and recounting their ancestors' achievements, many of whom had themselves been educated and knowledgeable. By the fourteenth century in particular, formal rules of poetic composition were drawn up to complement the lengthy apprenticeship which poets had to serve in order to become masters of their craft. In a mainly unlettered society bardic knowledge of genealogy was also indispensable in matters of landholding, precedence and inheritance. In this respect, in the first millennium, they shared a crucial oral tradition with the lawyers who transmitted knowledge of traditional, distinctive Welsh law from generation to generation until it was eventually codified. At the same time, a fund of knowledge was crucial to successful tilling of the soil, animal husbandry, the production of utensils for eating and drinking, building work and the arts of war. The associated crafts, sometimes embodying high levels of both skill and art, were passed on orally in the time-honoured tradition of learning by doing under the tutelage of a skilled practitioner.

Formal Latin-language scholarship, after the Romans departed, was the preserve of the clergy of the Church who spread the Christian religion in the fifth and sixth centuries so zealously that this has been traditionally called the Age of the Saints. Not only was the area of Wales a vital link with scholarly Celtic communities in Ireland, Scotland and Brittany, but also some of its monks were among the most famous of scholars, with a complete mastery of biblical scholarship and the Latin language. The best known is Illtud, who attracted disciples such as Gildas to study with him at Llanilltud Fawr (Llantwit Major). While the monastic settlements in other parts of Wales were less famous for their scholarship, they were all expected, through their abbots, to be communities of learning as well as mission, and to provide adequate education for their clergy. These traditions of learning, teaching and copying of manuscripts managed to survive even the depredations of Viking raiders who, from the ninth to the eleventh centuries, raided monasteries for treasure and wrought havoc in the contemplative existence, with St David's a particular target.

With a relatively scant residue of artefacts and manuscripts from the Celtic society of the first millennium AD it is not easy to be sure of the details of educational and cultural transmission. The picture becomes a little fuller from the first century of the new millennium. The history of Wales was orientated, along with other parts of Europe, both by Norman conquest and by a more general economic, political, social and cultural revival in Europe. The two were, of course, closely linked in that Norman influence in Wales, particularly ecclesiastical developments, brought Wales into closer contact with European influences, of the greatest significance because the centrality of the Church to educational activity in its widest sense remained.

In the second millennium, as in the first, formal education for the vast majority was both unavailable and not required. Indeed, it was not essential for even the highest in lay society, though this was gradually to change, particularly in terms of some kind of legal education. Social organization in the Middle Ages did become ever more complex. As administration in Norman Marcher society was consolidated, towns grew around castles and as market centres, and the administration of the king's justice, especially from the reign of Henry I, depended increasingly on written record, so that more professional bureaucrats, and clerks in particular, were required.

For most of the population, life continued to centre on the land, and required skills were passed on orally and practically from one generation to the next. However, the crafts needed to provide the whole range of farming requirements, including agricultural implements, became increasingly sophisticated, particularly in the growing numbers of small towns where, for example, blacksmiths and saddlers proliferated. In the towns the function of the guilds was crucial, since they exercised a virtual monopoly over the crafts which were a staple of medieval society. Restricting access to the learning of such crafts as leather working, coopering, haberdashing, tanning, metal crafts, or the making of wheels, and enforcing a rigorous seven-year apprenticeship system, they were largely responsible for supplying the technical education of the time.

The skill exercised in some crafts was of the highest level. The architectural and building achievements of medieval stonemasons, for example, were extraordinary. By the twelfth and thirteenth centuries, the construction of such castles as Caernarfon and Beaumaris in north Wales, or Caerphilly in the south, and cathedrals such as St David's in west Wales, is evidence of outstanding engineering and artistic skill in a period before drawing-board, let alone computer, simulation was even a figment of the imagination. The ubiquitous influence of the Church over all aspects of life is again manifest. Church building, from parish churches to cathedrals, drew on the skills of stonemasons and woodcarvers in particular, but the artistry which went into the making of stained-glass windows and the paintings and other colourful decoration which were a feature of pre-Reformation churches, is evident in some of those examples which survived Reformation and Puritan spoliation.

A literary education remained a virtual monopoly of the Church, and clerical education was of a very different order. It was normally available to an elite, though there were some from humbler backgrounds. The purpose of this education was to provide a literate manpower to service the ecclesiastical and administrative needs of an increasingly complicated diocesan hierarchy. During the Middle Ages, as indeed in the Tudor period, the early education of those with aristocratic backgrounds might be by a private tutor but, for most aspirants to a career in the Church, it started in grammar schools, usually connected with cathedrals, and was based on the classical education of the quadrivium and trivium, seven areas of study comprising grammar, dialectic and rhetoric, arithmetic, geometry, music and astronomy. The language of this education across western Christendom was Latin.

The monastic church, too, particularly in the orders introduced into Wales in the post-Norman period, provided some education and training for its own novitiate, though this aspect of its work has been exaggerated. Monasteries also continued to act as custodians of high culture. In particular, monks copied the great manuscripts of medieval Wales, thus preserving much of its early literary heritage. For a small minority, education was available at the universities of Europe. The oldest was the University of Bologna in Italy but, from the twelfth and thirteenth centuries respectively, there were universities also in Oxford and Cambridge. The former in particular was popular with Welsh students but we know that long before their foundation some Welshmen attended university in Paris. The most famous of these was Gerald of Wales (born in 1146) whose father, the lord of Manorbier, was of Norman descent and whose grandmother, Nest, was a princess of a Welsh royal household. He was a fine scholar who served for ten years as a clerk in the household of two kings of England.

His scholarship has contributed immeasurably to our understanding of the geography, topography and society of twelfth-century Wales. In 1188 he went with Archbishop Baldwin on a tour of Wales to recruit troops for the third crusade. We know from Gerald that Wales had a particular reputation for excellent warriors, which doubtless prompted this tour which Gerald recorded in 1191 in his *Journey through Wales*. This was complemented three years later by his *Description of Wales*. These are works of acute observation, historical skill and high literacy. Gerald was a cleric, as was Geoffrey of Monmouth who lived just before Gerald and whose *History of the Kings of Britain* was only the most famous of his literary works. The influence of Geoffrey's history was extensive both at the time and in subsequent centuries because it provided Wales with an ancient, if fabricated, historical pedigree so essential to national pride and consciousness.

Much of the literary culture of the Middle Ages, therefore, was bound up with the Church and the writings of clerics. They were responsible for recording the most significant events of the time, for investigating the past to view it from a religious perspective and, of course, for furthering theological and biblical study, including lives of the saints of the Church. But it was not only in matters relating to the Church that its near-monopoly of literary education was manifest. The role of clerics, particularly bishops and abbots, in administration at the highest level and in the law was crucial to the smooth working of administration and justice. Before the conquest of Wales in 1282 the princes of Wales needed high-ranking churchmen, as well as lay administrators, lawyers and diplomats, in their service, as did the Norman state after the Conquest. Indeed, as the state developed in its administrative and judicial sophistication, particularly from the thirteenth century, rulers appointed men to the highest offices of the Church in order to serve this secular purpose. While opportunities for Welshmen to achieve high office were much more restricted after the Norman conquest of Wales, kings and Marcher lords were forced to use the service of a well-educated and influential Welsh aristocracy. So the need for people who could read and write, and these were preponderantly clerics, became increasingly felt. They were not only responsible for the law of the Church, canon law, but also the development and codification of state law in England and Wales. Literacy could now confer considerable power and influence.

As the state, in both England and Wales, developed its law, administration and financial organization it relied increasingly on those with a legal training. Until the end of the thirteenth century this applied to the independent parts of Wales, particularly Gwynedd. Then, in the thirteenth and early fourteenth centuries, three disasters crucially affected the politics, economics and society of Wales. Education in all its aspects, but particularly formal education, was deeply affected.

The first of these calamities, for so it was seen by the poets of the day, was the conquest of Wales in 1282 by the English king. The administrative structure which prevailed from the Statute of Wales of 1284 until the Acts of Union of 1536 and 1542 was, in general terms, a duality of Principality and March, with the Principality subject to the administration and justice of the English king, put into practice by his officials, and the March substantially subject to the authority of individual Marcher lords of Norman descent. There were many manifestations of conquest in this society, including the ousting of the Welsh from positions of authority for long periods. However, neither king nor Marcher lords could govern effectively without the cooperation and service, in all but the most senior offices, of educated Welshman. They remained, of course, an elite drawn from the ranks of the noble and princely households or the higher echelons of the Church who had been educated sometimes in the universities, sometimes at a later stage at the Inns of Court.

The second calamity, occurring in the mid-fourteenth century, was the Black Death, no respecter of rank or nationality. The spread of this plague across Europe is calculated to have killed as many as one-third to one-half of the population, with disastrous effects on economic activity and social prosperity. Inevitably, the Church, which was central to the provision of, and the demand for, education, was particularly badly hit in that the surplus wealth so often channelled to it in the form of endowments was much reduced and the numbers of monks and friars drastically diminished, so reducing the wealth of the monasteries and friaries even further. The result was that the provision of clerical education and the patronage of the Church for young scholars was adversely affected. On the other hand, the greatest of medieval Welsh poets, Dafydd ap Gwilym, wrote in the mid-fourteenth century.

The third disaster to befall Wales was the defeat of the rebellion against the English king led by Owain Glyndŵr. In a society already weakened at the roots by depopulation and depression, the further dislocation caused, at least to some parts of Wales, between 1400 and 1415 was considerable. Allied to this was the subsequent legislation of Henry IV which ostensibly forbade Welshmen from holding office under the Crown. Owain's brief period of control sheds some interesting light on the educational priorities of rulers of the period. He himself is reputed to have been a student at the Inns of Court in London. Like any medieval ruler, he required the services of clerks, administrators and lawyers to work the bureaucracy of the state – administering its law, collecting taxes and conducting foreign affairs. In this respect two of Owain's policies were intended to work in tandem. He proposed a Welsh Church independent from that of England, and the establishment of two universities, one in north Wales, one in south. This structure would have supplied him with the educated elite which he required. It was not to be. Owain's defeat by the English king, together with the economic dislocation associated with the Black Death, meant that the prospects for education for the top echelons of Welsh society were badly affected. This was reflected in the fact that far fewer works of theology originated from Welsh scholars in this period and the main activity in the monasteries was copying of existing manuscripts.

During the course of the fifteenth century the legal impediments to the Welsh were increasingly ignored, and a social structure based more on the accumulation of land into consolidated estates began to emerge. Gradual economic recovery resulted in more active patronage of the bards. These trends were particularly noticeable from about 1450, and it is evident that our definition of formal education as being the province of the Church is being similarly changed. There had been various portents of this in the fourteenth and early fifteenth centuries. In terms of formal education, a Welsh lawyer, David Holbache, had founded a grammar school in Oswestry early in the fifteenth century. Most significant, there was a growing demand for education among more prosperous landowners in particular, and an appreciation of the importance of the kind of secular and legal knowledge, especially knowledge of English and Latin, helpful in public and private administration.

Essentially, the Welsh economic base, structured around farming and its associated crafts, changed little during the course of this century but Welsh society was substantially modified, with consequent effects on the supply and demand for education. Economic recovery eventually followed the depredations of the Black Death and the Glyndŵr rising. This meant that traditional crafts, whether literary or manual, revived. Indeed, from the time of the Carmarthen eisteddfod in 1450, when the rules governing both the training of poets and the poetry which they wrote were radically revised, the craft flourished greatly in what Glanmor Williams has called the golden century of Welsh poetry. Similarly, Welsh masons and carpenters, for example, were in greater demand as secular and Church buildings once more had surplus wealth devoted to them.

This cultural recovery was predicated on economic revival. The Church was again at the forefront of scholarship, both in terms of its leadership within Wales and the extensive copying of manuscripts. Highly significant in the long term was the gradual consolidation in Wales of a class of landowners bent on building up estates which they could pass on intact to their heirs. Although the great majority were less wealthy than their English counterparts, emergence of this gentry class in the fifteenth century was of the utmost importance.

They were to dominate life in Wales from the sixteenth to the nineteenth century, during which period it is possible to paint some general picture of the gradations in Welsh society, divisions which gave rise to different educational needs. The major economic divides were between landowners, their tenants and landless labourers, of whom landowners, in particular, had sufficient surplus wealth to expend some of it on education. Wales was overwhelmingly a rural society. Its population in the early sixteenth century was about a quarter of a million, scattered across Wales, so that any formal provision for education, even if there had been demand for it, would necessarily have been confined to the small towns. These were generally market and administrative centres, like Carmarthen and Wrexham, and were the location for the crafts and trades which serviced outlying rural areas. The basic social structure which had emerged in the second half of the fifteenth century was, especially in the sixteenth century, to blend with Europe-wide changes which were to have a major impact on the demand for education.

Three influences, in particular, form the backcloth to the formal educational endeavours of the period. The Renaissance both reinforced the emphasis on the classical languages of Latin and Greek as the vehicle for conveying the best of the European cultural heritage, and at the same time stimulated the development of vernacular languages, including Welsh, if they were to accommodate these ideas and develop their literature accordingly. This had a particular impact on Wales as William Salesbury translated the New Testament and, eventually, William Morgan the Bible into Welsh in 1588.

A second strand of Renaissance thinking had some influence on the newly consolidating class of gentry in Wales. The ideal to emerge was epitomized in Castiglione's *The Book of the Courtier*. His perfect Renaissance gentleman was highly educated, endowed with wit, intelligence, appreciation of music and painting, as well as the virtues of magnanimity, bravery and articulacy. The influence of such ideas on formal education in Wales was limited, but it did provide an ideal for which at least some of the wealthier gentry families of Wales could aim, as they assumed an increasingly obvious role as leaders of society in Wales.

A third element in Renaissance ideas proved to be abortive. Although the medieval scholastic tradition was modified, grammar-school and university education was to be centred on the classical languages and did not incorporate the new scientific ideas which some influential educators advocated. There were outstanding Renaissance humanist thinkers, like Erasmus, who were particularly critical of the aridity associated with the study of formal Latin and Greek grammar as the staple diet of education. During his brief stay in England in 1509 Erasmus tried to put into practice at St Paul's School in London his ideas on extending the curriculum to geography and history and even mythology, but these ideas had little impact. In the seventeenth century, Francis Bacon and Harrington, both prophets of the new experimental sciences which stressed the investigation of real life and the importance of testing and experimenting with natural phenomena, deplored the concentration of the grammar schools on the old masters of the classics. But there was no equivalent in Wales of the Mathematical School opened at Christ's Hospital in 1673, for example, which included navigation as a subject.

So, despite attempts in England to set up academies which would teach more modern subjects, arguments from Comenius in the seventeenth century, for example, that education should more directly be related to real life, criticisms that grammar schools trained only for the professions and, towards the end of the eighteenth century, John Locke's indictment of the narrowness of the curriculum and constant repetition as a method of teaching, Tudor, Stuart and Georgian grammar schools concentrated on Latin and, to a lesser extent, Greek.

If the Renaissance gave rise to ideas which affected the education of the wealthy, the Reformation required that attention be given to the instruction of the population as a whole. One of the revolutions of the sixteenth century assisted the dissemination of these ideas – the widespread development of printing. Printed books, of course, were expensive and, in general (though by no means exclusively), were read by those in wealthier families, but they did eventually make a more widespread education, both formal and informal, possible. The New Testament had already been translated into English by Tyndale in 1526 and, as a result of the new technology, was published in pocket size. So the invention of printing, and its impact on the dissemination of religious books and tracts, had the most profound implications for both religious observance and the relationship between the state and its subjects. As more such literature circulated from the reign of Henry VIII onwards, against a background of change in religious observance, the government became increasingly worried at the implications of the Bible and religious literature being available to those able to read, or prepared to listen as others read to them. So it was that Henry VIII decreed that the Bible should only be read by aristocracy, gentry and prosperous merchants. Nevertheless, succeeding Reformation changes, dramatically contradictory in the reigns of Henry VIII, Edward VI, Mary and Elizabeth, and the increasingly desperate attempts of the Roman Catholic counter-reformers, meant that the printed word was an essential tool in a fundamental battle for people's souls. There was a substantial Catholic literature in Welsh and English circulating in Wales to counteract the tracts produced by the reformers to justify what seemed to the mass of the people to be revolutionary changes. This was a world of secret printing presses – like the one on the Great Orme near Llandudno – and remarkable historical claims such as that of Bishop Richard Davies in his introduction to the Welsh New Testament, in which he argued that the Church of England represented the restoration of the true British Church of ancient times.

While the printed word now became the chief weapon in the hands of both reformers and counter-reformers, the Reformation changes of the reigns of Henry VIII and Edward VI changed for ever the educative process for the mass of the population. As the interiors of cathedrals and churches were whitewashed, images and statues torn away for destruction, and sites of pilgrimage despoiled, the visual depiction of stories from the Bible, conveying the deepest theological truths in art form, which had been the staple means of interpretation of organized religion for the majority of the population in Wales as elsewhere, no longer performed its educative function.

The Reformation had practical educational effects in various parts of Europe. For example, Luther's belief that all children should have some kind of education had some impact on the establishment of city and state schools and the *gymnasium* in Germany. Nearer to home, the influence of Calvinism impelled John Knox in Scotland to draw up a blueprint for a unified system of national schools taking in the stages of elementary and grammar schools, colleges and universities to provide education for all. The plan was rejected but it influenced the eventual establishment of a network of parish schools in Scotland, so that by 1646 the Scottish Parliament enacted that a school be founded and a schoolmaster appointed in every parish in which none had yet been established. This emphasis on education stemmed from the centrality to the reformers of an under-standing of the Bible and belief in the priesthood of all believers. It was essential, therefore, that the masses should be able to read the Bible.

It was partly as a consequence of the political implementation of Reformation changes in England and Wales that major modifications took place to the government of Wales which, in turn, had an impact on the provision of education. As a result of Union legislation between 1536 and 1542 the structure of Welsh administration was radically modified. The division between the counties of the Principality, governed by the English king, and the area under the control of the Marcher lords, gave way to a united Wales and England. The whole of Wales was divided into twelve counties, with Monmouthshire in an anomalous position. These counties had their own administrative and judicial structure with extensive legal and military functions. Each county and its county boroughs were given parliamentary representation. The county itself was essentially governed by local officials – deputy lieutenants, sheriffs and justices of the peace. Another provision of the Act of Union, of the utmost significance in the long term, was that English was to be the official language of administra-tion and justice in Wales. In the early part of the sixteenth century many court records were still kept in Latin but later in the century it gave way to English. The advantages of learning English, as well as Latin, had been apparent to the Welsh gentry in the previous century. By the sixteenth it was essential. The great majority of the population below the rank of gentleman remained monoglot Welsh, a fact which was to impact on the provision of formal education for centuries.

This social, religious, economic and political background determined the demand for increased formal secular education from the sixteenth century. A combination of private interest – as estates needed more efficient record-keeping in the inflationary sixteenth century – and public responsibility in law and administration, combined with notions of the educated Renaissance gentleman, prompted landed families and an expanding group of merchants, traders, lawyers and other professionals to pursue their education in unprecedented numbers.

The more wealthy of Tudor and Stuart gentry, in Wales as in England, could afford to employ private tutors for their young children. Lord Herbert of Cherbury recounted that 'my schoolmaster in the house of my said lady grandmother then began to teach me the alphabet, and afterwards grammar and other books commonly read in schools'. The Revd Richard Lloyd was tutor to the children of the Wynn family of Gwydir, and in 1607 received a pension for 'the services, pains and travail . . . in training and bringing up in learning diverse of the sons of me the said sir John Wynn'.

Some of these tutors educated children, both boys and girls, from other gentry families and, occasionally, even the children of tenants. There were a few elementary schools run by clerics, associated with those chantries which survived the dissolution of the 1540s. They were, however, very far removed from comprising the network of elementary schools which historians of education once depicted. Some of the Welsh grammar schools also taught reading and writing, and employed a writing master for the purpose, although this was not their function and they would only have done so from necessity. There were other, sporadic ways in which a few children might acquire the rudiments of reading and writing. Some parish priests taught scholars at their home or in the church precincts and there are numerous examples of parish schools in Wales which provided an elementary or grammar type of education. A number of lay men and women taught the little they knew to local children, very often to relieve their own penury. Examples are few, but we are told that in 1574 Alice Carter turned her shop in Denbigh into a schoolroom. In 1603 the burial of the son of Richard Price, schoolmaster, is recorded. In 1615 the upper room of a house in Chepstow was used for a school and there were schools also at Llandenny and Llanarth in Monmouthshire. A few examples exist of endowments for the rudimentary teaching of poorer pupils. However, during the sixteenth, and indeed much of the seventeenth, century opportunities for learning to read and write were unavailable for the majority of children. Occasional charitable enterprises did not begin to provide an opportunity for the mass of Welsh children but, of course, there was as yet no demand for such education when the material advantages of literacy were minimal for most of the population. Including the grammar schools, it has been estimated that there were probably about a hundred schools of all kinds in Wales just before the Civil War, and Malcolm Seaborne has listed thirteen elementary schools endowed between 1660 and the end of the century which, unlike the grammar schools, may well have admitted girls as well as boys.

There was already in place an element of state control through the Church which decreed that 'none [was] to teach school without a licence', though this could not be enforced. We know of fifteen such licences being granted in Monmouthshire in respect of schools other than the grammar schools but there was little demand. So the supply situation was only to be modified when concentration on the importance of knowledge of the Bible focused the minds of Puritan divines on providing more opportunity for children to learn to read. There were some, like Knox in Scotland, who believed that to this end it was the responsibility of the state to provide a system of elementary education whatever the lack of popular demand.

Of course, it was in the interest of Puritans to paint the worst picture, but their statements still echo their worries. For example, in 1595, Gabriel Goodman, dean of Westminster, wrote to Queen Elizabeth bemoaning the fact, according to him, that there was only one school in the whole of north Wales which educated children in their duty to God and the queen. Such apprehensions were echoed in Wales in 1623 by Vicar Prichard in one of his famous simple verses, penned to try to bring an understanding of scripture and salvation to more people. He referred to the lack of bibles in houses, compounded by the inability of people to read them. Given the expense of bibles this was inevitable, but it does give an insight into the lack of rudimentary education, and Puritan worries about the situation. His strictures about people's ability to read are also not surprising given that only about 20 per cent of the population, about 60,000 people, were literate in either English or Welsh.

In respect of the more affluent, the most significant development in the sixteenth century was the creation of a network of grammar schools in Wales, in response to the increased demand for education among the middling sort of people – merchants, professional people, shopkeepers, tradesmen, freeholders, skilled craftsmen and lesser landowners. This development was common to Wales and England, as a rash of grammar schools formed the staple provision of that urban education which was to last substantially unmodified until the middle of the nineteenth century. The accepted interpretation, until relatively recently, was that the provision of grammar-school education was at its apogee in England, at least, at the end of the medieval period and that the dissolution of the chantries, with their associated guilds and fraternities, brought an end to a system of education which was widely available. This distortion exaggerates both pre-Reformation provision and the effect of the disappearance of the chantries. In fact, the Chantries Act of 1547 did allow for the extension of a whole range of charitable concerns, including schools, and, it has been argued, marked significant state intervention in the education system. This resulted in the widespread creation of urban grammar schools to supplement those already in existence.

Not surprisingly, the development of such schools in Wales lagged behind their establishment in various parts of England. In England, it is mistaken to regard late medieval education as the province only of the monasteries and Church – there was sufficient demand to foster the creation of grammar schools. If we exclude Oswestry, only one such school was set up in fifteenth-century Wales. However, given the more settled social context of the early sixteenth century, with a landed hegemony resembling that of England in structure if not in wealth, together with the administrative settlement of 1536–42, a similar demand resulted in grammar schools being founded in many Welsh towns.

The sons of the more affluent Welsh gentry were usually sent to the more prestigious and expensive English grammar schools. Sir John Wynn of Gwydir's sons were sent to Eton, Bedford, Westminster, St Albans and Lichfield. Shrewsbury, established in 1552 with money from dissolved chantries, was particularly popular with both landowners and leading clergy. None of the Welsh schools came close to the size and reputation of Shrewsbury, which had four ushers. The smaller Welsh schools had only a master, while some, like Brecon and Bangor, had a master and usher. Even so, as a result of the efforts of concerned educated clerics, gentry, merchants and lawyers, there had been founded, before the Civil War, grammar schools in Carmarthen (1538, refounded 1573), Brecon (1541), Abergavenny (1543), Bangor (1557), Margam (1558), Presteigne (1565), Ruthin (1584), Harlech (1590), Caerleon (1592), Wrexham (1603), Chepstow (1605), Northop (1606), Hawarden (1608), Cowbridge (1608), Beaumaris (1609), Botwnnog (*c.*1609), Llanrwst (1614), Haverfordwest (1614), Monmouth (1615), Ruabon (1618), Usk (1621) and Defynnog (1624). Grammar schools continued to be founded and endowed during and after the Civil War – at Llanegryn (1650), Cardigan (1653), Llantilio Crossenny (1654), Dolgellau (1665), Swansea (1682) and Deytheur (1690).

They supplied what were then the more populous parts of Wales and depended for their continuation on endowment income from land and tithes. The majority of the early schools were held in parish churches or defunct ecclesiastical buildings. The school in Bangor, for example, was held in buildings formerly belonging to the Dominican friary. Later schools tended to have purpose-built accommodation, usually modelled on the late medieval single-storey, unceilinged hall house.

Grammar schools concentrated on teaching the classical languages, especially Latin, the indispensable language for the educated gentleman. There was little respect paid to the Renaissance ideal of going beyond the classics to the study of music, painting, geography and even sports. In general terms, if more modestly, the schools in Wales resembled those in England – Bangor and Ruthin were consciously modelled on Westminster, one of the best English schools. They were financed by individual endowments and were usually small, varying in pupil numbers from about twenty to the 120 of Ruthin. For those not able to live at home, some schools, such as Monmouth, had boarding facilities, though more usually pupils took lodgings in the local town.

Age of entry was as low as eight, the leaving-age varying from twelve to nineteen, although there was usually some rule governing length of stay. For example, in Bangor the course was not to extend over more than six years, and no pupil could remain at Ruthin beyond the age of nineteen. The low age of entry was complemented by the fact that the majority of students who went to university did so between the ages of fourteen and sixteen. The general ethos of this type of school is evident from the words of Lily, first High Master of St Paul's School in London:

> Be thou there avoiding idleness when thy school shall call thee . . . let a penknife, quills, ink, paper, be implements always ready for thy studies . . . but thou shalt not commit the Latins or verses to loose papers which is meet to have written in books . . . see that thou learnest the most famous writings of ancient men. Thou shalt give or sell nothing: thou shalt change or buy nothing . . . leave money, the enticement to evil, to others . . . let noise, battling, scoffing, lies, thefts, scornful laughter be far from you, and fighting far off. Thou shalt speak nothing which is filthy or not honest.

The grammar schools, for boys only, were an indispensable step to a university or a profession. Pupils were taught largely by rote, and the regime of at least eight hours' work each day except Sundays was a demanding one. They were expected to be able to read and write and have a knowledge of English by the time they were admitted to the grammar schools at Ruthin and Bangor, but at Oswestry, Caernarfon and Carmarthen there were either reading or writing masters. Their education was through the medium of English or Latin, but there were complaints that many pupils had not yet mastered sufficient English before they were admitted.

Once the horn book and the alphabet had been dispensed with, pupils were plunged into the mysteries of Latin grammar which was to be the staple diet of the rest of their school lives. Indeed, the emphasis by the sixteenth and seventeenth centuries was far more on grammar than the dialectic of the medieval period. The Renaissance ideal was that Latin grammar should be the means to the end of studying classical literature, with all the wisdom that it encapsulated, but this tended to degenerate into arid and passive acceptance of vast amounts of Latin and Greek committed to memory. By this time, also, the method of learning was far more by means of the written Latin theme in prose or verse than disputation.

Nevertheless, there was a moral and practical purpose in this classical education, epitomized in the stated purpose of education in Presteigne's statutes as 'virtue and learning'. Lily's Latin grammar, for example, staple diet for the first year, communicated the rules of Latin by means of moral maxims. Erasmus's colloquies, similarly, contained high moral content. A complete programme might involve study of Ovid, Plautus, Terence, Virgil, Horace, Cicero, Sallust and Caesar.

Teaching methods tended to be common. By the time they started their work at grammar school, pupils were expected to be able to make their own quills with a penknife and their ink with a mixture of vinegar, gall, gum and alum. At Ruthin, a boy's first lessons were to recite parts of speech and verbs, followed by a reiteration of the previous day's lessons. Sentences were then set for translation in the lower forms. After breakfast the sentences were completed and the master and usher read to their respective groups from the set authors, while pupils hurried to select phrases to copy down. After an 11 a.m. lunch there was a session on parts of speech and a recapitulation on the morning's reading. A half-hour break at 3.30 p.m. was followed by an hour's reading of the set authors. There was very little variation on this structure, although on Saturdays, when school finished at 2 p.m., there was revision of the week's work and a declamation by three or four of the senior pupils. The school year was punctuated by three holidays, three weeks at Christmas, two weeks at Easter and two weeks at Whitsun. Discipline was severe – the birch was not only used for bad behaviour but also for inability to learn. At least at Ruthin the statutes stated that 'boys shall not be struck in the ears, noses, eyes or faces'. The most vital pupil attribute was a good memory because Latin was basically taught by reading passages and learning them by heart.

Not surprisingly, there were many criticisms of such regimented learning which was, at best, comparatively narrow and, at worst, utterly arid, despite the geographical and historical horizons incidentally invoked by the classics. The best schoolmasters objected on psychological grounds that this diet of the rules of grammar was wholly unsuited to the capacity of young children. In the seventeenth century, Comenius argued that education should be more closely related to real life, while Sir Francis Bacon criticized the domination of the authorities of the past and the fact that education was geared entirely to the professions. Such criticisms had virtually no impact on the practice of either the Welsh or the English grammar schools.

The established Church, while no longer the ubiquitous benefactor of so much education, still exercised a hold over all schools. Edicts of 1559, 1571 and 1604 tried to determine that no unlicensed person should teach, and the licence was dependent upon a mastery of the classical languages and a good name: 'Know ye that we have examined . . . whom we find to be sufficiently instructed for his knowledge and learning in the Latin and Greek tongues and likewise of good and honest behaviour . . . wherefore we have admitted and authorised him to teach in any place throughout our whole diocese of . . . as long as he shall honestly behave himself and bring up in virtuous education the youth of your parishes . . .' Licences were issued only to those loyal to the established Church and, after 1662, to the liturgy of the Church. Teacher quality varied enormously. Some schools required that the master had to have an MA degree, but many staff were just required to have a general proficiency and good name.

Even though the original endowments of the grammar schools often stipulated a number of free places, the schools were available to only a very restricted segment of the population, with total numbers of such pupils in Wales very small. Bangor, for example, provided free lodging and education for ten pupils, while Brecon had twenty free places, but there were more extensive expenses involved – pens, ink, books and candles – which usually debarred all but the prosperous and effectively restricted most admissions to sons of landowners, clergy and some tradesmen.

The school at Ruthin was means-tested, so that a gentleman worth £30 per annum had to pay 2s 6d to the master and 8s per year in fees, while the son of a person worth £2 per annum was required to give the master 6d, and one shilling in fees. Such fees were originally intended to supplement money provided by the original endowment but financial problems were never far from the surface. This is evident at Friars' School, Bangor, for example. The intention was to pay a master and an usher £20 and £10 per annum respectively, for teaching up to 100 boys, ten of whom had grants of £2 per annum for 'their finding and education in learning'. Then, in the 1620s, the dean of Bangor refused to pay £52 to help with much-needed repairs, and the bishop of Bangor refused to hand over £100 he had received for the education of three poor boys. Only after the bishop's death did the school receive the money. The school continued during the Civil War on revenue of £58 per annum from rents, but it was only after 1688 that confidence was fully restored due to the interest taken by John Jones, dean of Bangor. It had been allowed to lapse into a bad state of repair through the neglect of the governing body (the dean and chapter of Bangor), the foundation service was not observed, school accounts were not audited and the annual survey of repairs was not taking place. A similarly chequered history befell many of the Welsh grammar schools in the seventeenth century. Monmouth School, founded by merchant William Jones through the Haberdashers' Company was, for periods in its early days and at least twice during the seventeenth century, blighted by the inefficiency of a master.

Generally, then, the financing, governing and staffing of the Tudor and Stuart grammar schools were susceptible to periods of poor teaching and administration, as well as the occasional maladministration of funds, to the extent that these were more disruptive overall than the Civil War and the Interregnum. Indeed, the famous Shrewsbury School, a favourite of a number of Welsh gentry families, experienced a riot in 1607 when the fourth master was not promoted to third master, apparently on suspicion of Roman Catholic sympathies, while early in the seventeenth century a Chancery suit accused the town bailiffs of taking money from the school chest.

From the start, the Welsh grammar schools had an Anglicizing influence, so tending to reinforce social divisions. English was the initial language of teaching, as were the grammars statutorily employed. In at least three schools the Welsh language was specifically debarred from playing any part in pupils' education. Nevertheless, these schools provided an unprecedented extension of educational opportunity in Wales, though only for boys. Opportunities for girls were far more restricted, with, inevitably, the daughters of the more affluent families best catered for. Where there were tutors in gentry households it is likely that the daughters profited as well as sons. But there are very few examples of endowments for the formal education of girls.

For the vast majority of the Welsh both the language and the experience of this formal education were entirely alien. Their day-to-day existence continued to be determined by harsh economic conditions and a constant struggle for survival. They were skilled farmers and possessed a knowledge of their animals and crops which was passed on from generation to generation. There were respites from work on feast days and numerous saints' days or holy days in pre-Reformation times, during which they might dance to the harp or get involved in mass games like football or *cnapan*. Their spiritual education, until the Reformation, was by means of churches, where they would encounter stained-glass windows, statues and other icons of the Virgin Mary and a variety of biblical figures, wall-paintings in profusion, images and pilgrimages. Even the spoken word was largely ineffective, since services were in Latin and many parish priests were able to do little more than recite them without understanding. A whole range of popular superstition underpinned both day-to-day life on the land and knowledge of religion.

After the Reformation the visual images which sustained an element of religious knowledge were almost wholly done away with. The growth of Puritan influence in Wales towards the end of the sixteenth and the beginning of the seventeenth centuries, and especially from the 1630s, meant that a new significance was attached to bringing the mass of the population to some knowledge of the Bible. The doctrines of the leading theologians of the Reformation, Luther and Calvin, inevitably led to a concentration on the education of the masses. The central tenets of Roman Catholicism, especially that of salvation by good works, were replaced by the notion of salvation through faith, which involved, in the famous phrase, the priesthood of all believers. Such a concept of individual responsibility for personal salvation led inevitably to the necessity for a knowledge of religious teaching which, to the reformers, was available through the Bible. The emphasis on the importance of education, with the Bible as text, was as significant for Puritanism in Wales as in Germany, Geneva or Scotland, though without such far-reaching results in terms of formal schooling.

In Wales, as in England, there was concern over the lack of education, the inability of the majority to read, the paucity of texts to read had they been able, and the best way of alleviating these situations. When the Puritans were in a position to use the authority of the state, during the Interregnum, to address these problems they tried radical measures. They were guided for a short time by the ideas of one of the greatest seventeenth-century educationists, Comenius. He was invited over to England by the Long Parliament to implement some of his ideas on universal learning, but his stay of only six weeks was curtailed by the worsening situation which led to the Civil War. His concerns in his native Sweden were of a piece with those of Puritan reformers in Wales – providing sufficient literature in the native language and providing universal education as one of the fundamental human rights. He believed that education should be provided from infancy, first in the home, then in the village school, then in the city *gymnasium* and finally at university, and he shared with Luther the notion that this education should not be grounded in narrow classicism but be a preparation for life. He was only one educationist – Hartlib and Dury were others – to have an influence on educational debate in the Long Parliament. A notion of universal education was being built up. Pre-eminently, the motives were religious – the saving of souls – but education was also seen as a safeguard against the sins of idleness and profanity.

Puritan educational efforts in Wales therefore followed predictable lines. There was an attempt to provide religious literature. In this context by far the most significant event, particularly in the long term, for education and the Welsh language was the translation of the Bible into Welsh in 1588. The expense of William Morgan's Bible meant that it was intended for use in churches rather than for private consumption, but eventually, in 1630, a small Bible was published which intended for wider use. To complement the scriptures, and to facilitate teaching by means of the staple method of the catechism, there was a range of devotional literature. In the same year which saw the publication of the small Bible, Lewis Bayley's *Practice of Piety* was translated into Welsh, and Vicar Prichard's *Canwyll y Cymru* (Candle of the Welsh) provided a quantity of homely and morally impeccable verse.

It was in a context of Puritan anxiety over the inadequacy of educational provision that the Long Parliament discussed the matter of schooling for Wales in 1641. However, it was not until the Puritans achieved power in 1649 that they were in a position to act. Cromwell's government was particularly conscious that not only was education in Wales even more deficient than in England, but also Wales had provided the strongest support for royalist efforts during the Civil War. Something needed to be done. In 1650 an Act for the Better Propagation and Preaching of the Gospel in Wales, and Redress of some Grievances, was passed. More than seventy commissioners were appointed to act for north and south Wales with the fruits soon to emerge.

An ordinance for the establishment of a school at Lampeter indicates what was envisaged:

> By the commissioners for propagation of the gospel etc: Swansea 2 August 1652. Lampeter: it is ordered that a free school be created and settled in the town of Lampeter in the County of Cardigan for the education of youths in English and Latin tongue – and that the yearly sum of £20 be allowed for the keeping of the said free school. And Mr Thomas Evans is hereby authorised to keep the said school and to receive the said stipend till the commissioners shall take further order therein, and John Price esq. treasurer for South Wales is hereby enabled to pay and allow the said sum of £20, at such time and seasons as the same shall grow due and payable, the first quarter to commence the five and twentieth of March last past.

The ordinance is signed by seven of the commissioners.

Sixty such schools were set up, concentrated mainly, though not exclusively, in the towns, and their significant features are evident from the ordinance. They were free schools, with their curriculum reflecting that of the established grammar schools, in so far as Latin was taught, although there was elementary education in English. There was no provision for education in the Welsh language. Upkeep of the school and its master were paid for from the revenues of ecclesiastical livings. According to Vavasor Powell, one-third of tithes went to these free schools. The commissioners were responsible for paying salaries of up to a very respectable £40 per annum, though certainly one schoolmaster, in Llanrwst, was paid only £8 per annum.

The state, this time in the form of a Puritan government, continued to exercise control over teaching by means of certificates issued by the commissioners. However, not only were some clergy who had been ejected from their livings given certificates to teach but also others taught privately – like Hugh Gore of Oxwich and Francis Davies of Llangan –

with the result that the system of Church/state control was less effective than under the bishops.

The ambitious scholastic experiment was to be short-lived. In 1653/4 the Commission for the Propagation of the Gospel disappeared and, under the Approbation Act of 1654, trustees and Triers were charged with carrying on the work of the commissioners. The numbers of schools dwindled, so that by 1660 only twenty-one remained in existence. The new regime was not wholly to blame. Some of the original schools had been located in remote rural areas and stood little chance of success from the outset. In Breconshire nine schools had been established; only two survived. Movement of personnel from school to ecclesiastical living – as in Welshpool where both master and usher were affected – could result in school closure.

At the same time, it would appear that the Triers were more stringent in their standards than their predecessors. For example, some schoolmasters accused of papistry, drunkenness and ignorance in 1652 gave up and their schools disappeared with them. David Evans of New Radnor and Hugh Jones of Glamorgan, both accused of drunkenness, and Hugh Powell of Brecon, accused of Catholic sympathies, stopped teaching. There seems also to have been a more stringent attitude towards ejected clergy who had been allowed to teach in Propagation schools. Only three of the eight approved by the original commissioners survived into the Protectorate period. Confusion over the payment of schoolmasters (arrears of as much as two years had been allowed to build up) did not help. Some, such as Griffith Jones of Dolgellau and John Evans of Bala, were paid retrospectively but the master and usher of Newtown school, for example, were refused payment and the Triers opened only one new school: that in St David's.

This highly significant experiment in extending educational opportunity, if mainly in the towns of Wales, was therefore fraught with problems even during the Protectorate. With the sea change of the Restoration in 1660 there was little hope for survival. The Commonwealth schools had made little difference. They were a forced growth, without any tradition. In 1662, the bishop of Llandaff complained that the county of Glamorgan was 'utterly destitute of schools', but there is no evidence of widespread demand from below for the kind of education on offer in the Puritan schools, while the Restoration and the penal legislation of 1662 reasserted Anglican control through a licensing system, imposing fines of £40 for teaching in an unlicensed school. Only one Interregnum foundation survived in the long term: Cardigan Grammar School.

It was significant that the Propagation schools in Wales were sponsored by the state, the first example of such direct patronage. Private endeavour, even among royalists, continued during the Interregnum. The most famous, a small boarding school, was that at Golden Grove, in Carmarthenshire, lasting from about 1645 to 1657. It was run by Jeremy Taylor, former chaplain to William Laud and Charles I, who had sought refuge under the patronage of the earl of Carbery. One of the teachers at this school, William Wyatt, wrote both a grammar and a catechism – a reminder that this technique of question-and-answer was one of the staple methods of teaching and gave rise to a genre of text book.

There was no formal post-school education available in Wales. The only facilities for Welshmen with the means and the desire to continue their education were the English universities at Oxford and Cambridge and the Inns of Court, although some did attend continental universities. The number of students from Wales proceeding to university was inevitably even smaller than that attending grammar schools. Between 1200 and 1500 about 400 Welsh students attended the University of Oxford and about forty the University of Cambridge, though this number does not take account of those who did not register. Not since the days of Owain Glyndŵr had the idea been mooted of a university in Wales, but Welsh students went to Oxford or Cambridge in greatly increased numbers in the sixteenth century, especially to Oxford. W. P. Griffith has estimated that there were about 200 Welsh students at Oxford in the first forty years of the sixteenth century, with an average age of entry of eighteen, although this masked very substantial variations. He has calculated that in the century after 1540, registrations from Wales at Oxford, Cambridge and the Inns of Court came to over 3,000 and, as a proportion of the total student population, increased significantly over the following thirty years. Cambridge continued to attract very few students from Wales – only about twelve between 1500 and 1540.

In the medieval period and in the early sixteenth century the majority studied canon and civil law, although later in the century most Welsh graduates took degrees in arts. The 50 per cent of students who graduated took about four years for a bachelor's degree and another three to become a master of arts, which intending clerics would be ambitious to complete. The course which they followed still depended in the sixteenth and seventeenth centuries on a close study of Aristotle, but the curriculum widened in this period to include more concentration on Greek and Hebrew texts. Study was still structured to a great extent around the trivium and quadrivium. Those proceeding to the MA studied ethics, physics, natural philosophy and metaphysics. Here, it was the faculty of divinity which was of the highest status, rather than those of law, medicine or music.

Oxford and Cambridge Universities continued in the sixteenth century to be essentially ecclesiastical institutions and initially the main source of endowments from Wales tended to be from clerics. But both intake and organization were changing. Increasing numbers of lay students were admitted and the universities were developing their collegiate tradition, based on substantial endowments, with the university body itself becoming of limited significance as the colleges assumed the widest autonomy from the sixteenth to the nineteenth century, even over syllabuses and examinations.

While the universities remained the training ground for clerics they also became an accepted part of a gentleman's education in the sixteenth century. There is some debate as to how seriously many such students took their studies, but numerous examples occur in Wales of serious and highly successful scholars. For example, Edward Carne of Ewenny in the Vale of Glamorgan had an extremely distinguished legal career, became principal of Greek Hall, Oxford, and ambassador to Rome in the reign of Mary I. The progress of Welsh students to Oxford was helped after 1571 by the endowment of Jesus College, and there were some endowments in Cambridge for the benefit of Welsh students by means of which a few intending clerics from poor backgrounds were able to go to university.

The Inns of Court, for the training of lawyers, were more restricted to the affluent. During the sixteenth century they continued to attract relatively small numbers of students from Wales, as they had done earlier, though the proportion did rise during the first half of the seventeenth century, especially during the 1630s. Between 1570 and 1609, 259 students from Wales attended the Inns of Court, half of whom had previously attended university. Those who intended to be called to the bar faced a training of between seven and ten years.

The expansion of higher education in the sixteenth century resulted partly from the increasing secularization of education but also from the increasing importance given to education as a prerequisite of administrative and professional service. A legal education was not only functional for those becoming professional lawyers. As local government and justice were revolutionized in Tudor Wales, justices of the peace in particular, drawn from the ranks of the gentry, became the linchpin of the administration of justice, and increasing numbers received a higher education – about 40 per cent in the early decades of the seventeenth century.

Although some of the expansion of the universities generally from the sixteenth century is accounted for by an influx of sons of professional and commercial families, this was not true of Wales, where the social origin of students was rather different from that in England. About 60 per cent of students from Wales in the sixteenth and early seventeenth centuries were designated as being from non-gentry families. They were the sons of clergy and common people, although a proportion of the latter were of lesser-gentry origin. Some were also of the poorest, taking on a role as servitors and sizars, which allowed them to act as servants in their colleges or to individuals in return for remission of fees and some element of subsistence. For the sons of gentry, attendance at university involved substantial expenditure on fees, accommodation and subsistence. Not surprisingly, some students ran up considerable debts.

As a proportion of the population of England and Wales the Welsh were significantly under-represented at the universities. Nevertheless, those members of landed families, in particular, set apart by their participation in an extending state bureaucracy of administration and justice and a more affluent lifestyle, now benefited from an exclusive education. Education reinforced their power and integrated them more closely with their social peers in England, and eventually played its part in accentuating the division in Wales between those in authority in the community, generally the gentry, and their social inferiors, which was to become so marked in the eighteenth century. This was less true of the university-educated clergy from Wales who, in the later seventeenth and early eighteenth centuries, were responsible for much educational endeavour, providing elevating literature in the Welsh language and scholarly investigation into Welsh history and language. Even so, close involvement with English universities and European culture contributed to the Anglicization of the Welsh gentry, as did the predominance of English-language books published by Welsh authors. Even those books published in Welsh were mainly translations of English works, although those humanists at the forefront of the movement to endow the Welsh vernacular language with the capacity to adapt to all the new demands of the Renaissance were themselves university-educated.

Links existed between some of the Welsh grammar schools and Oxford and Cambridge colleges. For example, Friars' School, Bangor, maintained a scholarship at Magdalene College, Cambridge, and associations with St John's College. But it was Jesus College, Oxford, with which the Welsh were most closely associated, with 230 Welsh students attending between 1570 and 1622. It had been founded by a Welshman, Dr Hugh Price of Brecon, who petitioned the queen to found the college in 1571 'that he might bestow his estate for the maintenance of certain scholars of Wales to be trained up in good letters'. Its first principal was David Lewis from Abergavenny. Although supplemented by benefactions from some Welsh gentry who took more interest in this college than any other, Price's endowment was comparatively small. Then, in the seventeenth century, the college's greatest benefactor was Sir Leoline Jenkins who had himself been a student at the college and returned after a period in exile during the Interregnum to become fellow and principal from 1661 until 1673, before he went on to a distinguished legal career. He also endowed Cowbridge Grammar School and established its close links with Jesus College. As a result, the principal of Jesus chose five boys who were given their school education free and the chance to take up one of three exhibitions at Jesus College. Jenkins also established close ties between the college and the grammar school at Abergavenny.

A fellow of Jesus, Dr John Ellis, was a chief mover in a scheme to establish a university in Wales in the seventeenth century. The negotiations, not surprisingly, were the product of the ferment of the Protectorate period and an idea mooted by John Lewis of Glasgrug, Cardiganshire, a commissioner for the Propagation of the Gospel in Wales, and Ellis, a minister in Dolgellau. Lewis pressed the idea on Richard Baxter, one of the most eminent of Puritan divines, who had considerable sympathy with the scheme, since its purpose was to provide Puritan ministers for Wales. There was discussion about the location of the university, with Aberystwyth, Cardigan and Machynlleth all suggested, although Baxter was in favour of Shrewsbury, which, at that time had the strongest of links with both north and south Wales. The inevitable stumbling block was money. It was calculated that £1,000 would be needed for the building and £200 minimum as a yearly income. In any case, appeals to some Puritan gentry in Wales were unavailing and the project was doomed even before the Restoration.

More positively, Baxter provided 120 copies of one of his books to be distributed in north Wales in 1666 and, in so doing, may have had some influence on the work of Thomas Gouge's Welsh Trust. The Trust, along with other religious initiatives of the later seventeenth and eighteenth centuries, was to move the emphasis far away from university education to providing education for the mass of the people of Wales.

CHAPTER TWO

⋈

The Religious Motive Redefined, 1670–1847

For much of this period the Welsh economy and the social structure associated with it remained fundamentally unchanged. Essentially, this was still a landed economy dominated by the nature of the terrain, the seasons and the weather. There was a substantial increase in population, particularly in the second half of the eighteenth century, from about 380,000 in the mid-seventeenth century to approximately 490,000 a century later, and 580,000 in 1801, though no previous surge began to compare with the doubling of population in the following half-century. Improvements in agriculture, particularly in animal husbandry and the cultivation of crops, catered for some of the increased demand. But the food riots of the 1790s are sufficient indication that the poorer tenants and the landless, in particular, were as near to subsistence level as they had been in Tudor times, and just as susceptible to climate, when two or three bad harvests brought, if not starvation, then certainly malnutrition and increased vulnerability to disease.

The discrepancy in wealth and lifestyle between the poorest in society and the richest remained. After the upheavals of the Interregnum, the restoration of the monarchy in 1660 saw a swift reversion to the old order. While some of those families who had come to the fore during the Cromwellian period managed to integrate and prosper in the new system, the traditional landed families consolidated their hold on large estates, populated by a dependent and deferential tenantry. Effortlessly, they took over the reins of local government which, in essence, remained largely unchanged from the structure which had been put in place at the time of the Acts of Union.

There were modifications in the early decades of the eighteenth century. Some gentry families, often with genealogies originating with Norman Marcher lords or Welsh princes and their advisers, died out, so that extensive estates reverted to English or Scottish families. At the same time, there was a tendency towards estate enlargement, and the disparity between the wealthiest landowners and the rest of agrarian society became even greater. This gulf was accentuated by the tendency of the wealthiest to model their lifestyle on polite society centred on London and Bath. A house in the capital was crucial for those for whom the social and political implications of meeting their peers were a consolidation of status or preferment. Absence from Wales for lengthy periods therefore became far more common and at least some of the traditional involvement of the Welsh gentry in local leadership of their communities, economically, administratively and politically, was lost.

The divide was consolidated by disparities in language and religion. In the Tudor and early Stuart period the members of many leading gentry families had spoken Welsh, but this was less so in the eighteenth century, and patronage of Welsh culture and poetry diminished as the status of the Welsh language among the gentry class declined. In religion, too, with the growth of Dissent and Methodism, particularly among the solid sections of tenant farmers and prosperous tradesmen, there was an accentuated divide between them and the Anglican gentry. Of course, it is possible to exaggerate the extent of this communal rupture, particularly in the more remote and poorer counties, but essentially Welsh society of the eighteenth century was more fragmented than that of the sixteenth. It has even been argued that the resulting psychological dislocation was instrumental in making the mass of the Welsh population more open to the appeal of Nonconformity and to the educational initiatives evident from the 1730s.

By the 1780s, in retrospect at least, we can see the beginnings of a revolution. From the 1750s, iron production increased and within decades the great ironworks of Dowlais and Cyfarthfa, for example, were part of a chain of manufactures from Cardiganshire to Monmouthshire which was to bring Wales to the forefront of the world economy. This was only the start of the expansion of heavy industry, chiefly in metal and coal production, which was to transform Wales in the nineteenth century. If changes in the structure of agrarian society had caused an element of dislocation, this was as nothing compared with the impact of increasing population and the disproportionate location of this population in towns like Merthyr Tydfil which expanded, in an inhospitable part of the country, from a parish of less than a thousand to 24,000 in 1831and 70,000 in 1861. While the 1790s were characterized by food riots, the most notable manifestations of popular unrest in the nineteenth century were protests located in the new industrial towns of the south Wales Valleys, most notably that of 1831 in Merthyr Tydfil. These protests, too, arose out of a breach of what were taken to be the traditional rules of the moral economy. But, in the newer urban context, in which structures of local government and justice had been undermined, they took on a new and complex political and social dimension. By the 1840s, therefore, the milieu in which popular education was provided had dramatically altered and, as we shall see, the massive report of the commissioners into the state of education in Wales in 1847 bore witness to the scale of the transformation.

For the bulk of the period covered in this chapter, however, the motivation for the provision of popular education remained religious, a matter for philanthropy rather than the state. Indeed, those who wish to take Wales as a case study in the ongoing debate as to whether the industrial revolution required a substantial level of literacy might conclude that Welsh industrialization, occurring early and depending so substantially on iron and coal, does not support the thesis since literacy levels, if measured by the ability to write, rather than to read, were at the time substantially below those of England. Indeed, what emerges so graphically from the 1847 education commissioners' report is the disruptive effects of industrialization, not any associated opportunities. It has been persuasively argued that the main benefit to employers of widening elementary education was not improved literacy but an inculcation of ritual, discipline, punctuality and acceptance of authority which was then translated to the workplace.

One of the more remarkable features across Europe in the eighteenth century is the discrepancy between educational theory and its practice. In this revolutionary period education was certainly important to intellectuals in their approaches to theories of government, science and the natural world. It was the century in which Rousseau propagated influential ideas about the stages of development in children and young people, and stressed the significance of the adolescent years. He was one of the chief apostles of the idea of treating the child as a child rather than a miniature adult. Towards the end of the century, Pestalozzi put into practice some of Rousseau's theories and those of the philosopher Kant, in providing education through the sensations and experiences of a peasant home environment.

Significant too was the discussion about the relationship between the state and educational provision. This was integral to the Enlightenment because the notion was beginning to emerge that individuals were the product of their education, and therefore society could only be reformed by education. Such ideas were promulgated particularly in France, where La Chalotais, for example, argued for state provision of education – admittedly only for the upper classes – because of what he regarded as the faults of Jesuit education.

It was Prussia, however, which became the first of the European countries to embrace the principle of substantial state intervention. By 1717, Frederick William I had made attendance at village schools compulsory, although the schools were under the control of the Lutheran Church. By the second half of the century, national schools would be established and, by 1803, a national system of education, completely independent of religious influence, had emerged. That this had occurred in a country yet to industrialize makes once popular theories that state intervention in education was brought about by industrialization difficult to uphold.

Enlightenment theories, as they applied to education, had relatively little practical impact in Wales or England, and even commentators like Wordsworth, who accepted that the state should provide universal education, or Adam Smith who, in his *Wealth of Nations*, stressed the advantage to be gained by the state providing a minimal education for all its members, were exceptional.

Theories of direct state intervention had little impact on the provision of education in Wales until well into the nineteenth century, and notions of adapting educational provision to the different needs of children at different ages were of even more remote consequence. Even so, during the eighteenth century, Wales did make a highly distinctive contribution to addressing the problem of how the mass of a population might be furnished with at least an ability to read. Indeed, such provision must dominate an account of formal education in this period because the system which had emerged and consolidated in the sixteenth and seventeenth centuries was rather less vibrant in the following century.

Although there is some dispute over the extent to which grammar schools generally in Wales and England fared in the eighteenth century, their decline has sometimes been exaggerated. There were, after all, eight new foundations in Wales during the eighteenth century, although all these took place before 1762 and most found it difficult to prosper. They continued to emphasize Latin, the key to the clerical and other professions as well as the universities, but there was some extension of the curriculum. There seems to have been increased demand, although this was met by extending fee paying and boarding at the expense of free scholars. For example, Seaborne records that of the seventy-six boys in Friars' School, Bangor, in 1721 all but thirteen were fee-paying sons of smaller landowners and clergy, merchants or prosperous farmers. Some of the older foundations, for example Ruthin and Cowbridge, were substantially extended, while Queen Elizabeth Grammar School in Carmarthen was completely rebuilt in 1797.

Even so, the grammar schools grew increasingly out of kilter with a changing Wales. They faced diverse problems – some disappeared, others degenerated to elementary status. The remoter schools in particular were increasingly ill adapted to Welsh society. From the beginning, as we have seen, the more prosperous of the Welsh gentry had tended to send their sons to English schools even though they supported the smaller and less affluent Welsh schools. By the eighteenth century, as the landed elite became more exclusive, Anglicized and distant from the base of the society in which theoretically they were at the apex, they became increasingly antipathetic towards Welsh institutions which had once prompted at least some sympathy. They had recourse to the great public schools such as Eton, Harrow and Winchester, only one of which, Shrewsbury, was near to Wales geographically, if far away aspirationally.

As the endowments of the sixteenth and seventeenth centuries proved more and more inadequate, grammar-school fee payers became increasingly essential. Since lesser landed families had been squeezed as the consolidation of larger estates proceeded in the eighteenth century, the pool of potential fee payers for a Welsh, as opposed to an English grammar-school education, was inadequate. So headmasters were attempting to maintain the classical curriculum, usually stipulated in their foundation statutes, with a diminishing resource. In some areas there was insufficient support from minor landowners and tenant farmers who were not convinced of the need for the education which was on offer, so that many of these schools struggled with relative penury and were sometimes forced into elementary status.

The headmaster of Hawarden Grammar School, Flintshire, for example, complained that children were being sent to his school to learn elementary English, in violation of the foundation statutes of the school. It was decided that no boy should be admitted who was unable to read the New Testament. Even so there was a decline. Hawarden still called itself a grammar school but had, in some senses, forfeited that status if an advertisement of 1789 is any indication. An usher was required at the low salary of £20 a year. The qualifications were that he 'writes a good hand, reads well, and has a competent knowledge of vulgar and decimal arithmetic, mensuration, merchants accounts etc'. In grammar schools proper the predominantly classical curriculum was as entrenched as ever, partly through apathy but also because this was the kind of instruction laid down in foundation statutes. When some schools did attempt to widen the curriculum this itself caused problems. The grammar school at Beaumaris employed a writing master and, eventually, masters for modern languages and music, but these subjects were only available at extra cost. There was, therefore, an unfortunate distinction between those who could afford the extra subjects and those who could not, and such costs, in any case, only added another deterrent for poorer parents.

University education across much of Europe lost its dynamism. The University of Paris slumped to depths unprecedented in its history, for example, though the German universities, at the same time, made substantial progress in establishing principles of academic freedom and teaching. In the universities of Oxford and Cambridge, normally the only ones attended by students from Wales, there was academic torpor in the eighteenth century. Numbers of admissions fell and the practice of private tutoring became more common. Both universities became increasingly the preserve of the rich as opportunities for poor scholars became fewer. Classical humanism had lost its ability to inspire. The amount and quality of the teaching were usually inadequate and there were many examples of fellows, who until 1871 had to be Anglican and forced by declining numbers to become resident, being lazy and self-indulgent. Even less teaching took place at university, as opposed to college, level. Regius Professors of Modern History at Cambridge delivered no lectures between 1725 and 1773. The curriculum perpetuated the disputation and the syllogism of medieval times. There was no rigorous system of examinations, and undergraduates could qualify for their degree even if they spent only thirteen weeks of the year in residence. Although reforms were mooted in the second half of the eighteenth century – Cambridge instituted a written examination in 1780, Oxford in 1800, and there were new chairs, some of which, in Cambridge in particular, were in science – there were few opportunities for Welshmen (the universities were open only to men) to attend. Not until 1856 did both Oxford and Cambridge allow Nonconformists to graduate. There was no plan for any such institution in Wales, though St David's College, Lampeter, was established in 1827 as a degree-granting institution to train Anglican clergy.

Nevertheless there was an advanced education available in Wales. The origins of the Nonconformist academies lie in the repressive legislation of the Cavalier Parliament of 1662, subsequently reinforced. Numbers of ejected clergy, bereft of their livings as a result of this legislation, and with a clientele of Dissenters barred from the universities, set up academies. These were founded and conducted by serious and intent men, mainly at first to train ministers of the gospel. They had a four-year curriculum and, in the various institutions, taught a range of subjects – classics, logic, Hebrew, mathematics, natural sciences, modern languages, even medicine. The academies acquired a reputation for high standards, so attracting not only Dissenting students but Anglicans who preferred their quality and breadth of curriculum to Oxford and Cambridge. Of the twenty-three academies founded in England and Wales, originally by individuals but run later by boards, the most famous in England was the Gloucester/ Tewkesbury Academy which provided tuition in Hebrew, Chaldee and Syriac, although Warrington Academy could boast John Dalton (teaching mathematics and natural philosophy) and Joseph Priestley as tutors. Science teaching also featured in the best-known of the academies in Wales, the Presbyterian Academy at Brynllywarch, which later moved to Carmarthen. It was founded, probably in 1672 or 1673, at a farmhouse near Bridgend by Samuel Jones, former fellow and tutor at Jesus College, Oxford. Jones was rated by contemporaries as 'a great philosopher, a considerable master of the Latin and Greek tongues, and a pretty good orientalist'. An Anglican vicar, he had been ejected from his Llangynwyd living in 1662 and became a staunch Nonconformist, but he attracted many Anglicans to the academy, including a member of the Mansel family of Margam, one of the richest estates in Glamorgan. By the end of the seventeenth century, Jones was getting support from both the Presbyterian and Congregationalist denominational boards. This support became more extensive in the eighteenth century when, after a peripatetic existence, the academy was established permanently in Carmarthen. An insight into the education which trainees for the Nonconformist ministry were expected to receive at the academy is contained in the Presbyterian Board regulations for 1725:

> that none of the managers of this fund will encourage their being employed anywhere as ministers . . . unless it appears upon examination that they can render into English any paragraph of Tully's offices . . . that they read a Psalm in Hebrew, translate into Latin any part of the Greek Testament . . . give a satisfactory account of their knowledge in the several sciences they studied at the Academy and draw up a thesis upon any question that will be proposed to them in Latin . . .

One of Samuel Jones's students at Brynllywarch was James Owen, founder of the Oswestry and Shrewsbury Academy which operated from 1676 in Oswestry and 1700 in Shrewsbury. The curriculum there consisted of logic, metaphysics, physics, geometry, astronomy, chronology, ecclesiastical history and theology. For some part of the eighteenth century, the contribution of the Welsh Nonconformist academies to higher education was more dynamic and learned than that of the ancient universities, and from humble beginnings – the academy at Llwynllwyd started life in a barn – these institutions were the origin of theological colleges run by all the denominations in Wales in the nineteenth century.

The history of education in the late seventeenth and the eighteenth centuries is most noted for repeated and substantial voluntary effort to provide the mass of Welsh people with a basic literacy. What prompted this remarkable series of educational experiments? First, they must be seen in the context of a similar pattern of activity in Ireland, Scotland and England. The charity-school movement of the period is part of a general pattern of involvement of the wealthier class of society in a range of welfare movements prompted by both religious and social motives. Philanthropy was a feature of the eighteenth century, inherited from the growth of individual concern with charitable effort in the sixteenth, and reinforced from philosophical, religious and financial bases. The Puritan ethic, from which, it is argued, much of this philanthropy stemmed, was a two-edged sword. Following the Weber thesis, it often impelled believers to a material prosperity signifying a Calvinist conviction of election. But for the faithful, so steeped in biblical notions of moth and dust, as well as the temptation which accompanied wealth, their expiation through philanthropy became almost *de rigeur*, as it did in the Dutch society of the mid-seventeenth century. John Locke's emphasis on education as a means of disciplining mind and body, as well as it being a prime prerequisite of acquiring healthy moral and uplifting habits in response to the correct stimuli, provided some of the philosophical justification for the emphasis on education.

Such theories meshed with the religious ideals of those who promoted charity-school movements. If the association of Puritanism with the development of capitalism has been questioned, it was certainly associated with an ethic of material progress and the accumulation of wealth. The virtues inherent in these ends have been seen as sobriety, thrift and hard work in a useful field of employment. Education had to reflect the usefulness embodied in a Puritan life. Certainly education was a crucial prerequisite to reading the Bible and thus to salvation, and this became the dominant feature in Wales. But there was also a crucial social purpose, more pronounced in England and Scotland than in Wales, requiring for all sections of society an education which would inculcate what the Puritans believed to be the behavioural and social virtues of good living.

In Wales, in particular, the clergy were often leaders in these philan-thropic educational endeavours but they depended on the massive financial support of members of a Puritan class who, though not neces-sarily able to afford the large single endowments characteristic of former foundations, were perfectly well able to participate as shareholders in the financing of education based on the joint-stock-company principle. Respectability was maintained both in the object of the philanthropy and in its financial machinery.

If Puritan benefactors in Wales and England shared similar ideals, the practical effects in Wales were very different. In Wales the religious motive far outweighed the utilitarian, though it by no means excluded it. Souls had to be saved. Since this depended so much on the ability to read the Bible, a minimum of education was essential. That members of the Anglican clergy figure prominently in providing leadership for the education of the mass of the population in the eighteenth century might seem surprising, given the view which historians took for so long of the lack of effectiveness of the Anglican Church in Wales in the period. It is true that this was not a glorious century for the Church, with its absentee bishops unable to speak the language of most of the people, and many parish clergy having little education. Nevertheless, the Puritan wing of this Church provided some of the great educational innovators and administrators of the eighteenth century in the persons of Griffith Jones and, in his early days, Thomas Charles.

This was not to be foreseen at the beginning of the eighteenth century. The Church of England did not provide a national system of education, though some in its ranks aspired to this. There is little evidence that the Welsh desired such an education or that sufficient finance could be found for it. The comparative lack of success of the Welsh Trust and the Society for Promoting Christian Knowledge (SPCK), as we shall see, does not indicate great demand, and the paucity of numbers of that social group which provided the bulk of finance in England did not provide a secure financial base for this scale of philanthropy. It is only when that demand burgeoned that the circulating schools became so successful.

We have seen that the sixty or so schools founded during the Interregnum had a short and troubled history. It seemed as if the Restoration and the Clarendon Code of 1662 would reassert the iron grip of the Anglican Church on educational provision and stifle new initiatives. This was not to be. Even before the Welsh Trust had got under way, unlicensed schools in the dioceses of St David's and St Asaph, at least, outnumbered those licensed by the bishops. Some of the teachers employed under the Propagation Act taught once more in Trust schools and two of the commissioners under that Act, Sir John Trevor and Sir Erasmus Philipps, were to be members of local committees of the Welsh Trust.

It is with the beginnings of the Welsh Trust that we embark on the long eighteenth-century phase of the charity-school movement, with its origins in the late seventeenth century. The idea of charitable investment in, for example, concern for the poor and for education for those for whom there were no opportunities was firmly rooted in the notion of private benevolence which developed in Tudor and Stuart times, though adapting now to more modern business methods. The successive movements in Wales were all dependent on financial support from outside, particularly from London, and the SPCK, in particular, provides an early example of how approaches relevant to the Home Counties had limited effectiveness and had to be substantially adapted when applied to Wales.

The three names particularly associated with the work of the Welsh Trust were Thomas Gouge, Stephen Hughes and Charles Edwards. Gouge was an Englishman, educated at Eton and Cambridge, who had held a living in the diocese of Southwark for almost a quarter of the century but became a victim of the Clarendon Code and was ejected. He proceeded to devote his attention to alleviating the poverty and ignorance in those around him which had troubled him all his life. That these conditions prevailed in Wales had been brought home to him by his reading, and he was greatly concerned. After a first visit to the border counties in 1671–2, when he preached to the people and gave some money for teaching, he set about the work of providing Wales with religious literature and schools in the rather more liberal atmosphere of the post-Indulgence period. To this end, he established the Welsh Trust in 1672. Because of the respect in which he was held, the trust contained people of a wide spectrum of opinion including, although Gouge was an ejected cleric himself, Anglicans like the future Bishop Tillotson.

Stephen Hughes was another ejected vicar, from the parish of Meidrim, who was stirred to similar activity by the ignorance he saw around him. His was the organizing brain behind the work of the trust, and he was especially concerned with providing the Welsh with religious literature.

Charles Edwards, like his colleagues, was spurred on by a sense of crisis over what he witnessed. He had a sense of mission, believing that he was an agent of Providence. He considered that the translators of the Bible in the sixteenth century, and the great divines, had come to prepare a way for great works, and lead the people of Wales out of darkness. He believed that God would bring spiritual greatness to Wales once more and that his role in the work was to supervise the printing of religious literature for the trust.

The two major thrusts of the trust's activities were the provision of schools and the supply of books. Schools were established from 1672, but their impact was short-lived and ineffective. Resources were limited so that teachers were very poorly paid and transient. The language used was English in an attempt to make literate in that language a largely monoglot Welsh population. Moreover, the trust did not survive Gouge's death in 1681. As with the establishment of schools, the provision of books was hampered by lack of funds, and many were reissues. But the remarkable aspect of this work was that the books were intended for the poorer section of society and that the material provided in them, like Vicar Prichard's verses, was intended to be at a level which they could understand. The trust also printed the Welsh Bible and distributed over a thousand copies.

Its work may have been short-lived and, in the scale of its grand purpose, highly inadequate, but it represented a significant breakthrough in the nature and organization of providing a religiously based literacy for the lower orders. It set a precedent; the trust was the parent society of the better-known Society for Promoting Christian Knowledge, even bequeathing money to it. The trust also indicated to its successor body the nature and extent of the difficulties it would face.

The Society for Promoting Christian Knowledge was an Anglican organization established with similar aims to those of the Welsh Trust – to teach children to read and write, and to provide literature. The SPCK was, of course, a far wider organization than the Welsh Trust, covering England as well as Wales, but its promoters were well aware of the debt which they owed to both the achievements and the inadequacies of the trust. Additionally, there were strong Welsh connections. One of the founder members was Sir Humphrey Mackworth of Neath, one of the most innovative entrepreneurs of the late seventeenth and early eighteenth centuries, whose industrial exploits in the metal and coal-mining industries brought him great wealth until he overextended himself and went bankrupt. An early recruit to the society was Sir John Philipps of Picton Castle in Pembrokeshire, a philanthropist who was involved with movements in London for the improvement of morals and regularly presented Bills to Parliament on related subjects. He was a stern, upright, godly man, immensely rich, the mainstay of the foundation work of the SPCK in Wales. Not surprisingly, given this kind of commitment, the society was well organized through its central committee and its control of the localities in which it worked. Its ultimate object was to save souls.

A purely voluntary organization, its secret was that, where individual endowments were inadequate, it modelled its finances on the joint stock company, relying on large numbers of individuals donating relatively modest sums. The scope of its plans was ambitious. It was flexible in the kind of schools it established. In addition to day schools for children and adults there were night schools and works schools, though the latter were few in Wales. We know that Mackworth was patron of one in Neath and one in Cardiganshire. The works schools are particularly interesting in that they manifest the interest of at least some members of the society in the enhanced industrial activity of the period, though on a far more limited scale than was the case later. But the more widespread works schools of the nineteenth century were certainly not unprecedented.

Where day schools were established, the hours of formal schooling were as lengthy in Wales as in England – 7 to 11 a.m., 1 to 5 p.m. Inevitably the parental sacrifice of forgoing a wage, however small, so that children might attend school was substantial and well known to the society, which did what it could to provide clothes and help maintain the poorest children. The religious focus was reflected in the texts which were used to make children literate – the Bible, the Prayer Book, such uplifting texts as *The Whole Duty of Man* and, of course, the Catechism. Ideally, however, the curriculum was richer than this because members of the SPCK were inevitably drawn to linking proper religious observance with a personal code of morality and acceptance of the social hierarchy which, as members of their class, they deemed essential to good social order. So, for example, the pattern in England was for girls to be taught needlework, knitting, weaving and spinning, an aspect of their education which was enthusiastically received in Wales where these were available. This emphasis on training pupils for later life extended to arranging apprenticeships for boys and even attempting to keep an eye on them subsequently, and there are examples in Wales of training for occupations in agriculture and at sea. The hidden curriculum of social conditioning by means of inculcating virtues of meekness, gratitude and humility, crucial for learning one's position in society, were equally significant, although less overt than in England.

It is generally accepted that there were substantial differences between the movements in Wales and in England, resulting from different social and political considerations. The government's fear of Jacobitism was particularly strong in Wales and, although this was based rather more on image than substance, it impelled the school organizers in Wales to concentrate far more on the religious aspects of their work. More fundamentally, the structure of society in the two countries reinforced this distinction. Wales was a less prosperous country than England, with fewer towns and poorer markets. There was, proportionately, a far smaller and less socially influential middling and professional population. Predominant were small tenant farmers and landless labourers, but in scattered populations and generally lacking political influence. In the circumstances, the leaders of the SPCK diagnosed a more fragmented society, less in need of the social conditioning deemed necessary in England. However, without the spur of providing rather more socially exclusive charity schools for the elite of the poorer classes, intended to differentiate them from the more irresponsible and feckless poor, it was difficult to centre SPCK attention on the Welsh situation.

All the educational experiments of the eighteenth century, and many of the nineteenth, found a major impediment to be the lack of suitable teachers. The society insisted that they be drawn from the Church of England, sober and upright citizens and obviously literate themselves. Many came, therefore, from the ranks of vicars and curates. There were some notable scholars among them: William Gambold, author of an English–Welsh dictionary; Thomas Jenkins, the first missionary to go abroad from the diocese of St David's; Lewis Evans, a translator. But Sir John Philipps reached the conclusion long before the days of Kay-Shuttleworth in the 1830s that the only real answer was to found a training college for teachers, an aspiration not realized by the society. Nevertheless, a remarkably well-structured system was erected, to the extent of building in an inspection procedure. As with the Welsh Trust, English was normally the medium of instruction in the schools, although there was no attempt to suppress the speaking of Welsh. But there was a little more flexibility than was usual in that a dozen schools in north Wales were conducted in the Welsh language.

Up to a point this wholly voluntary, philanthropic effort was, within the terms of its religious and social purpose, remarkably successful, at least in its early years. Between 1699 and 1714, ninety-six schools were established in Wales. Although growth slowed after this, there is evidence of 157 schools in Wales between 1699 and 1740, not all of which had been founded by the SPCK.

As always, tensions were evident in a voluntary organization. There were worries that children of the lower orders were being overeducated, and the commercial view was that education of such children was a mistake. The High Church and Low Church factions within the society struggled for control. Some of the leaders of the movement were suspected of Jacobitism at a time of political upheaval and the first Jacobite rebellion in 1715. All these ideological and political clashes could easily be used by self-interested factions to generate dissent and suspicion about motives. But from the perspective of those for whom the education was provided there were also innate weaknesses. Apart from some of the practical elements of their schooling there was very little which would make a difference to the earning potential of those who attended. There were endless demands on children other than attendance – jobs to be done on the farm and siblings to be helped, so that short stay and absenteeism were perennial problems.

The leaders of the SPCK were as aware as those of the Welsh Trust that educational progress was dependent on the supply of reading material. This alone could provide the necessary stimulus to the spread of literacy and ensure the establishment of a tradition of a reading public. John Vaughan of Derllys was a leading contributor to the committee which organized the reissue of Welsh Trust books, written in easily accessible language for the mass of the people and including two editions of the Welsh Bible. Diocesan libraries were also set up for clergy and their parishioners at Cowbridge, Carmarthen, Bangor and St Asaph.

Here, then, was an educational effort similar to that of the Welsh Trust, though with greater resources and extended ambition. Of course the ambition was greater than the achievement. The subsequent work of Griffith Jones was indication enough of how much remained to be done for those who wished to bring the means of salvation to the mass of the Welsh population. Nevertheless, the work of the SPCK, significant in itself, reinforced the tradition and thrust of voluntary effort, and aided a new mass voluntary effort launched in the 1730s.

Griffith Jones was rector of Llanddowror in Carmarthenshire, a man motivated by the continuing ignorance of less affluent contemporaries and its consequences on their eternal souls. He was also well aware of both the achievement of the SPCK and its limitations. It was obvious that there would never be sufficient finance for school buildings, so logic decreed spending the available money on teachers. He therefore suggested to the organizers of the SPCK that a new type of school be established in Wales which would be free, conducted in Welsh and teaching only the essentials for the purpose in hand: a basic ability to read. The teaching of writing, arithmetic and manual skills was to be prohibited, although in practice this was not always observed. These conditions would allow the education on offer to operate with the minimum possible income and therefore reach out to the widest number of people. The schools would stand a chance of being effective because of the common language and limited parental sacrifice involved. His idea, not to be gainsaid within his own terms of reference, was that it was far better to educate a large number of people than to provide extended education for a few. The schools themselves were to be held for about three months at a time when demand for both child and adult labour was least, particularly over the winter months. The need for accommodation was to be met by existing resources, the vestry of a parish church, a hired room or, if there was no alternative, a barn or outhouse.

There is no evidence of a shortage of teachers, although many of them were unable to read themselves until taught by Griffith Jones. Recruits were given a few weeks' training at a cottage in Llanddowror and then sent off to run their schools. Although they were paid very little – £5 per annum was not untypical – many were very able. Their objective, as with the SPCK schools, was religious, but more restricted in terms of curriculum. The basis of teaching was reading, particularly the Bible and the Catechism. Indeed, within the limited time-span of each school, even the effective teaching of reading was an ambitious undertaking. But the saving grace – literally, for those who believed – was that teaching was in Welsh and therefore had the greatest chance of being effective.

Another similarity with the two former educational movements was that effectiveness was predicated on the availability of books in the Welsh language. Since this was an entirely voluntary movement, both the payment of teachers and the provision of books was wholly dependent on the generosity of patrons of the circulating school scheme, and Griffith Jones's indispensable role lay in his constant quest for funds from sponsors who were informed of the progress of his schools through the publication of *Welch Piety*. This was an annual report which appeared between 1737 and 1761 and contained a prefatory letter from Griffith Jones, together with statistics of the schools. The proverb on the title-page was reminiscent of Jesuit philosophy: 'Train up a child in the way he should go and when he is old he will not depart from it.'

The purpose and philosophy of the schools are amply elucidated in the successive reports, and the religious objective of the schools made perfectly clear: '[the Catechism] was designed to fix better in their memories the doctrines and duties such texts of Scripture contained in them.' Griffith Jones argued that the SPCK schools had had limited success, so that the mass of the population remained in ignorance because they could not read:

> can you good Sir verily believe that most of those . . . who came to be instructed in the Welsh charity schools knew neither the creed, the Ten

Commandments, nor as much as the Lord's Prayer before? . . . will not these poor wretches (unless some or other pity their blindness) continue to walk according to the course of this world and according to the Prince of the power of the air, the spirit that now worketh in the children of disobedience.

Jones ascribed this ignorance partly to the state of the Anglican Church in Wales – his own Church – and its lack of effective preaching.

Welch Piety also provides a comprehensive overview of how the schools were run, how the money was spent, teaching methods, attendance, staffing, books used, the age of the pupils and their poverty. Jones had to confront the language problem and the objections of his English benefactors to the use of Welsh, but he was able to counter such objections by pointing to the lack of success of the SPCK schools as a result of their using English.

Sir John Philipps had been his earliest, very generous, benefactor but he died in 1737 and Jones's most constant helpmeet was Madam Bevan of Laugharne who carried on the movement after Griffith Jones's death. But Jones would have made little headway had he relied solely on Welsh patrons. He managed to attract the interest and donations of a range of English philanthropists, doctors, members of the aristocracy, Church divines and bankers, many with Methodist connections, despite con-temporary attitudes to the Welsh language which were distinctly unflattering.

The circulating schools were among the most important educational experiments anywhere in Europe in the eighteenth century. Between 1731 and 1761 it has been estimated that 3,325 schools were held and as many as 250,000 scholars – something like half the population of children and adults – taught to read. Within this limited definition, it is hardly an exaggeration to say that the schools were responsible for making Wales a literate nation, and the fame of the schools was widespread throughout Europe. The system obviously enabled a mass reading of the Bible and access to the means of salvation. However, the spread of reading skills on this scale not only rested on the provision of religious literature in Welsh but also fostered a demand for it, so pointing once again to the centrality of the purity of biblical Welsh to the preservation of the spoken and literary language. The Bible became a desired and precious possession in innumerable households across Wales, among even the poorest sections of society. It was this widespread biblical education interacting with the Methodist revival in a mass movement, rather than the more restricted social appeal of traditional Dissenting denominations, which prepared the way for the vastly increased demand for pious denominational literature which reached its apogee in the mid-nineteenth century. It also prepared the way for the success of the Sunday schools. Here, then, was a major educational experiment, and it was a unique to Wales, covering parts of all the regions, although more concentrated in the south. Itinerant teachers were not a wholly new concept – there had been examples in the Scottish Highlands – but there had been nothing like this scale of endeavour.

Given their limited objectives, the success of the circulating schools as an experiment in mass education was unprecedented. They remain the only educational initiative on such a scale unique to Wales, and must place Griffith Jones in the forefront of eighteenth-century Welsh educational organizers, if not theorists. It remains the fact that none of the conventional explanations of effectiveness in educational experiment sufficiently explain it. The more Whiggish interpretations, in their Welsh context, would indicate that this was a concomitant indication, with Methodism, of an inherently spiritually inclined and moral population satisfying an inner religious hunger. This, of course, only raises the larger question of why Methodism experienced such dramatic growth in the eighteenth century. Again the Whig interpretations highlight the inadequacies of the Anglican Church – absentee bishops, the insistence on the use of the English language, poverty and lack of education amongst the priesthood – against the dynamic, inspirational, native Welsh-language leadership of Methodism. However, the simplicity of such an explanation has long been shown to be more the product of Methodist hagiography than strict historical accuracy and, for it to have any credence, the interpretation must be substantially widened.

It is certainly arguable that both the success of Methodism and the enthusiastic reception for the circulating schools rested at least partly on an inchoate sense of the dislocation of traditional Welsh society in the eighteenth century. This was certainly not on the scale caused by industrialization at the end of the century, but there were substantial changes in traditional rural society. In the first quarter of the eighteenth century, as the incidence of bachelordom and childlessness among traditional gentry families increased in unprecedented fashion, we have noted that many English and some Scottish families took over estates in Wales. There was increased polarization between the wealthier gentry and smaller landholders who often found their land eaten up by the great estates. Given that all the Welsh counties were dominated by a small number of landowners, with vast resources of wealth and property, who had been the traditional leaders of their communities as landlords, administrators of justice and the Poor Law, the objects of deference and loyalty on whose economic position and good management the mass of the population, tenant farmers and labourers depended, the void created by Anglicization and absenteeism of the traditional leaders of society was bound to create strains and breed uncertainty. It may well be that it was this social vacuum that Methodism and the circulating schools helped to fill.

The counterpoint provided by the traditional Marxist explanation for the success of the circulating schools is even more obviously inadequate than the notion of a natural progression based on the innate inner enlightenment of the Welsh. The idea that the education on offer from the circulating schools, or from the Sunday schools later in the century, was an attempt by the social elite to foist their own values and views of the traditional social structure on those below them is untenable. It is, of course, true that, as with the SPCK, the philanthropists who supported the circulating schools had every interest in replicating the social mores and structure which safeguarded their own position, although this, too, is a complex issue, since correspondence to the SPCK and to *Welch Piety* expressed anxiety about the effects of educating the poor beyond their station. What is certain is that the circulating schools, in particular, were not forced on the poorer sections of society but met a pent-up and unprecedented demand. The mass of the Welsh people were very keen to be provided with at least this level of education. They shared the objectives of the providers.

The contemporary spiritual, and consequent educational, hunger of the Welsh has generated its own folklore. In 1800 a young girl of sixteen set out from the remote village of Llanfihangel-y-Pennant in Merioneth to walk more than twenty-five miles to the town of Bala. She had informed her worried, poverty-stricken parents that she was determined to acquire her own copy of the Bible, and she had heard that a man by the name of Thomas Charles was distributing them. Her inadequate shoes were soon worn out on this long trek over the hills and she completed her journey barefoot. She arrived in Bala, eventually found Charles and was ushered into his presence. She told her story, only for Charles to tell her that such was the demand, and so inadequate the supply to meet it, that he did not have a Bible to spare. After her epic journey it seemed as if Mary Jones would have to return home disappointed. She burst into tears, and Thomas Charles was so moved that he took one of his own copies so that Mary returned to her village the proud possessor of one of the great man's Bibles. Charles was determined that such devotion had to be rewarded in future and was spurred into urging the founding of the British and Foreign Bible Society on his London colleagues. The society came into existence in 1804 with the mission of providing Bibles not only for Wales but also for the whole world. By 1806 the supply to Wales was deemed adequate. Mary Jones's Bible is still in the society's possession.

There has been much discussion ever since about the veracity of aspects of this story, told in regular reprints and still distributed as a Sunday-school prize as late as the 1950s. The consensus is that in essence the story is true and that it is certainly evidence of a wider truth, one we have already encountered in the history of the circulating schools, that there was a vast demand for the Bible in Welsh in the eighteenth century and for the education which would allow people to read it. The Bible occupied a place of honour in countless simple farm cottages across Wales. It is no accident that Thomas Charles is regarded as a Welsh hero. His statue, Bible in outstretched hand as if on offer to the supplicant, dominates the main street of Bala. In Charles, the interdependence of religious literature and educational endeavour is more explicit than ever.

Charles was born in the village of St Clears in 1755 and his parents determined that he should enter the Church. He attended school in Llanddowror, the centre of Griffith Jones's pioneering work, thence to the Presbyterian Academy in Carmarthen, one of those pioneering institutions of advanced education which provided some opportunity for those of humbler means in Wales. At the age of eighteen he heard Daniel Rowland, one of the triumvirate of the greatest Methodist leaders in Wales, preach in Pembrokeshire and was inordinately impressed.

He was then given sufficient money to attend Jesus College, Oxford, the college most associated with Wales. One of the hagiographical stories has it that he walked from his home in St Clears, west Carmarthenshire, to Oxford because he did not have the stagecoach fare. He graduated in 1778 and took up a curacy in Somerset for six years before returning to Wales as a curate near Bala, a post from which he was dismissed because of his Methodist leanings. He then became an itinerant preacher, something which, as a curate, should have been denied him because of the restriction of preaching to one's own parish. His work was then concentrated in two areas. First, he became the leader of Methodism in north Wales, particularly significant because its strength hitherto had been concentrated more in the south. Second, sharing the contemporary concern among Methodist leaders for education, he experimented with setting up different types of schools. In 1785 he tried circulating schools on the Griffith Jones model, training teachers in his own home, then sending them into neighbouring villages to teach. The schools were generally held in the evenings but gradually changed to Sunday afternoon sessions. This was a considerable benefit to parents in not requiring them to forgo the pittance which children might earn in order to allow them this modicum of education. Nor, of course, was adult attendance inhibited by loss of wages.

This notion of holding schools on Sundays had first been tried by Robert Raikes in Gloucester in 1780, and a Baptist minister in south Wales, Morgan John Rhys, whose revolutionary fervour had first emerged in his idea of being a missionary to revolutionary France, set about planning Sunday schools in his area. He produced a comprehensive plan for their organization in his journal, *Y Cylch-grawn Cymraeg*, though his effectiveness was blunted by his revolutionary ideals, which led to the suppression of the journal. So it was Thomas Charles whose name has always been associated with the Sunday-school movement in Wales.

Like all his forerunners who tried to educate the ordinary people of Wales, Charles faced enormous difficulties. The hills and mountains of north Wales made journeys hazardous. As always, there was great difficulty in accumulating funds to establish a sufficient spread of schools. As we have seen, the supply of Bibles, the staple reading matter, was inadequate. Teachers were paid poorly, perhaps £12 a year, little more than an agricultural labourer, although they might be provided with food by those they taught. Charles also had to face vehement criticism for holding schools on a Sunday, which for his opponents, including many in his adopted town, constituted breaking the Sabbath.

Nevertheless, by 1787, a small network of very successful schools had been established, and by 1789 was properly organized. Raikes had provided a template for these schools, with the simple objectives of learning to read through study of the Bible and learning by rote the simple truths of the faith through preordained question and answer – the Catechism. However, the Welsh Sunday schools differed in that they continued to cater for adults as well as children and, of course, were held in the Welsh language – crucial to their success. Furthermore, the context was different in that, while there were Anglican Sunday schools, the majority were to be particularly associated with the Nonconformist denominations, so much stronger in Wales than in England in the nineteenth century. The shortage of Bibles was inevitably highlighted by the success of the Sunday schools. Much of Charles's energy was devoted to acquiring Bibles and distributing them around the circulating and Sunday schools.

Charles, like Griffith Jones, was an organizing genius and, within the terms of a mission entirely appropriate in its context, extremely successful. His object was not education for its own sake but, as with Griffith Jones, the saving of souls through knowledge of the Bible. His objective was the same in Scotland where he helped to establish Sunday schools, or in Tahiti, because Charles was instrumental in organizing foreign missionary ventures including that of John Davies, one of his former pupils and a teacher employee, who sailed on the first British and Foreign Bible Society missionary ship, the *Duff*, to Tahiti.

Within Wales, Charles's Sunday-school initiative proved to be profoundly significant and enduring. As with Griffith Jones, we need to accept a limited definition of literacy because the overwhelming concentration was on learning to read. But the combined effect of the circulating schools and the Sunday schools was to allow the majority of the people of Wales to read their own language and to attain, for members of their class, an unprecedented knowledge of theological issues and the ability to deal with them in an intense and mature manner, unlike anything achieved by their peers in England. We have the evidence of the 1847 report of the education commissioners to testify to that. Relying on the Methodist dynamic for their early achievements, they became inextricably bound up with fostering Nonconformity and its associated chapel-founding zeal in the first half of the nineteenth century, so that soon the newly built chapels were able to provide accommodation for the Sunday schools in their schoolrooms, a tradition which has continued to the present day. They played a major part in defining Wales as an overwhelmingly Nonconformist country by the mid-nineteenth century. By 1847, 80 per cent of pupils who attended Sunday schools in Wales went to Nonconformist establishments, while nearly half of those who attended day schools went to Anglican day schools. The Sunday schools were all-age religious communities which were, in the nineteenth century, to branch out into social and leisure activities centred on the chapels of all the Welsh denominations.

The historiography of eighteenth-century educational initiatives in Wales has taken on a life of its own. During the nineteenth century, Charles Edwards pressed the notion of Wales as a chosen race, deserving the protection of the Deity, which manifested itself in the translation of the Bible into Welsh in 1588 and its distribution across Wales by Thomas Charles. Stories with a far less secure base than that of Mary Jones centred on the extension of divine protection to Charles himself. On one occasion he is supposed to have been returning across the mountain to Bala, a journey which took many hours because of the snow. In holding the reins, a thumb had been exposed and he got frostbite. The thumb had to be amputated and Charles fell seriously ill. A meeting of his friends prayed that he be granted fifteen more years of life to pursue his providential work. From that moment Charles improved and lived exactly that further period.

One stage on, as we have seen, is a more acceptable Methodist interpretation: in the context of the economic exploitation, social prejudice and injustice inherent in the Anglican Church, educational initiatives of the eighteenth century were a distinctively Welsh response to an alien, unsympathetic and ineffective religious order unable and unwilling to meet the needs of a spiritual people. Such historiography is distorted but, for whatever reason, the messages of Dissent and Methodism had their own receptive constituents. The latter encompassed an unprecedented number of the poorer members of society, though of course many were left out.

The success of the circulating schools and the Sunday schools reminds us that popular education was not the product of formal, state-sponsored schools. These voluntary efforts were inevitably of limited scope and reflected a rigidly demarcated society. The concept of education for gentry and aristocracy remained that of classical humanism, though with the Renaissance ideal of the educated gentleman substantially diluted in what was on offer in public schools and universities. It was certainly not a vocational education, but the vestiges of a philosophy of enlightenment and good breeding provided a rationale. Some of the philanthropists, land-owners and professional people who provided the money to run Griffith Jones's circulating schools had reservations about educating the mass of the people at all, fearing that they might rise above their station in life, and be introduced to subversive ideas – particularly towards the end of the eighteenth century.

Private philanthropy nevertheless continued, to the extent that seventy-nine elementary schools in Wales were endowed between 1700 and 1800. They were usually lay endowments, spread across all the counties, with most in Denbighshire. Some were provided by women, and mark a limited extension of educational opportunity for poorer girls in the eighteenth century. As with other charity schools, the motive behind these elementary-school foundations was religious and moral. They did not require lavish facilities and were still normally held in one schoolroom, though two-storey, purpose-built accommodation became commoner towards the end of the eighteenth century. Most schools were still held in churches, church vestries or in buildings on Church property.

Long before state intervention, therefore, it proved possible to construct an educational system which meshed with the desires of ordinary people without impinging so far on their economic limitations as to nullify its impact. The ideals of the providers and the demands of the masses in the eighteenth century synchronized in a way which proved impossible without compulsion in the following century.

In 1761 Griffith Jones died. By that year, four ironworks had been established in the environs of Merthyr Tydfil, a small parish of about 900 people at the head of the Taff valley in Glamorgan. These ironworks, along with those at the heads of the Monmouthshire Valleys, particularly in Blaenafon, were to herald the beginning of the greatest social trans-formation which has ever encompassed the Welsh people. Early on, the great ironworks were visited by the best artists of the day, attracted by the primeval industrial power which had been unleashed. By 1830, Merthyr had become the largest town in Wales, its scale unprecedented. Ultimately, the population balance between the regions of Wales was transformed, with the majority living in the two counties of Glamorgan and Monmouthshire. The social dislocation accompanying this transforma-tion, as well as an unprecedented growth in population generally, is a well-known feature of the history of Wales – overcrowded housing, inadequate sanitation breeding disease, lack of recreational facilities, sporadic unemployment without any state or communal support. The conditions in the countryside, under the impact of rising population and pressure on land, were, if anything, worse. Social strains here found expression in traditional responses of fighting against injustice. In the 1790s there were sporadic riots against the price of corn, and there were risings in industrial Merthyr in 1813 and, most famously, in 1831.

Successive governments, in the context of a war of independence in America and a revolution in France, accompanied by the spread of revolutionary ideas in Britain by, for example, the London Corresponding Society, were worried, particularly after the outbreak of war against France which lasted until 1815. There was a genuine fear of revolution. Inevitably, the state was concerned with social control in a society in which traditional means of achieving it were outdated. At its most draconian this took the form of using troops to quell riots and risings, complemented by penal legislation. But there had always been far more subtle means of social conditioning, particularly by means of religion and education. It might seem inevitable in retrospect that state intervention in education must be the consequence of industrialization, but the process was not linear and, in the form it took, by no means inevitable. Popular state education across Europe was not the predetermined outcome of the Industrial Revolution – we have seen that Prussia had a state system long before it industrialized – and the interplay of secular and religious, private and public solutions produced in England and Wales had no parallel elsewhere. Mass education and compulsory attendance were eventually to be common in the industrial world, as were substantial elements of the curriculum, but the structures were, and remain, different.

Since the sixteenth century the established Church had seen itself as having the central role in providing education. The original intention of the SPCK was to provide a school teaching Anglican doctrines in every parish. This national system of voluntary mass education was never realized, and the SPCK gave up the idea, certainly after 1725. The social changes consequent on the mass movement of population, particularly apparent in Wales, ensured that any such provision would in any case be totally inadequate. At the same time, Wales was more a Nonconformist than an Anglican nation, which ensured that any attempt to impose an Anglican-based system would meet stern resistance from Nonconformist leaders. But there were no constitutional means, even if there had been the will, by which the Welsh could devise a system appropriate to their situation because Wales was at the mercy of the religious persuasions and predilections of the Westminster Parliament. The religious difficulty had been apparent in the work of the eighteenth-century charitable societies; it was to bedevil the deliberations of the early nineteenth century as well.

Only in retrospect is it obvious that, by the end of the eighteenth century, voluntary efforts to make the mass of the people literate, whether for religious or social reasons, were inadequate. It was certainly not accepted at the time. At the beginning of the nineteenth century, in a changing social context, came a new burst of voluntary activity. Not only was the state unprepared to view the provision of education as anything other than a philanthropic activity, but also there was a deep suspicion among all the religious denominations of any hint of state provision and the trend towards a secular education which that denoted. This was coupled with a belief among the majority in government, which reflected the views of the upper and middle classes, that a religiously based education would be most likely to inculcate respectability, deference and acceptability of the social order, and avoid the danger that the working classes would be educated above their station by being provided with the means to try to better themselves at the expense of their social superiors. Even so, the clerical lobby was not the only protagonist in a debate changed out of all recognition by industrialization and urbanization. For example, by the 1830s there was a complex alliance of followers of Bentham's argument that the state should provide a secular education for its citizens, though their objective was the same – the preservation of the social order in the face of such social disharmony as was represented by trade unionism and Chartism.

At the beginning of the nineteenth century a Quaker, Joseph Lancaster, set up schools in Borough Road, London, dependent on benefactors, open to all, and non-denominational in the sense that the only religious text was the Bible. Additionally, he trained men and women to teach and employed a system, the monitorial system, which allowed the schools to be run as cheaply as possible. This method of instruction was associated with a system of rewards for achievement in the shape of, for example, books and caps. The curriculum of the schools centred round the teaching of reading, writing and arithmetic, largely by rote, to be supplemented by non-denominational religious instruction.

Lancaster himself played a leading role in disseminating his ideas all over England and Wales. His planning was detailed and included specifications for the ideal school building, for example, accommodation of 70 by 32 feet for 320 pupils. Such purpose-built schools were rare in Wales, where they were more likely to be held in adapted single-storey stone buildings in which children would sit on benches facing the master, who would supervise monitors.

Schools on Lancaster's model were established in only a few places in south Wales. In 1806/7 Lancaster visited Cardiff, Neath, Swansea and Carmarthen. His links with Swansea were close, given that Richard Phillips, born in Swansea in 1756, and an ardent London Quaker, was closely involved in the management of Lancasterian schools. In 1806, representatives of some of the best-known and wealthiest Swansea families with strong Quaker connections set up the Swansea Society for the Education of the Children of the Poor on Lancasterian lines. The objective was to establish two schools, one for boys and one for girls, to teach the three Rs, together with moral and social responsibility. The school for boys opened in Swansea in 1806, the first outside London, and was replaced by a new school in 1808. Subscriptions led to the founding of a girls' school in 1808, replaced by a much better building in 1811. The curriculum for the girls was similar to that of boys, although in addition they were taught needlework. The objective was to produce good domestic servants.

Quaker industrialists organized the establishment of a school in Cardiff on Lancasterian lines in 1808 and another associated with the ironworks in Neath Abbey. There was less interest in the Lancasterian method in north Wales but schools started in Wrexham and Tremadoc. Schools on the Lancasterian model, but with local organization and subscription, were set up in Brecon, where there was a separate school for boys and girls, Usk, Abergavenny and Machen. There are instances, therefore, of girls being catered for, though the majority of schools were for boys.

Lancaster resigned in 1814 but had taken the initiative which led in the same year to the founding of the British and Foreign Schools Society in London. The movement, intending to cater for children of parents unable to buy their children an education in any kind of fee-paying school, did not have a major impact in Wales, despite its non-denominational stance, at least until the 1840s. Its ambitions were sorely restricted by lack of money, with the result that its sponsorship of new schools in Wales, despite requests for funds and information from various parts, was negligible. Indeed, its chief contribution to schools connected with it was to supply subsidized equipment such as books, pencils and slates. The limited impact of the British Society is evident from its report in 1820 that, since 1806, fifteen schools had been set up in Wales, and a few teachers had been trained in Borough Road. Essentially, this was because the society was a purveyor and coordinator of information about a teaching structure and teaching materials rather than a body with the means to found schools. The money for the establishment and running of schools in a locality was largely dependent on local philanthropic activity, particularly from the local Quaker community, and this was limited.

The boys' school in Swansea, itself a centre for training teachers in the Lancasterian system, was a pre-eminent example of what might have been possible in terms of its free, non-denominational appeal and its efficiency in teaching reading and writing, but funds were so limited that the rival Anglican school movement made far greater headway across Wales.

Swansea also provided a less edifying example of the religious tensions which could be generated within these voluntary movements. The girls' school, founded by Richard Phillips, one of the staunchest of Lancaster's allies, alienated him by leaning strongly towards the teachings of the established Church. Phillips responded by founding another girls' school in Swansea which was wholly non-denominational. There were other associated schools, such as those in Newport and Carmarthen, opened in 1814, but there were also retrograde steps, such as the charging of a 2d per week fee in the Neath Abbey schools from 1828, a practice which was repeated in a number of other British Society schools in Wales as financial difficulties mounted.

The Church of England had always believed itself to be the ordained provider of charity-school education for the masses, and that tradition continued into the nineteenth century. The Anglicans established the National Society for Promoting the Education of the Poor in the Principles of the Established Church in 1811 to counteract Lancaster's non-denominational initiative. This led to unseemly bickering between Anglicans and supporters of Joseph Lancaster as to who had instigated the monitorial system, because it was an Anglican clergyman, Dr Andrew Bell who first used it in India in 1789.

The National Society shared the original aim of the SPCK – to provide an Anglican school in every parish – and used reading materials supplied by that body. The objectives in the schools were similar: to teach boys and girls the rudiments of the scriptures and religious instruction, to teach them to read the Bible, to master simple writing and arithmetic and, in some schools, to provide craft instruction. The other crucial element was that the schools should instil in pupils good behaviour, self-discipline and a respect for their betters, along with an acceptance that so many were their betters in a highly hierarchical society. Although this blend of religious and social purpose varied between different areas in Wales and England, it was central to the purpose of all charitable education.

The essential pattern in Wales, as elsewhere, was for private individuals or diocesan committees to establish schools, often financed from parish funds, which were then affiliated to the National Society and run on monitorial lines at least until the 1840s and the advent of the pupil-teacher system. The first in Wales were those in Penley and Talwrn Green in Flintshire, starting in 1812. In that year, too, the dynamic Dean Cotton of Bangor was the driving force behind setting up the first diocesan organiza-tion for establishing National schools. By the end of 1814, ten schools had started work in Wales, twenty-three by 1816, though many of these were existing parish schools which now affiliated to the National Society. Nevertheless, the National Society had galvanized diocesan committees into strenuous and productive fund-raising which was increasingly complemented by the society's grants, with the resulting education concentrated just as much on girls as on boys. Not only did the National schools provide weekday education, but also many opened on Sundays to provide an Anglican alternative to compete with the highly successful Nonconformist Sunday schools which were attracting children from Church of England families.

There were many parallels between the two societies. The demand from the central body for funds outstripped supply. While there was a tendency in the early days for the schools of both societies to be free, most soon charged fees. Schools affiliated to both societies employed the monitorial system, which meant that a school could be run by one master, sometimes employed in conjunction with his wife. After the provision of the school building, paying the master was the greatest expense, even though remuneration was so poor. In Carmarthen Boys' National School, for example, the master was paid £40 per annum, supplemented by what he could obtain from pupils. Another common element was that many teachers were still not trained.

In one respect the National Society had enormous advantages over the non-denominational society in its capacity to raise funds and therefore establish schools. Compared with the British Society's handful of schools started by 1833, National schools numbered 146, educating nearly 100 pupils each. By 1846, of the 1,100 Church schools in Wales, 377 were affiliated to the National Society. The Church of England, of course, had something of a start in the provision of schools, but the disparity between the numbers of Church and Nonconformist schools in a country with the weight of religious observance favouring the Nonconformists is an indication of the tensions inherent in the politics of educational provision.

Even so, many rural parishes did not have their own school, and in the maelstrom of the industrial south-east of Wales, in particular, neither society had the resources to make a concerted attack on the lack of educational facilities. They were beset by the perennial problems of limited resources, shortage of adequately trained teachers, and absentee children. Even if education was free, the incidental expenses, particularly those of forgoing the tiny wage which even the youngest children might earn in the most appalling conditions underground in the coal mines or in dangerous ironworks, were often too great. Especially after the publication of the 1847 education report, rivalry between Anglicans and Noncon-formists was exacerbated, particularly so when the Anglicans insisted on teaching their Catechism in all National Society schools.

The result was that day-school education reached proportionately far fewer children in Wales than in England in the first half of the nineteenth century. On W. B. Stephens's figures, in 1818, 4.8 per cent of the total population attended day schools in Wales compared with 6.6 per cent in

England and 10.9 per cent in Scotland. The Welsh figure had risen to 8.7 per cent on roll in 1851, though 7 per cent were in attendance on census day.

What other criteria might be used to judge the success of voluntary effort before 1870? The circulating schools and the Sunday schools allowed the majority of the Welsh population to read. Writing was another matter. The ability of brides and grooms to sign their names in marriage registers, though these figures are only available reliably from the 1830s, tells a different story. The figures for 1855 bear out the picture of day schooling in Wales depicted in the Blue Books of 1847. In that year the figure for Wales was only 46 per cent, compared with that for England and Wales of 65 per cent and Scotland's 83 per cent. By 1870, the gap between Wales and the collated figure for England and Wales had lessened – 65 per cent in Wales compared with the combined figure of 76 per cent.

It was the middle classes, in alliance with both the Anglican and Nonconformist churches, who had infused enthusiasm and capital into day-school provision in England. That is why the absence of a populous middle class in Wales was the focus for comment. The most extensive sections of the population of Wales by 1846 were iron and coal miners, metalworkers and rural labourers, occupational groups at the bottom of the literacy tables across England and Wales, when this was measured by the ability to write. If the jump were to be made from mastery of reading to the ability to write, vastly greater effort would be needed in Wales than in England to compensate for these social differences through efficient and ubiquitous day schooling.

The schools established under the auspices of the two societies are often seen as a link between the charity-school movements of the previous century and the state system of elementary education which now seems an inevitable consequence of the 1870 Education Act. In fact, the schools of the two societies were firmly in the former camp, although they differed in important respects from their predecessors. In particular, the maximum number of children were taught with the minimum expense by means of the monitorial system, whereby the master taught the most able senior pupils who, in turn, taught the younger pupils. This was not a new idea, but it was now elevated into a system which encompassed not only those schools affiliated to the societies but also many existing schools, particularly those run by Anglicans. In Penley National School in Flintshire, for example, there were three classes. The lowest committed the Lord's Prayer and the alphabet to memory and learned the National Society's work cards. In the next class the children learned to write on slates, read a religious text and learn the Catechism. The top class read from the Bible and did simple number work. Institutionalized rote learning as a method of instruction was particularly ineffective in Wales because the language most used was English, resulting in the incomprehension which formed such a significant element in the indictment of Welsh education made by the 1847 Report of the Commissioners into the State of Education in Wales.

By the time that report was published there was an embryonic state system of elementary education in England and Wales because, in 1839, all those schools which received some grant from the government became subject to government inspection. A new era for both politics and education had dawned in Wales. The first tentative steps had come in 1833 in the shape of a government grant of £20,000 for school building under the approval of either the British or National societies. At the time, this was intended to be a limited initiative, and so it turned out as far as British Society activity in Wales was concerned. Local money had to be raised for any area to qualify for a grant, and the poverty of the mass of the population, combined with the indifference, even hostility, of the great majority of landowners, militated against this. The result was that there were few requests for assistance with school building in Wales during the following decade. Between 1835 and 1840, for example, only fourteen localities across north and south Wales received building grants to open British Society schools, though numbers of applications increased in the following three years.

At this point, also, the social impact of industrialization was becoming increasingly evident and worrying to the government. The Merthyr rising of 1831 and Chartist activity culminating in a march on Newport in 1839 which was almost certainly intended to herald an attempt at revolution, concentrated government thinking on attempts to exert greater social control, particularly on south Wales. The involvement of the state in education in the shape of its annual grants, and the establishment of the Committee of Council in 1839 which took over the administration of grants and provided a mechanism for assessing the spending of state money, began to produce a mass of evidence about the impact of industrialization. The most extensive, of course, came in the report of the Education Commissioners in 1847 which will be analysed in the next chapter. But already, in 1839/40, Her Majesty's Inspector Tremenheere had outlined the parameters of the problem in the most fraught area, the mining districts of south Wales. He found that British Society schools were in a very small minority. As a result, the government, through the Committee of Council, became more proactive in attempting to influence industrialists into sponsoring schools under the auspices of either of the societies. There was also preferential treatment for the mining areas. For example, a long-delayed application to build a school at Ynyscedwyn, near Ystradgynlais, was now approved by the Committee of Council which provided a very substantial £250, an unprecedented 50 per cent grant.

Even so, by 1843, there were still probably fewer than thirty British Society schools throughout Wales.

It was not only the state which was concerned about trends in the provision of education in Wales. Nonconformist leaders, in particular, were extremely apprehensive over the educational alliance between government and the Anglican Church which seemed to be enshrined in Graham's Factory Bill of 1834. There was also an awareness, generated by inspectors' reports in particular, of the inadequacy of provision in so many parts of Wales, rural as well as industrial. In much of rural Wales there was a virtual monopoly of Anglican schools while, in industrial areas, the speed and extent of social change had made it impossible to provide sufficient schooling. The religious divide, coupled with utilitarian and idealist theories of society which generated considerable debate, particularly among London Welshmen, about the provision and place of universities and schools in society, found its most obvious individual expression in the work of Hugh Owen, a prominent Welsh civil servant working in London. His 'Letter to the Welsh People' in 1843 was the practical expression of the apprehensions of his group about the state of education, and he saw the answer at school level as a network of British Schools across the whole of Wales. In many ways, the kind of organization he envisaged resembled that which, at the end of the century, successfully resulted in the intermediate school system. He hoped for a British School Society in every county, with local committees in every district responsible for finding funds, building a school, appointing a master and running the school. There was a massive response, and the British Society financed a local agent, the Revd John Phillips, to work in neglected north Wales. Certainly the pace quickened. By 1846, north Wales had seen the establishment of thirty-one schools, with another forty-eight across the whole of Wales by the middle of the following year.

A parallel Nonconformist movement based on true voluntaryist principles, resulted in a conference in Llandovery in 1845 which proposed establishing non-denominational schools in Wales, entirely free of government aid, to be in the charge of teachers trained not under the aegis of the British Society at Borough Road but in Wales. In 1846 a Normal school for the education of children and the training of teachers was set up in Brecon. Owen followed this up in 1846 when he was instrumental in founding the Cambrian Education Society in London to formalize the setting up of British Society schools in Wales. In many ways it was a Welsh version of the British and Foreign School Society in that its objectives were to help organize and coordinate local efforts to build, staff and run schools on the British Society model, but it had an uphill task.

To Griffith Jones and Thomas Charles it was as crucial to save the souls of adults as of children. Later in the eighteenth century and into the nineteenth, changing economic contexts, particularly industrial growth, combined with traditional philanthropic concern with poorer members of the population who were prepared to help themselves, brought into existence a different kind of adult education from that of the circulating schools, the Sunday schools or the Nonconformist academies. The mechanics' institutes originated in Scotland, starting with John Anderson's lecture programmes, continuing with George Birkbeck's lectures to audiences of over 500 mechanics each week, and eventually developing into the Glasgow Mechanics' Institute, complemented by the Edinburgh Society of Arts. In 1823 the London Mechanics' Institute, the first in England, was established, Birkbeck being one of the founders. Although most of the money came from the wealthy middle class, two-thirds of the committee of managers had to be working class. Three years later, now Birkbeck College, the institute became part of the University of London.

In that same year of 1826, a Trades and Mechanics' Institute was established in Swansea, with precisely the same objectives as the London Institute, that is, instruction in the various branches of science and useful knowledge by means of books, machines, model workshops, lectures and elementary schools for adults where they might be taught arithmetic, algebra, geometry, trigonometry, architecture, mensuration and navigation. The Swansea experiment had a fitful history, closing in the 1830s, with attempts to revive it only partially successful. Indeed, the mechanics'-institute movement spread far more slowly in Wales than in either England or Scotland. Of nearly 250 in Great Britain by 1840, only five were founded in Wales – at Swansea, Bridgend (1829), Dowlais (1830), Pembroke Dock (1832) and Llandeilo (1839).

They were entirely dependent on charitable funds, supplied mainly from well-to-do members of the middle class and strongly supported by Nonconformists. Although Nonconformity was such a strength in Wales, there was a less substantial professional body of manufacturers, merchants, bankers, doctors and journalists to emulate England and Scotland. Nevertheless, industrialists and businessmen did become involved, the Swansea institute being founded largely through the influence of Matthew Moggeridge, businessman and later mayor of Swansea, and Lewis Weston Dillwyn, Fellow of the Royal Society, naturalist, owner of the Cambrian pottery works and a Member of Parliament.

In the 1840s a working men's institute was set up in Swansea, inspired by a local minister, in which lectures in English grammar, arithmetic, geometry and chemistry were given 'gratuitously by gentlemen eminently qualified and heartily disposed to communicate instruction to the working classes'. Such experiments in adult education survived only into the 1850s in Wales, whereas the doyen of Swansea's cultural societies, the Royal Institution of South Wales, survives to this day. Although part of its remit was 'the general diffusion of knowledge', it was less a mechanics' institute than a philosophical and literary society, and was complemented by literary and scientific institutions founded in Neath, Carmarthen and Cardiff. There was a dichotomy between respectable serious middle-class interest in science and technology – as, with photography, an appropriate interest for gentry and industrialists alike – which coexisted uneasily with the training for a trade, however scientific, believed appropriate and increasingly crucial for the skilled working class. It continued to be reflected in the nature of different types of provision throughout the nineteenth century and, indeed, much of the next.

By the 1840s, the social context of this and more extended educational concerns had begun to be modified more dramatically than at any time in the history of Wales. A population explosion (in unlikely locations) associated with the iron industry, the dramatic concentration of that population in the south-east of Wales particularly, and consequent urbanization with its concomitant social strains, had begun to fashion a new kind of Wales. One of its characteristics had to be a rapidly changing and adapting way of providing education for its people.

CHAPTER THREE

✄

'Treason' and its Aftermath, 1847–1870

By 1840 the population of Wales had doubled since the beginning of the century, major towns appearing where previously there had been only scattered farms and hamlets. The largest of these was Merthyr Tydfil, home of some of the biggest ironworks in the world; but the Welsh iron industry reached its zenith in the 1850s, and only a few works successfully converted to the new product, steel. The age of iron was over; it gave way to the age of coal. Until the 1830s the production of coal had been largely geared to its use as a fuel for industry, but the discovery in 1837 of excellent steam coal in the Aberdare valley, followed later by the discovery of superior seams in the Rhondda Valleys, led to an ever-increasing world demand for Welsh coal; its export precipitated the growth of Cardiff, which quickly overtook Merthyr Tydfil in size, its docks eventually forming the greatest coal-export port in the world. While south Wales was increasingly identified with coal, steel, copper and tinplate, coal and tinplate were vital to the economy of the Wrexham region, and there was a thriving woollen industry in mid-Wales and an expanding slate industry in the north-west.

Welsh industries had attracted entrepreneurs from many parts of Britain, some with money to invest in establishing industrial concerns, others with technical 'know-how' acquired elsewhere. From London came the wealthy Anthony Bacon and Richard Crawshay to begin iron smelting in Merthyr Tydfil. Also to Merthyr Tydfil came John Guest from Shropshire and Samuel Homfray from Staffordshire, both of whom already had experience of iron smelting. Many stayed and raised families in Wales, the iron industry especially being noted for dynasties such as the Baileys, Crawshays, Fothergills, Guests, Hills and Homfrays. Meanwhile, the copper industry in the west had attracted Charles Neville from Clapham, and John Vivian and Pascoe St Leger Grenfell from Cornwall. While the potential of steam coal continued to attract Englishmen, such as the Corys and Insoles, it was also noted for the contribution of Welshmen, figures such as David Davies of Llandinam and the Davis family of

Aberdare, David Alfred Thomas (later Viscount Rhondda) and Sir William Thomas Lewis (later Baron Merthyr). Nonetheless, for most of the century it was English and, to a lesser extent Scottish, entrepreneurs who dominated all towns of any size in the industrial areas of Wales experiencing an influx of incomers. The Industrial Revolution in Wales, as elsewhere, had generated a new type of social and political leader, the industrial magnate, who took his place alongside the traditional leader, the landowner, indeed, the parvenu industrialist quickly emulated the lifestyle and shared the social, if not political, values of the gentry.

Wages in the new industries were generally higher than in agricultural districts, and most of the labour force was composed of Welsh-speaking workers, largely Nonconformist, migrating from the farms, a trend which continued throughout the century. Others came from the border counties and from Devon and Cornwall, while frequent potato famines resulted in successive waves of Irish immigrants, committed to their Catholic religion.

The population of Wales was nearly to double again in the second half of the century, and its relocation to the new industrial areas, especially Glamorgan and Monmouthshire, continued. Industrialization also brought about profound changes in the structure of the population. Middle-class groups expanded significantly in number as did the lower middle class of shopkeepers, agents, commercial men, industrial technicians, clerical and other officials who augmented farmers and professionals. Furthermore, the industrial areas now became a potent mix of nationalities, languages and religious denominations. While the great majority of the people of Wales in the eighteenth century had been Welsh-speaking, that was no longer the case in several parts of the country by the end of the nineteenth. At the same time, the increase in population generated by industrial development led ineluctably, in the absence of any social planning and legislation affecting working practices, to appalling living and working conditions. Poverty, unparalleled social dislocation, industrial unrest and conflicts between employers and workers created a simmering atmosphere of discontent which occasionally exploded into violent outbreaks such as the Merthyr riots of 1831, the Chartist riots of 1839, and the activities of the Scotch Cattle.

The social and political turbulence in Wales in the 1830s and 1840s was viewed with alarm by central government, the belief growing that a principal underlying cause was the deplorable state of education, and, in particular, the ignorance of the English language among Welsh people. We have seen that, following the Chartist insurrection of 1839, a survey of the mining areas by Seymour Tremenheere revealed appalling social conditions, though they differed little from those in many industrial areas of England. Only 70 per cent of children between the ages of three and twelve attended school, while many boys and girls as young as seven years of age were sent out to work.

In a largely voluntary organization of schooling, Nonconformists feared that extension of state aid would lead inevitably to greater control of education by the state and the established Church. The voluntaryists, largely Congregationalist, abjured all state grants while putting their faith in self-help. Other Nonconformists believed that the way forward was to work for more non-denominational schools under the auspices of the British Society with the assistance of government grants. This approach lay behind Hugh Owen's 'Letter to the Welsh People' of 26 March 1843 which resulted in an increase in British-school numbers, particularly in north Wales.

Although school provision in the early 1840s improved, it failed to keep pace with the expanding population. The dismal state of education depicted by school inspectors prompted William Williams (1788–1865), the Radical MP for Coventry, to move an address in the House of Commons seeking a government inquiry. His claim that an improved system of schooling was the best means to bring about 'law and order' struck a chord with his listeners, so that the government agreed to 'an inquiry into the state of education in Wales, especially into the means afforded the labouring classes of acquiring a knowledge of the English language'. The names of the commissioners were announced on 10 October 1846; they were three young English-speaking law graduates of Oxford and Cambridge, only one of whom had so far been called to the Bar. Their very names, Robert Wheeler Lingen, Jelinger Cookson Symons and Henry Vaughan Johnson, must have seemed to Welshmen redolent of middle-class England. Knowing no Welsh, they were advised by Dr Kay-Shuttleworth, secretary of the Privy Council Committee on Education, to seek assistance from Welsh-speakers. This they did, but in a predominantly Nonconformist country, eight of their ten assistants were Anglicans, among whom five were young students at the Anglican foundation, St David's College, Lampeter. Furthermore, of the 334 witnesses questioned, over 80 per cent were members of the established Church, many being Anglican clergy. Even before the commission report was published, therefore, there was sufficient evidence to arouse suspicion and prejudice among Welsh Nonconformist leaders. Its appearance in 1847 caused a furore because the commissioners were scathing in their condemnation of the Welsh people on the grounds of their alleged intemperance, immorality and egregious social behaviour; the Welsh being portrayed as ignorant, given to drunkenness and loose morals, the women, especially, exhibiting a want of chastity. The observations contained in the report included those of assistants and witnesses as well as those of the commissioners themselves.

It was not only the commissioners' strictures on the morality and social behaviour of the Welsh people which caused deep resentment and offence; ignorance of the English language was pinpointed, as it had been in earlier inspectors' reports, as holding back the population, while the prevalence of the Welsh language was held to be a baneful influence. Lingen reported that his area of investigation, Pembrokeshire, Carmarthenshire and Glamorgan, 'exhibited the phenomenon of a peculiar language isolating the mass of the people from the upper portions of society'. The Welsh element, whether in rural areas or among the furnaces, was never found near the top of the social scale. The Welsh workman 'may become an overseer or a contractor, but this does not take him out of the labouring and put him in the administration class'. His language 'keeps him under the hatches, being one in which he can neither acquire nor communicate the necessary information. It is a language of old-fashioned agriculture, of theology and of rustic life, while all the world about him is English'. Such criticism of the Welsh language stemmed from the contemporary English middle-class belief that it was essential for everyone to be able to speak and communicate in standard English, for the English working class was likewise criticized in educational reports for its regional dialects, which, like Welsh, 'were symbols of backwardness reflecting uncouth behaviour, and inadequate for proper communication'. The language used by the commissioners was typical of their class, both in its vocabulary and its tone. As a recent study has pointed out, there was an implicit arrogance and underlying condemnation inherent in such an Oxbridge-fostered middle-class pedigree. Inevitably both tone and content were anti-Welsh, but this was not a racially based animosity, more a genuine contemporary middle-class endorsement of standard English as the language of civilized society. Those who could not aspire to a mastery of it, whether in Wales, England or the rest of the Empire, were disadvantaged citizens.

The commissioners therefore viewed ignorance of standard English as an obstacle to the modernization and secularization of Welsh society. Most Welsh literature, too, was found wanting in terms of modernizing society. Johnson, responsible for reporting on the north Wales counties, found that books in circulation in his area, while rich in theology and poetry, were 'obsolete and meagre in secular aspects'. Periodicals were almost all denominational and devoted exclusively to religious matters. Similarly, the Sunday schools, which had become a central feature of Welsh community life, limited knowledge to religious matters. 'Most singular', wrote Lingen, 'is the character which has been developed by this theological bent of minds isolated from nearly all sources, direct or indirect, of secular information.' At the same time, Lingen conceded that the Sunday school performed a beneficial role in at least creating a population literate in the Welsh language. Whereas English was the language of the day schools, that of Sunday schools in the majority of cases was Welsh. 'These schools', he reported, 'have been almost the sole, they are still the main and most congenial centres of education. Through their agency the younger portion of the adult labouring classes in Wales can generally read, or are in the course of learning to read, the Scriptures in their mother tongue.'

The report of the commissioners, a translation of which was soon produced, was examined minutely by the Welsh, who vented their anger through highly critical ripostes in journals, pamphlets and newspapers. Nonconformists interpreted the report as an English and Church-inspired attack on the Welsh, and it was soon to be known as *Brad y Llyfrau Gleision* (The Treason of the Blue Books). But moderate churchmen, too, such as Dean Cotton of Bangor, and Sir Thomas Phillips, knighted for his part in the defence of Newport against the Chartist insurrection in 1839, felt compelled to protest at the tone of the report.

In the brouhaha aroused in Wales over the commissioners' comments on immorality and the language issue, the educational aspects almost took second place. But here the commissioners were on safer ground, for, although equally outspoken, the criticisms, albeit somewhat exaggerated, were generally merited. Schools were too few and inadequate, teachers were largely untrained and unqualified, too few children went to school – and, among those who did, attendance was irregular, while only a minority stayed for any length of time. The majority of the children knew little English, and often neither did the teachers. 'In the day schools, the teachers are often most inadequately acquainted with English themselves and employ Welsh for all colloquial or explanatory purposes.' Inadequate attempts were made to teach English, while fewer than one-third of children were learning arithmetic, partly because a penny a week extra was required in addition to the normal school pence. An extra penny had to be paid for instruction in writing, too – little wonder that Lingen reported that the great majority of the labouring classes were unable to write.

Private adventure schools abounded in the industrial areas and towns. Of 196 schools in Cardiff, Swansea and the mining districts of Glamorgan, no fewer than 149 were private schools. Anyone was entitled to open a school, no experience or training being required; they were often owned by individuals who had failed in other walks of life, or by widows attempting to make ends meet. The standard of these schools on the whole was deplorable. Of thirty-seven schools in Merthyr, not more than three were judged moderately good, twenty-six inferior and eight poor.

Of the remaining schools in the mining districts, twelve were under the auspices of the National Society and nine of the British Society, while no fewer than nineteen were attached to various works. The best of these were the Kilvey schools in Swansea for boys, girls and infants, which had been started as early as 1806 by Pascoe St Leger Grenfell in classes attached to his copper works, and the schools in Dowlais established by Sir John Guest, owner of the Dowlais ironworks, the largest of its kind in the world. Lady Charlotte Guest was closely involved in this initiative and extended provision after Sir John's death in 1852. Both Grenfell and Guest insisted on employing trained teachers, taking pains to select them from the London training colleges. Both churchmen, they ran their schools on non-denominational lines in deference to the wishes of their workmen, the majority of whom were Nonconformists. The Guest schools, in particular, were a model of what was possible: they embraced a wide curriculum, employed trained teachers, catered for infants and had an elaborate system of night schools. Some other works schools also attempted to provide evening instruction, with a limited degree of success; this was largely similar to what was provided during the day, but a few even attempted instruction in technical subjects. Works schools were important in Glamorgan and Monmouthshire, and, to a lesser extent, in Carmarthenshire and north-west Wales. A major factor in impelling industrialists to establish such schools was the need for a literate and numerate workforce, the best pupils being promoted to good positions in the works. But so also were considerations of sobriety, obedience and deference to the social order, improved attitudes to which could be inculcated in the schools; 'fear of the mob' which had been engendered by the traumatic events of the 1830s was also a powerful factor. Whatever the motives involved, some thirty schools were founded in the 1840s, mostly by large companies in Glamorgan and Monmouthshire. The method of financing them consisted of the owner providing a site and building, while a levy (usually 1d a week) was imposed on each worker's wages, which paid for books and covered the teacher's salary. Some schools accepted the children of non-employees for a fee of 2d or 3d, if space was available.

Symons, the commissioner responsible for Monmouthshire, reported similar findings to those of Tremenheere six years earlier, and to those of Lingen in Glamorgan. The population of the county of Monmouthshire, 45,582 in 1801, had grown to 134,355 by 1841, while a flood of in-migrants had helped to double the population between 1821 and 1841. Only 62 per cent of boys and 58 per cent of girls were found to be attending schools, in which teachers were untrained and unfitted for the job, their ranks including farmers, miners, blacksmiths, labourers, dress-makers and shopkeepers. In view of the many adverse factors in industrial regions, it might have been expected that education would be more successful in rural areas. That such was not the case is borne out by Johnson's investigations in Montgomeryshire and Lingen's in Pembroke-shire. Johnson found unsuitable buildings that were damp, cold and insanitary; of 125 schools, twenty-eight were private day schools, most of which were 'truly worthless'.

In Montgomeryshire he found totally inadequate accommodation. Of 125 'schools' only thirty-five were in schoolrooms set aside for that purpose – others were located in churches, chapels, shops and cottage kitchens. Johnson believed that there was a connection between damp, cold and insanitary conditions in the schools and the widespread prevalence of disease among both children and teachers. Twenty-eight of the schools were private-venture schools, most of which did no work of value. Teachers, whose wages were often less than those of able-bodied labourers, included shopkeepers, weavers, soldiers and former labourers. Just over a third of children between the ages of five and ten were in school; of those, half attended for less than a year, only 13 per cent remaining longer than three years.

There is no reason to doubt the commissioners' assessment of the poor provision for schooling in Wales. Such a state of affairs may have surprised and shocked the young and inexperienced graduates, ignorant of life among the lower orders, but they were no worse than those to be found in many parts of England, particularly the industrial areas. Notwithstanding its offensive tone, the 1847 report was a formidable document that recorded in great detail the level of schooling in Wales. Many agencies and individuals were involved in its provision, and there is a clear divide between rural and industrial Wales in respect of providers. Schools associated with the Church of England, by no means all of which were in alliance with the National Society, were more numerous in rural parishes. In Glamorgan, there were marked differences between the industrial areas, where works schools played an important role, and rural areas such as Cowbridge, where the Church held sway. In most parts of Wales, British schools and schools run by voluntaryists were in a minority, despite the population increasingly turning to Nonconformity. Private adventure schools were widespread and, although often charging exorbitant fees, were successful because Nonconformists, in the absence of non-denominational schools of their own, wished to avoid local Church schools.

In spite of their trenchant criticisms of schooling in Wales, the commissioners were of the opinion that the Welsh had a strong desire for education; they deserved better, the existing provision was inadequate and instruction unsuitable to their needs. Indeed the mythology surrounding the Blue Books, which has assumed a life of its own in the historiography of Wales, has distorted the educational message which the commissioners conveyed. A recent study of Symons, in particular, has seen him rehabilitated to a degree, wholly justifiably. It is rarely observed that the commissioners complimented the Welsh on their hunger for education and noted the sacrifices that many were prepared to make to acquire it, the intelligence they brought to bear on theological matters, bred in the

Sunday schools, and their quickness in mathematics. Although not trained in education, the commissioners were astute enough to realize the educational implications of fostering the English language among a predominantly Welsh-speaking population, so many of whom were desperate to master English. They insisted that rote learning was not the answer, and that a bilingual approach provided the only path to successful teaching of English.

The grim state of education portrayed in the 1847 report galvanized the agencies responsible for school provision. It also sharpened the competitive struggle between the Church authorities and Nonconformist bodies. A religious census in 1851 revealed the extent to which the established Church was losing out to Nonconformity, but, under two reforming and progressive bishops, Connop Thirlwall of St David's, and Alfred Ollivant of Llandaff, the Church responded to the challenge of Dissent; in a mini-renaissance the bishops stimulated a programme of church building and renovation in some 350 churches, and associated with many of these were Church schools. The voluntaryists' initial response to the report was to claim that it revealed the extent to which state aid had failed, prompting them to take action. Within a few years, however, even they came to realize that state funding was necessary; their strong opposition weakened, and in 1853 an agent (the Revd William Roberts of Blaenafon) appointed by the British Society soon brought more schools to south Wales.

Even so, in 1870 across Wales, schools in receipt of government grants provided only 59.3 per cent of places required by the population, provision in most places being dominated by Church schools. In all there were 1,164 schools, British schools comprising only a quarter of the total and 27 per cent of the places available. Between 1840 and 1875, 318 parochial and National schools had applied for building grants, whereas only 110 applications had come from British schools. Although provision had improved immeasurably it had not kept pace with the increase in population, especially in certain areas; while the population of Wales had increased by 22 per cent between 1851 and 1871, that of Glamorgan had increased by 70 per cent, largely due to in-migration. Little wonder that 78 per cent of children in Flintshire had access to a school place compared with only 22 per cent in Glamorgan.

The promotion of schools by a number of different agencies, employers and individuals resulted in a lack of homogeneity in the system and a wide variation in fee levels. Elementary schools were intended in the main for the lower middle classes and the working classes, but, as Marsden has pointed out, in England the differentiation in fees involved catering for different groups within these sectors. In Wales, a much less class-structured society than England, there was an element of differentiation, though this was not nearly as pronounced as in secondary education. Even in the works schools, providing education for workers and their children, there was a range of fees from ½d a week to 9d a month, although the majority imposed fees of ½d a week for boys, 1d a week for adult workers and 2d a week for others if accommodation was available. Fees in Wales were low compared with England, with British schools generally imposing lower fees than Church schools.

Schools were available at different costs, therefore, but there were not nearly enough of them. It is debatable how many working-class children could avail themselves of this provision, though it may be assumed that skilled artisans, for example, if they were in work could afford the fees. On the other hand, inspectors' reports regularly complained of early withdrawal from school. There were a number of reasons, including a lack of appreciation of the value of education by parents and the attraction of extra wages to supplement family income. But an inability to maintain payment of school fees, especially in the case of large families, was an important deterrent. As late as 1875 children were being sent home from some schools in Merthyr Tydfil for inability to pay fees as low as 1d a week. For those at the bottom of the social scale, the destitute, vagrants and paupers, there were Ragged schools. One was founded in Swansea in 1847 by the medical officer of health and financially supported by leading industrialists, but there were very few in Wales.

In 1870 there was no compulsion on parents to send their children to school. Later, successive measures attempted to enforce attendance, but irregular attendance continued to pose problems throughout the century. In industrial areas, children were often kept at home to look after smaller children or take food to other members of the family at work, while in the rural areas the agricultural requirements of harvests and potato picking took priority. Sometimes, social events, such as fairs and circuses, were a sufficient excuse for children to stay away from school. Frequent epidemics of childhood illnesses took a heavy toll. But there were also frequent interruptions to school routine, as recorded by George Kovachich, master of Upper Rhymney School around 1870; they included tea parties, eisteddfodau, colliery explosions and riots.

Many of the factors affecting schools were common to Wales and England. One feature was unique to Welsh society – the Welsh language. From the time of Tremenheere onwards, most official opinion held the prevalence of the Welsh language in Welsh life to be an obstacle to schooling and learning, with ignorance of English holding back advancement at work and the extension of social acculturation. With few exceptions, English was the medium of instruction in schools; in 1846, for instance, Symons found that in Brecon, Radnor and Cardigan only at one school was some of the instruction in Welsh. He claimed that parents were responsible, desperate for their children to learn English to advance their prospects. Instruction in English was often given by Welsh-speaking teachers with an insufficient grasp of English, to pupils who knew no English, or very little.

In the revised School Code of 1862 Welsh was not included as a grant-earning subject, and for many years there was no encouragement from any quarter for a place for the Welsh language in education, the widely held view being that the basis of secular knowledge was English, while in any case the abundant Sunday schools provided religious instruction in Welsh. In 1868, George Berry Kovachich wrote in his diary: 'I found the Welsh language a hindrance to the progress in English as it is Welsh in the home, in society and chapel.' There was no mention of Welsh as a class subject in his school before 1895, when it was taught in the two lowest standards.

One constant theme running through the 1847 report was the utter inadequacy of those who taught in the schools; untrained, in no sense did they constitute a professional body embracing uniform standards, a shortcoming equally characteristic of English schools. Realization of this had led to the founding of a private training college at Battersea in 1840 by Dr Kay-Shuttleworth, which prompted the establishment of several other training colleges. The first in Wales was a Church college, Trinity, at Carmarthen in 1848, another being established at Caernarfon in 1856. Two years later, the Nonconformists, prompted and led by Hugh Owen, established a non-denominational college at Bangor, though all admitted only men. There was no training college for women until Swansea Training College opened in 1872, under the auspices of the British and Foreign Schools Society.

Of equal significance to young Welsh men and women was the pupil-teacher scheme established by the government in 1846. Pupil-teachers were offered a five-year apprenticeship from the age of thirteen, at the end of which they could compete for a Queen's Scholarship which enabled them to spend two to three years at a training college. This scheme was of enormous benefit to Welsh children from mainly lower middle-class and even some working-class backgrounds; a new career in school teaching opened up which did not involve an expensive education in grammar school or university, so necessary for entry to the law, medicine and the Church. As a result, buttressed by this degree of financial support, teaching became the most popular profession for Welsh boys and girls. Already by 1859 there were 484 male and 258 female pupil-teachers in Wales, though 'payment by results' had an adverse effect on recruitment, particularly of men, so that ten years later numbers of men had fallen while numbers of women stood at 391. Not surprisingly, given the all-male nature of the training colleges, numbers of male certificated teachers in 1868 exceeded women by 546 to 230.

The education of the majority of Welsh people at mid-century was confined to a few years of elementary education; it was only a small minority who were able to take advantage of secondary education available in twenty-eight small grammar schools and in a plethora of private schools of variable quality. The most successful of the Welsh schools at the time of the Aberdare Report of 1881, Llandovery College, had been established only in 1847, exclusively for boys. It was an Anglican foundation, the brainchild of a wealthy surgeon, Thomas Phillips, built on land given by Lady Llanover and marked out by its excellent building and progressive curriculum, which included Welsh and emphasized science.

The aristocracy and gentry had traditionally looked to the English public schools or to private tutors, the former practice emulated by the new industrial plutocracy in the nineteenth century. With the coming of the railway age after 1840 and the rapid spread of new foundations in England, increasing numbers of the lesser gentry and the wealthier professional and middle classes turned to one of the burgeoning number of English boarding schools, while the Welsh grammar schools in the main continued to serve the sons of smaller landowners, clergymen, farmers, professional men, shopkeepers and tradespeople.

The Schools Inquiry Commission under Baron Taunton in the late 1860s found twenty-eight grammar schools in Wales with a combined total of 1,100 pupils; sixteen of the schools were described as classical and eight as semi-classical. The commission singled out Prussia as a state with an advanced system of secondary education with sixteen pupils per 1,000 of the population in secondary schools. For Wales, however, it recommended a figure of ten per 1,000, owing to the 'special circumstances' of the country; at the time the figure was only 0.77 per 1,000! The endowed grammar schools had been founded in small market towns such as Brecon, Llanrwst and Ruthin, at the time thriving centres of trade and commerce. By 1870 these schools were largely isolated from the new centres of population, while the exodus from rural areas had deprived them of potential day pupils. Most of the endowed schools had survived and a number of them were rebuilt, remodelled or extended in the mid-nineteenth century – for example Bala, Abergavenny, Cowbridge, Swansea, Brecon and Monmouth.

However, in a changed Wales their contribution to education was limited. They were invariably Anglican. Only in the 1860s were children of Nonconformist families entitled to avoid Anglican religious instruction in them and, as a result, some, like the grammar school in Bala, became predominantly Nonconformist by the 1880s. The staggering growth of population in the south-east of Wales, in particular, highlighted the desperate inadequacy of endowments in these areas. They were therefore supplemented by a large numbers of fee-paying private schools of varying worth. In some areas of rural Wales the population was best served by using the limited endowments for elementary education, and by 1870 ten endowed schools had either been transformed into elementary schools or had ceased teaching classical subjects.

Wales in 1870 was woefully defective in terms of the provision of secondary education compared with England, which in turn compared unfavourably with the Continent. Whereas in England there was one school per 27,000 of the population, in Wales it was one per 47,000. The commission identified the lack of endowments in Wales as a key factor; endowments in England in relation to population being three times as great. Endowments in Glamorgan, Lincoln and Warwick were respectively £1,921, £48,294 and £63,446. The total gross endowment income for the whole of Wales was £9,936, of which £3,000 was assigned to the charitable foundation which supported Monmouth School. Net annual income for the whole of Wales after payment of repair bills, taxes and insurance totalled only £7,251.

The curriculum of the schools, largely restricted to classics and mathematics, had limited appeal for the new industrial and commercial classes. There was no attempt to adapt it to the Welsh economy, either agricultural or industrial, Wrexham being one of the few schools to plan a curriculum geared to the needs of the new communities. The relatively high fees, which ranged from six to ten guineas a year for day boys, and from twenty to forty guineas a year for boarders, were a bar to entry for many of the middle class, poorer in Wales than in England. This was especially true of Nonconformists who, in any case, distanced themselves from what they conceived of as being 'Church-controlled' schools; in most cases the governors were Anglicans, the Church Catechism was part of the curriculum and pupils were expected to attend the parish church on Sundays. Of some 250 non-Anglicans with formal higher education listed in the *Dictionary of Welsh Biography* who lived in the nineteenth century, thirty-four went to a Welsh grammar school; significantly, too, not one of the Nonconformist leaders of the Welsh education revolution that took place between 1846 and 1896 was educated in a grammar school.

Such was the position with boys' secondary education; for girls the situation was far worse. Some middle-class families employed governesses, though overall numbers are impossible to determine. There were only two schools providing a secondary education for girls – those of the Howell foundation at Llandaff and Denbigh respectively had been opened in 1860, financed from an original bequest of a merchant draper, Thomas Howell. They catered for both boarders and day girls and had fewer than 200 pupils, predominantly from Anglican families. Not until 1878 did a similar school open for Nonconformist girls, the Dr Williams School in Dolgellau.

The Taunton Commission found much evidence of the general indifference of parents to the education of their daughters. The widely accepted view of the role of middle-class women in Victorian Wales, as in England, was that of supportive wife and mother whose efforts in the home would serve to provide stability and moral uprightness for the family. Furthermore, there was an 'inveterate prejudice' against educating girls as they were thought less capable of mental cultivation and less in need of an academic education. The general view was that what was needed for girls was 'accomplishments', that which was 'showy and attractive', whereas 'more solid achievements are actually disadvant-ageous'. Only in the last two decades of the nineteenth century did a more enlightened attitude result in wider opportunities when the Welsh intermediate secondary schools provided equally for boys and girls. Before this, scholarship associations and the reform of existing secondary-school endowments had, to a limited extent, enhanced opportunities for girls.

In addition to the grammar schools, a plethora of private schools and academies, both day and boarding, catered for both sexes. Some of these, whose fees were beyond the reach of most of the population, were very good, for example the private Merthyr Grammar School run by James Kernick in which 'young gentlemen receive a very superior education and are prepared for the university'. For twenty guineas a year a pupil had the benefit of a curriculum which, as well as classics and mathematics, included philosophy, history, geography, natural history and physiology. The Merthyr Classical and Commercial School, run by the Revd C. Lunn, provided an extended curriculum which included French and commerce, and drawing schools in collaboration with the Government School of Design. All too often, though, these private academies were short-lived, ending with the death or relocation of their owners. Furthermore, the majority, especially those at the lower end of the scale with low fees, provided an inferior education. Nevertheless, the contribution of post-elementary private schools to Welsh education in the nineteenth century has been considerably underrated. Seaborne has calculated that in 1880, 30 endowed schools were catering for 1,803 pupils, mainly girls, while 152 private schools were catering for 2,287 boys and 1,871 girls.

One of the functions of the grammar schools was to prepare boys for entry to the ancient universities of Oxford and Cambridge. For centuries Welsh boys had been going to 'Oxbridge' colleges, especially to Jesus College, Oxford, many aided by 'closed' scholarships established out of property left to the college by another Welshman and former fellow, Edmund Meyrick (1636–1721). The first degree-granting institution in Wales was St David's College, Lampeter, opened in 1827 at a cost of £20,000. The prime mover in its foundation was Thomas Burgess, bishop of St David's, who wished to improve the quality of Welsh clergy; he contributed one-tenth of his income for several years, further financial assistance coming from a government grant of £600 and a donation of

£1,000 from King George IV. In the following year the college was incorporated by Royal Charter for 'the education of persons destined for Holy Orders'; further Royal Charters empowered the college to grant degrees in divinity (1852) and in arts (1865).

Nonconformists meanwhile were barred from Oxford and Cambridge until mid-century (only in 1871 were all religious tests removed), and few entered a grammar school, either due to poverty or because of hostility to the 'Church' character of the schools. Fortunately, Nonconformists were able to turn to one of the several seminaries for training ministers which appeared in Wales in the nineteenth century. The oldest of these began as the Dissenting Academy established by Samuel Jones, which eventually settled in Carmarthen. As the Carmarthen Presbyterian College it enjoyed an excellent reputation for classical scholarship, theology, language and mathematics, as well as providing instruction in elementary science. Run on a non-sectarian basis, it attracted students from all denominations, several of whom later pursued careers other than the ministry. Each denomination strove to establish one or more colleges out of funds provided by hard-pressed congregations: for instance, the Calvinistic Methodists contributed £26,000 towards a college which opened at Bala in 1865, while the Memorial College opened by the Independents at Brecon in 1869 cost £11,650 out of a fund created by contributions from 617 chapels. All were male preserves.

Nonconformist ministers in Wales generally came from poorer backgrounds than did the Anglican clergy; few received secondary, and fewer still higher, education. Often a minimum of elementary schooling was followed by years spent on a farm, in a pit or in ironworks, or apprenticeship to craftsmen or shopkeepers. Some began to preach at an early age, only later taking up the ministry as a full-time career. Many studied at the theological colleges, but by no means all of them ended up in the ministry, some taking up teaching or the law. The theological colleges were of immense benefit to young Welshmen, especially those from poor backgrounds, for, as witnesses to the Aberdare Committee testified in 1880, many students were from the 'common people' and paid 'little or nothing for their support'. Furthermore, preaching on Sunday and financial support from their home congregation helped to provide maintenance.

The theological colleges were invaluable, too, as stepping-stones into higher education, for a number of students subsequently went on to University College, London, to Owen's College, Manchester, or to a Scottish or German university. Of particular advantage were the regulations of the University of London. Established as an examining body in 1836 it was empowered to grant degrees to students attending an 'affiliated' collegiate institution, but by a statute of 1858 it received a charter which exempted postulants for external degrees from attendance at an 'approved' institution named in previous charters. It thus threw open all degrees, other than those in medicine, to those who cared to sit for them. The Scottish universities, too, proved to be of great help to Welsh boys of all religious denominations: no religious tests were imposed; they were less socially exclusive; and they offered a four-year course of instruction which could begin at sixteen years of age, a course which combined the provision of a general liberal education with training for the professions, including medicine. Above all, fees were low, and there was no requirement to reside in an expensive hall or college, students being free to obtain cheap lodgings. At Glasgow there were scholarships available to Welsh boys as a result of the will of Dr Daniel Williams (1645–1716), a seventeenth-century Presbyterian divine and former graduate of the university.

Wales was manifestly disadvantaged in the field of higher education. At mid-century it possessed no university of its own, unlike most countries in western Europe. In May 1857 an imaginative, if overambitious, scheme was launched in Neath to establish a higher-education institution which would provide 'an education in the practical application of Science to the management of Land, Manufactures and Commerce, to the Public Services, and the Professions and other pursuits'. However, by November 1857 the scheme had collapsed. Another initiative was taken at about this time which, though slow to take off, bore fruit later. Encouraged by the example of government subventions in the 1840s to establish a number of Queen's Colleges in Ireland as part of a federated University of Ireland, a group of prominent Welshmen met in 1854 to consider the possibility of a similar structure for Wales. A year earlier a young graduate of Glasgow, Benjamin Thomas Williams, later a Liberal MP for Carmarthen, published a pamphlet, *The Desirableness of a University of Wales*, in which he argued that all sects should unite to establish a non-sectarian university. A leading figure in the London group was the ubiquitous Hugh Owen, who led a subcommittee of three in drawing up a scheme for a Welsh university based on the Irish model. Little action followed this ambitious plan, as it was dependent on government finance at a time when the Crimean War was proving expensive, and Owen turned his energies to the establishment of a training college. It was several years before the movement once more gathered momentum, its ultimate success leading to the opening of the University College of Wales at Aberystwyth in 1872.

Prior to the final quarter of the nineteenth century, the education available in Wales, aided by superior facilities available in England, Scotland and Germany, had enabled a small and privileged minority to pursue careers in the Church, law, politics and civil administration, while others, thanks to the pupil-teacher system and training colleges, were

enabled to take up teaching as a career. At the same time, the Nonconformist ministry was open to those from humble backgrounds and little
formal education. Nonetheless, the education of the great majority of the
population who worked on the land or in one of the ever-expanding
industries was at best confined to a few years of elementary education. For
those with ambition this could be supplemented by attendance at an
evening class sometimes found in conjunction with a day school run by
mechanics' institutes or literary and scientific institutes, which, however,
were scarce in Wales. In any case, attendance at evening class imposed a
huge additional burden on those who had worked long hours on the land
or in mine or factory.

Of especial importance, therefore, to those who had received little or
minimal formal education was the fact that Welsh society was
characterized by a range of social, cultural and educative influences,
particularly Sunday schools and eisteddfodau. There was, too, a buoyant
Welsh press, while brass bands and choirs were popular elements in
musical culture. The chapel and Sunday school had a distinctive role in
the life of the people. Lingen had highlighted the importance of Sunday
schools in the 1847 report, while four years later the Census of Religious
Worship revealed that 2,771 Sunday schools catered for 269,078
scholars of all ages, far greater numbers in proportion to population than
was the case in England. Intended originally to promote a knowledge of
the Bible in Welsh, they provided very much more as each denomination
distributed articles and reviews of new publications with suitable reading
material. The Sunday schools were merely an element, albeit an important
one, in the overall cultural contribution of chapels and churches. At mid-
century, Nonconformity was the religion of the people; by 1870 the
chapels of Wales could seat 50 per cent of the country's inhabitants,
compared with only 23 per cent in England. There was a boom in church
and chapel building, especially the latter, each Nonconformist denomination having its chapel serving the local community, sometimes more than
one due to 'splits' among congregations. At the same time, each sect strove
to attract non-Welsh-speakers and English immigrants by establishing an
English chapel; by 1870 a feature of Welsh towns and villages was the
ubiquity of biblical names such as Zion, Calfaria, Tabernacle, Salem and
Zoar.

The chapel was a unique force in Welsh life for it went far beyond
the spiritual dimension. It was a social and cultural institution for all
the family, of especial significance to women in view of their limited
opportunities; the focus of community life, it gave people a true sense
of belonging. Self-financed and self-managed, chapel congregations
provided an education in democratic processes, although, as the century
progressed, leadership became increasingly dominated by the burgeoning

middle class. The political consciousness of congregations lay at the root of the alliance between Nonconformity and Liberalism which developed during the third quarter of the century, while the minister, a person of esteem in Welsh society, was not only spiritual guide but also social and political mentor and leader. Sunday was the most important day, with several services, children's worship and Sunday school, but activities also continued throughout the week, with prayer meetings, young people's meetings, Bible study classes and temperance meetings, with the chapels in the forefront of temperance movements such as the Band of Hope. A particular feature were Penny Readings, an important instrument of popular education. Prizes were given for reading prose passages from which all punctuation marks had been omitted, and also for recitations, essays and impromptu speeches. Throughout the winter, too, rehearsals would be held in preparation for the singing festivals (*Cymanfaoedd Canu*).

Another Welsh cultural institution, unique in Europe, was the eisteddfod. When cheap railway transport became available the National Eisteddfod attracted large crowds to support their local choirs, poets and writers. It was at the National Eisteddfod at Chester in 1866, (which impressed Matthew Arnold), that 'Land of My Fathers' ('Hen Wlad fy Nhadau' – composed in 1856 by Evan and James Jones of Pontypridd) was adopted as the Welsh national anthem. Perhaps of even greater significance to the cultural life of Wales were the widespread local eisteddfodau promoted with great enthusiasm by churches, chapels and Friendly Societies. They provided an opportunity for ordinary people of modest social standing to demonstrate publicly their literary and musical talents. As well as promoting the Welsh language and literature, many topics for prize essays were historical, philosophical and sociological, and were frequently won by colliers, ironworkers, cobblers and tailors, among others. Every town and village, too, had choirs, single-sex and mixed, sponsored by churches and chapels, Friendly Societies, industrial companies and, later in the century, by trade unions, which also sponsored brass and silver bands. The 'tonic sol-fa' system helped the members of bands and choirs to read music, with Handel, Haydn and Mendelssohn oratorios especially popular.

Socially and culturally it was a vibrant society. It may also have been a far more literate society than might be inferred from the school situation and the vilification of the 1847 commissioners, if we define literacy as the ability to read Welsh, though in 1851 there was a substantial readership for English newspapers, measured by circulation figures: *Cardiff and Merthyr Guardian*, 66,000; the *Cambrian*, 61,000; the *Welshman*, 36,000 and the *Swansea Herald*, 4,800. In 1866, Henry Richard, who two years later was to be elected the first Nonconformist MP when he won the Merthyr Tydfil seat, claimed that there were five quarterlies, twenty-five monthlies and eight weeklies in Welsh, with an estimated circulation of 120,000. Many of these newspapers and publications were available in the public libraries that were springing up following the Museums and Libraries Act of 1851. The fact that many were also available in the libraries of mechanics' institutes, a noted example being that at Llanelli, suggests that the literacy levels of adult workers were not as low as is sometimes thought. In 1865 there were 4,699 borrowings from the library of the institute, of which only 1,625 were fiction. The others included: Welsh literature (424); biography (421); history and antiquities (399); science and art (281); poetry and drama (223); essays and reviews (179); religion and philosophy (172); and natural history (170). The reading room held eight daily newspapers including *The Times* and the *Telegraph*, twenty-one weekly publications, and fourteen monthly publications, which included the *Musical Times* and *Art Journal*. In addition, there were eight Welsh periodicals, among which were *Baner ac Amserau Cymry*, published by the radical Thomas Gee of Denbighshire.

The Llanelli Institute, founded in the 1840s by the Neville family, colliery and copper works owners, was under middle-class patronage; its members in 1865 included four MPs and five justices of the peace. Nonetheless, of the 534 members in that year, no fewer than 239 were industrial workers, masons, carpenters and labourers. While publications such as the *Graphic Engineer*, the *English Mechanic* and the *British Workman* would no doubt have been of special interest to them, there is no reason to suppose that they were not also among the book borrowers and readers of the eclectic range of publications available in the reading room. Of middle-class members, agents, clerks, merchants and shopkeepers were the dominant groups, whereas teachers, solicitors and surgeons numbered only seventeen. Interestingly, there were twenty-one lady members, presumably also middle-class, for whom there were publications such as *The Lady*, *The Queen* and *Women's World*; by 1884 their number had grown to over eighty.

The institute's initiatives were not confined to the provision of a library and reading room. There was also a museum, lectures, classes in French, reading classes in English and Welsh, discussion groups, vocal and instrumental groups and, later, science classes in connection with the scheme of the government Department of Science and Art. The annual report of 1865 concluded with the claim:

> while the Institute is providing sources of valuable instruction and wholesale entertainment for all classes of the community, unlike most kindred institutes, it is gradually drawing within its influence larger numbers of those for whose more especial benefit it was originally founded . . . the increasing income is enabling it to establish . . . a centre

of intellectual life and recreation second to no other place of equal population.

Wales entered the final quarter of the nineteenth century with a confidence that few could have anticipated at mid-century following the scathing attacks of the education commissioners in 1847. The Reform Act of 1867 brought immediate change in the parliamentary election of 1868, when the Liberals won twenty-three seats to the Conservatives' ten, with Henry Richard being elected in Merthyr Tydfil. Nonconformity had grown in strength, and the election heralded the beginning of the end of the hegemony of the Tory landowning class in Welsh politics. An unprecedented degree of state involvement from 1870 changed the nature of elementary educational provision with legislation which affected Wales and England equally, but it was to be a radical transformation in secondary and higher education which had the most dramatic and profound impact on Welsh society. A burgeoning middle class, a growing sense of Welsh national identity and ambition, an alliance of Nonconformity and Liberalism and ever-extending state intervention were to produce an educational revolution.

CHAPTER FOUR

✕

The State and the Nation, 1870–1902

In the final quarter of the nineteenth century the Welsh economy exhibited remarkable contrasts, several of its industries experiencing changing fortunes. Iron gave way to steel, which was increasingly located on the coast rather then in the hinterland. The tinplate industry enjoyed boom years in west Wales until the American tariffs of the 1890s brought temporary depression. The copper industry, so dominant in the Swansea region for most of the century, declined. It was coal, though, especially the steam coal of the Aberdare and Rhondda Valleys, which predominated during these years, achieving a peak production of 56 million tons in 1913, 30 million of which was exported to all parts of the world.

Industrial development was confined to relatively small geographical areas in south Wales, Flintshire and Denbighshire, while in Caernarfonshire slate quarrying was of considerable importance. Most of Wales continued to be rural and engaged in agriculture. However, the agricultural depression of the 1880s and 1890s, together with changes in farming, led to lower prices for land and livestock. Consequently, farms closed and there was migration, especially of the young, to England and to the new centres of industry elsewhere in Wales. Whereas the population of Wales during this period increased by 43 per cent, that of the rural counties fell; in contrast, the population of Monmouthshire increased by 53 per cent while that of Glamorgan doubled, 80,000 being attracted from Herefordshire, Gloucestershire, Somerset and Devon. Industrial development had wrought a remarkable imbalance in the distribution of the population of Wales and was to have profound importance for educational provision.

The construction of roads, railways and docks also required labour, as did housebuilding. There was an increasing demand for clerks, railway workers, post office officials and commercial travellers, while the need for support services was reflected, for instance, in a huge increase in the number of shopkeepers and domestic servants. The professional classes, especially lawyers and accountants, expanded too. A more substantial middle class than Wales had ever known before resulted. Urbanization meant that whereas in 1851 less than 20 per cent of the population lived in Welsh towns, by 1891 50 per cent did so. The social structure had grown far more complex. An analysis of the occupations of fathers of pupils entering a sample of south Wales secondary schools at the turn of the century reveals no fewer than eighty designations, embracing unskilled labourers, skilled workers and craftsmen at one end through accountants, commercial travellers, clerks and shopkeepers to managers, owners of works and a growing number of professionals at the upper end of society.

Wales continued to be a less class-conscious society than was the case in many parts of England. The democratic ethos of chapel, Sunday schools and eisteddfod was a potent force. But it would be misleading to assume that members of the working class were a wholly respectable chapel-going body. Substantial numbers attended neither Church nor chapel, though their number is unknown for they have been largely overlooked. Drink was regarded as an endemic problem which temperance movements tried to alleviate. Religious leaders tried, in John Davies's words, 'by missions, revivals and a flurry of temperance activity to entice [the irreligious] to places of worship or, if they failed, to legislate them into respectability'. In all, for increasing numbers, there was vibrant social, cultural and sporting life spanning the spectrum of respectability and centred on the chapel, eisteddfodau, Friendly Societies, working men's institutes, choral singing, singing festivals, operatic societies, brass bands, drama groups, music halls, boxing, association football, and especially rugby, which though introduced by public-school men, had a popular following in south Wales.

Politics in Wales inevitably adapted to economic and social change. Following the Reform Acts and the introduction of the secret ballot in 1872 the hold of the landed class on parliamentary representation weakened. By the 1880s Wales had become a Liberal stronghold, with admiration for Gladstone knowing no bounds. Among a largely middle-class membership, Welsh Nonconformist lawyers were prominent. Partly as a reaction to the Blue Books of 1847 a new sense of national identity had emerged.

Inspired by the Irish movement for self-government, Welsh nationalist aspirations were exemplified in the Cymru Fydd movement. In the late 1880s branches sprang up throughout Wales. In 1886 talented young Cymru Fydd followers established Cymdeithas Dafydd ap Gwilym (the Dafydd ap Gwilym Society) in Oxford University to foster pride in the Welsh language and culture. By the end of the century many of its members were products of a greatly improved and structured education system extending from elementary school to university. Advances in Welsh secondary and higher education, in particular, owed much to the efforts of a relatively small number of Nonconformist Liberals, many of them MPs, aided by a few Welsh Anglicans and sympathetic English MPs. Middle-class-led, this revolution in Welsh education was intended in the main to benefit the lower middle classes, but when implemented it provided opportunities for advancement to considerable numbers of the working class too. The greatly improved education system was a powerful lever in upward mobility, in which school boards, the pupil-teacher system and training colleges produced generations of schoolteachers who were prominent as local leaders and in local government. Further enlargement of the middle class came, too, through university colleges founded in the 1870s and 1880s and a network of secondary schools established in the 1890s.

A marked feature of the education system, though, was its dissonance with the Welsh rural and industrial economy. In education, as in the wider society, a 'humanistic' culture largely prevailed, and careers in such highly esteemed areas as the ministry, teaching, law and other professions were most commonly pursued. Following the Revised Code of 1862, science largely disappeared from the curriculum of the elementary school, not to reappear until late in the century. Science was almost entirely absent, too, from the endowed grammar schools, while the new intermediate schools at the turn of the century emulated the 'liberal education' ethos of the grammar schools, science subjects lagging behind the humanities. One consequence was that the Welsh university colleges to 1914 had a far greater proportion of 'arts' students than did their English counterparts.

More serious was the neglect of technical education and its lack of attraction for young people. Attempts to introduce subjects such as agriculture and metallurgy in the intermediate schools generally failed, while the initiatives of the Department of Science and Art and of the City and Guilds of London Institute to foster science and technical studies in evening classes were less successful in Wales than in England, Scotland or even Ireland. Commercial education at higher levels was deficient, a move to fund a department of commerce at the University College of South Wales and Monmouthshire in the 1900s meeting with a totally negative response from the commercial sector, with only £15 being raised.

This situation was not unexpected in a Welsh context. For the majority whose first language was Welsh and who spoke it habitually, a career in technology required not only mastery of a foreign language, but also of the arcane technical language of science and technical studies. The language was a barrier to progress in the elementary schools in which, although it was the medium of instruction, many pupils and some teachers had an imperfect grasp of English. Furthermore, until the Welsh Intermediate Education Act of 1889, opportunities for secondary education were far fewer than in England, while science was almost totally absent from the curriculum of elementary and secondary schools until late in the century. Religious and cultural influences led to a reverence for the ministry as an occupation. Young men were attracted to a highly esteemed vocation attainable through attendance at one of the theological colleges which were accessible to the very poor. In the second half of the century the popularity of eisteddfodau, particularly the National Eisteddfod, gave prominence to literary and cultural activities. A further significant factor may have been the nature of the Welsh economy, based largely on smelting and extractive industries, and almost devoid of manufacturing, light engineering and shipbuilding; there were consequently few formal apprenticeship schemes and no overwhelming demand for skilled scientific manpower, much of which, in any case, could be drawn from Scotland and the north-east of England.

During the 1860s pressure grew inexorably in England and Wales for radical action to improve the provision of elementary education; the nation generally had not been as complacent as had the Commission to Inquire into the State of Popular Education under the duke of Newcastle, while several events in the 1860s added strength to the argument for greater state involvement. In America the northern states won the Civil War while on the European Continent, Prussia defeated Austria. Both victor nations had well-developed state systems of education, leading some to the conclusion that superior education had been a key factor in ensuring victory. At the same time anxieties were growing over the maintenance of Britain's pre-eminent industrial position, now open to competition from France and Prussia, both rapidly developing industrial nations with state systems of education. In 1867, the passage of the second Reform Act seemed to some to pose the threat of undesirable elements being elected to Parliament by an illiterate electorate; the response, in the oft-quoted if inaccurate epigram always attributed to Robert Lowe, was that 'we must educate our masters'. Finally, it was evident that provision of education through voluntary societies was simply not keeping pace with the increase in population. Department of Education inquiries in Birmingham, Liverpool, Manchester and Leeds revealed that two-fifths of working-class children between six and ten years of age did not attend school at all. Despite recent resurrection of right-wing attempts to argue that private effort was adequately meeting the need for places in elementary education, and that the agitation leading to the 1870 Act was artificially generated, it remains the fact that provision, particularly in predominantly working-class areas, was wholly inadequate, certainly in Wales. New organizations began to rouse and fashion public opinion: the Manchester Education Aid Society (1864) demanded increased government aid for education; in Birmingham the Education League (1869) under George Dixon MP as chairman and Joseph Chamberlain as vice-chairman, campaigned for an education system 'universal, compulsory, unsectarian and free'. An Education Alliance Society formed in Wales the following year adopted similar aims.

Following the election of 1868 Gladstone appointed William Edward Forster, mill owner and MP for Bradford, as Vice-President of the Department of Education. In February 1870, Forster introduced a Bill 'to cover the country with good schools' through 'filling the gaps' in the existing elementary-school structure with non-sectarian schools publicly financed and managed under elected school boards, with a period of grace to allow voluntary schools to improve their provision. Many were opposed to such radical changes: the Church wished to preserve, and even to extend, its grip on education; the Nonconformists fiercely opposed any additional financial support for Church schools; there was strong opposition to the imposition of rates to aid elementary education. Nevertheless, with an amendment introduced by William Cowper-Temple which restricted religious education to 'simple Bible teaching' and allowed parents who had conscientious scruples to withdraw their children from school prayers and scripture lessons, the Bill became law on 9 August 1870.

The establishment of school boards instituted a 'dual' system of elementary schooling: the voluntary schools were financed through government grants, subscriptions, endowments and school fees; the new board schools could raise additional money through the rates. In boroughs, councils had the power to decide whether to establish a school board, whereas in rural parishes it was decided at vestry meetings. Since the gentry and Church authorities were generally opposed to school boards, and Liberals and Nonconformists were largely in favour, the situation had the potential for acrimonious power struggles; and in some areas there were intense confrontations. Occasionally, landowners and industrial employers were guilty of intimidation and coercion in their attempts to force tenants and workers to vote against the formation of school boards. In Cardiff, the influence of the marquess of Bute delayed the formation of a school board until 1875. Opposition came also from the burgeoning ranks of shipowners, businessmen and industrialists resistant to the imposition of another rate levy.

Prior to the Act of 1870, there were places for some 60 per cent of children of school age in Wales, though the differences between rural areas – where the proportion was in the high seventies – and the populous industrial areas was especially marked: in Glamorgan as a whole it was below the national average, being as low as 22 per cent in Merthyr Tydfil. Fewer than a third of schools in receipt of government grants were British schools, provision in some rural areas being entirely in National or other Church schools. The creation of school boards was to bring a marked change. By December 1872, 129 boards had been established, a further 107 between 1873 and 1895; their distribution was not uniform, reflecting religious, political and administrative difficulties. Elections tended to produce boards dominated by middle-class members; in some instances landlords were made chairmen to make it easier to obtain land for schools.

Meanwhile, the announcement of Forster's Bill had galvanized the Church and the National Society into an accelerated building programme during a six-month period of grace, activity which continued after the advent of school boards as Anglicans strove to retain their dominant position. Nevertheless Church and National schools were gradually overtaken due to an extensive programme of building by school boards. They also took over many British and works schools. Between 1870 and 1900 the number of schools in Wales more than doubled; of the 1,709 schools in receipt of government grant in 1900, 893 were board schools, 687 Church or National schools and 51 British schools. However, there were far more school places available in board schools. In 1900 they accounted for some 65 per cent of school places. In the industrial south the proportion was far greater (Glamorgan 82 per cent, Merthyr Tydfil 74 per cent and Newport 50.4 per cent) than it was in the rural counties (Montgomeryshire 33 per cent, Flintshire 17.8 per cent and Radnorshire 16 per cent).

Swansea, a strongly Dissenting region, had its first school-board election as early as December 1870. It quickly took steps to remedy the deficiency of 4,055 school places, building eighteen large schools in the next ten years. It also took over some British and works schools, so that by 1884 there were more board schools than there were voluntary schools in the town. In Merthyr Tydfil, as in Swansea, there was a substantial deficiency of school places, a subcommittee set up by the school board 'to discover gaps' finding that for 10,434 children between the ages of three and thirteen (middle-class children were excluded) there were only 6,556 places available; the board soon took over the British schools and the Cyfarthfa ironworks school (later also the celebrated Dowlais school of the Guest family) as well as building new ones; by 1890 some three-quarters of children in Merthyr Tydfil were attending board schools.

Rural boards were not idle. In Montgomeryshire there were difficulties in purchasing land from hostile landowners, especially in the Anglicized parts near the English border. Nevertheless, twenty-five board and British schools were built between 1870 and 1902 compared with twelve Church schools. In Haverfordwest, landlords' opposition to a school board was overruled at a meeting of the town council, while at St David's, resistance from the cathedral clergy did not prevent a board from being set up. Gradually, board schools appeared throughout the county.

The advent of school boards laid the foundation for a nationwide system of elementary schooling in Wales as in England but serious problems remained at least until the turn of the century – defective buildings, lack of equipment, inappropriate teaching methods, and disciplinary problems.

Above all, there was the perennial difficulty of poor attendance. Compulsory schooling had been no part of the Act of 1870: the Act was permissive in that powers were granted to boards to make attendance compulsory between the ages of five and ten. Only some adopted this policy, and regulation to this effect was not made mandatory until 1880. Notwithstanding compulsion, elementary education in Wales continued to be bedevilled by poor attendance until the turn of the century.

Attendance was always proportionately lower than in England – 75.6 per cent in 1899 as compared with 81.55 per cent in England. There were many factors which accounted for this poor record: the ready market for child labour which brought families extra income, hostility towards compulsion, the indifference and apathy of some parents who saw little point in schooling, and the frequent epidemics of childhood diseases such as whooping cough and scarlet fever. There is little doubt, though, that payment of school pence imposed an often insuperable burden, especially on the large families common at the time.

Poor attendance affected examination results. Because the grant system was based on results as well as attendance records, this led to a loss of grant income and of fees. As it was to the advantage of teachers that attendance should be high, some boards insisted that teachers take some responsibility for persuading parents to send their children to school and for collecting fines. One such board was that at Swansea. In 1878 a scale of salaries was devised according to which 'an inducement . . . is offered . . . to collect school pence, with that care and exactness which the Board had never been able to secure under the previous arrangement, while carelessness in collecting the fees or keeping up attendance, is rewarded by corresponding deductions'.

The state of school buildings in Wales continued to cause major concern. At the time of the Act they were generally inadequate, and, despite the Education Department's insistence on better conditions, many remained cold, damp and lacking cloakrooms and lavatories. Generally, the voluntary schools were in a far worse state than the board schools with the private adventure schools being worst of all.

Some boards building new schools employed their own architects, while others invited professional architects to compete. Smaller and poorer boards often used local builders, the design and construction of their schools reflecting this. Most designs, however, were executed by trained, experienced architects. The resulting buildings varied enormously in style, from the vernacular to the simple Gothic.

Variations in size, style, and layout reflected local pride and competitive spirit among the boards, as well as the personal predilections of individual architects. In Cardiff, the schools usually comprised a single storey for infants with an adjoining two-storey building for boys and girls. The largest school was at Lansdowne Road, built at a cost of £14,800, to accommodate 1,484 children. In Swansea, there were three-decker schools with infants on the ground floor, the largest of which was the Manselton School, designed by a London architect and built at a cost of £23,500 for 1,200 pupils. More elaborate buildings were required for the higher-grade schools built in the 1880s. The largest in Cardiff, Howard Gardens, accommodated 800 boys and girls. It was a two-storey brick building with a central schoolroom and four classrooms on the ground floor for boys, and a schoolroom and three classrooms for girls on the first floor, while the ground floor also housed a laboratory. Trinity Place Higher Grade School in Swansea, built of stone, contained two manual instruction rooms, a gymnasium, two art rooms and a chemistry laboratory.

The extensive school-board building programme saw costs increase from £5–£10 per pupil place in the 1870s to between £10 and £15 per place in the 1880s. The expenditure of the Swansea School Board in 1883, 1884 and 1885 was respectively, £11,075, £15,544 and £16,064. When advocating his Bill, Forster had spoken of a 3d rate, but within a few months of the Act's coming into operation it was obvious that he had grossly underestimated the cost. Not surprisingly, many ratepayers opposed rates being constantly increased to support a building programme of schools to accommodate the lower-middle and working classes.

Income for school boards could be derived partially from fees, the maximum legally allowable being 9d a week. We have noted that Marsden has demonstrated how, in England, a hierarchy of schools developed within some school boards with a close correlation between fee levels and residential area; London School Board in 1873, for instance, had schools where fees varied from 1d or 2d in most areas to 6d a week in select areas. Fees in voluntary schools in England, too, were generally high, varying from 3d to 9d. School boards in Wales, on the other hand, generally imposed a uniform fee on all their schools. The scale of fees for all schools under the Ystradfodwg School Board (Rhondda), for instance, was, for Standard I pupils, 2d; Standards II and III, 3d; and Standards IV and V, 4d. Mindful of the needs of poor parents, it reduced fees in 1880: Infants, 1d; Standards I and II, 2d; Standards III and IV, 3d; and Standards V and VI, 4d. Consideration for parents of large families also led to the imposition of a maximum fee of 9d on any parent, irrespective of the number of children at school. Several boards remitted the whole or part of school fees for a period for parents who were unable to pay on account of poverty.

The success or otherwise of schools was heavily dependent on the quality of teaching, which, despite remarkable improvements after 1870, continued to be a matter of concern to the inspectorate and Education Department. In the 1890s the opening of pupil-teacher centres where pupil-teachers could spend half a day receiving instruction, the other half being spent in teaching in schools, brought improvements in the pupil-teacher system. Uncertificated teachers were gradually crowded out by the increasing numbers of students leaving the training colleges as well as those from the university day-training departments established in the 1890s. A rapid increase in numbers of teachers followed, adding another element to those educated sectors in Welsh society which could provide leadership in social, political and cultural life.

Life was not easy for teachers; constantly under pressure in very large classes, they had to deal with children of mixed ages and different abilities, many of whom were from poor homes. Teachers were faced with the task of coaching them rigorously with inadequate books, materials and equipment in order to attain the high examination pass rates required to obtain government grants. Against this background, discipline was always a vexed problem, with use of the cane widespread. Complaints against teachers for handing out severe punishments were frequent. According to Robert Smith, 'the press for this period is littered with references to assault charges against members of the teaching profession'; he cites a case in Mountain Ash in 1884 when one of the town's schoolmasters was fined 10s when magistrates decided that the punishment he had inflicted upon a pupil had been so severe as to constitute an assault (though probably only a minority of teachers were guilty of sadistic behaviour). Adding to teachers' difficulties were their relationships with both the school board and with the inspectorate. If a teacher crossed the school board there was no appeal available, added to which there was no standard salary scale, so it was essential not to cause offence to employers who had the power to set pay. Such a process was patently open to abuse, sometimes leading to nepotism and favouritism. Teachers felt that inspectors were more concerned to seek out failings rather than successes. A damning report from an inspector was very damaging to a teacher's career, for there was no means of redress through school board or Education Department.

Teaching was, nevertheless, a popular career in Wales. This may, however, have been more a reflection of limited career options than of the inherent attractions of teaching itself; against a background of agricultural depression and constant fluctuations in the fortunes of industries, teaching represented stability and a degree of status which offset low pay and unfavourable conditions of work. At the turn of the century between one in four and one in three boys and 30 to 50 per cent of girls leaving secondary schools in south Wales became teachers.

Between 1870 and 1900 the curriculum for elementary schools changed. Robert Lowe's Code of 1862, which had restricted grants to success in the three Rs, had encouraged uninspiring teaching, rote learning and cramming. Teachers and pupils prioritized plotting to outwit inspectors.

Gradually the curriculum was widened as grants became available for history, geography and science, and, following a recommendation of the Cross Commission in 1888, for domestic science for girls and woodwork and metalwork for boys. The curriculum in Welsh schools followed that in England, though one characteristic feature was the popularity of music, essentially singing.

Language distinguished Wales. In 1870 nearly three-quarters of the population could speak Welsh. For the majority it was their first language; for some, especially in rural areas, their only language. The Education Act was designed for England, with no special consideration for the people of Wales or the Welsh language. Welsh was not an official language. It was not the language of industry and commerce, nor of genteel society; it was associated with the working class and held in low social esteem. The mindset of the school inspectors of the 1840s and the 1846–7 commissioners that the Welsh language was an obstacle to personal and social development, as well as economic advancement, held firm, with increasingly notable inspectorial exceptions. Many of those sympathetic to the language felt that its care could be safely left to the Sunday schools.

There was, therefore, little attempt to teach Welsh initially. However, because many children knew little English, instruction in that language often proved a failure, the difficulties being compounded by the idiosyncrasies of English pronunciation compared with phonetic Welsh. There were critics who advocated the use of Welsh as a means of teaching English and other subjects; these included some school inspectors, although most were hostile to the Welsh language. General hostility among the influential, as well as landowners and clergy, created a cultural atmosphere that influenced teachers, many of whom in the 1870s were English. Some teachers forbade the use of Welsh in the classroom and on the school premises, usually from a desire to improve the spread of English. Whatever the motive, it led to anger and resentment over the 'Welsh Not', a wooden plaque tied around the neck of any pupil speaking Welsh and passed on from one offender to another; at the end of each day its wearer was punished. There is plenty of anecdotal evidence of its use, most famously from O. M. Edwards, but no firm statistics as to how widespread it was. There is no evidence that it was used in board schools.

During the national reawakening of the final quarter of the century, a revival of interest in Welsh language, literature and history influenced official bodies to adopt a more sympathetic approach to the language, as evidenced in the main and minority reports of the Cross Commission in 1888. In the same year the North Wales Liberal Federation committed itself to a campaign for greater use of Welsh. The feeling grew that the teaching of Welsh should be recognized in its own right, quite apart from any improvements effected in children learning English. Towards the end of the century some school boards attempted, not without difficulty, to introduce Welsh, changes in the elementary-school code in the 1880s having made that possible. By this time, however, the proportion of Welsh-speakers had fallen to a half. There were many reasons, quite apart from its absence from the curriculum: rapid industrialization had brought in waves of immigrants from England, and the building of roads, railways and houses had created a vast labour force, many of whom were English or Irish; the language of rapidly expanding commerce tended to be English; chapels and Sunday schools, particularly in industrial areas, were forced to accommodate increasing numbers of monoglot English; the theatre and music hall were increasingly popular; the language of play in the streets was increasingly English.

Apart from the language issue, Welsh elementary education to 1900 was similar to that of England. The various acts, codes and changes in regulations were designed to suit English requirements, with Wales of no greater significance than an English county. No specific Welsh ethos or view developed. The powerful alliance between Liberalism and Welsh Nonconformity had little direct impact on the provision of elementary education; for the influence of that formidable political force we will turn later to secondary and higher education.

The success of the new system of state elementary education can only be measured objectively in crude terms. Obviously, given compulsory attendance, all but a very few boys and girls obtained a basic formal education by the end of the nineteenth century, although absenteeism continued to be a problem. Literacy figures, if measured by the ability to write, indicate how much this was needed. In 1870 Wales lagged considerably behind England in numbers able to sign the marriage register – 65 per cent in Wales compared with 76 per cent in England and Wales as a whole, and there was an obvious correlation with the low school-attendance figures.

Another dimension of elementary education was evening-school provision. Most evening classes were held in day-school premises as private ventures by teachers and clergy, pupils being charged 1d a week. According to the education commissioners, 2,000 persons over the age of eighteen attended evening schools in Wales at mid-century, while a further 111,811 adults attended Sunday schools. The growth of evening-class work was hampered by restrictions which limited grants to the three Rs and imposed an upper age limit of twenty-one. The Cross Commission report (1888) recognized the need for further education, as education for the majority of the population often ceased at the age of eleven. Its vision of a new type of evening continuation school was reflected in the Education Codes of 1890 and 1893, which abandoned the upper age limit and offered grants on the basis of attendance figures, rather than on examination results in the three Rs, thus opening the door to an extended curriculum which included languages, sciences, handicrafts, domestic science, shorthand and bookkeeping. From this point on the conventional day-school subjects formed but a small part of the work of evening schools.

The codes and new regulations presented the school boards with exciting opportunities. As early as 25 September 1890 the Cardiff School Board set up an Evening School Committee which resolved that three evening schools be opened and classes held on not less than three evenings a week. By November there were six evening schools with an attendance of 669; by 1902, 1,628 men and 340 women and girls attended the board's classes. The impact of the new codes was felt at Merthyr Tydfil, where the board's first venture in 1886 met with little success, numbers quickly falling. In 1891 when the board tried again, several hundred enrolled for classes in a wide variety of subjects in six evening-class centres. Boards throughout Wales took similar initiatives.

Two years after the profoundly significant Education Act of 1870 had such an impact on the development of elementary education, the opening of the University College of Wales in Aberystwyth marked a new era in higher education. In its early years the college faced myriad obstacles, its experience exposing the deficiencies in Welsh secondary education, as many of the students, who ranged in age from fourteen to twenty-five, were inadequately prepared for university education, especially in the sciences. The college had little appeal for headmasters of the grammar schools, who continued to send their more able pupils to Oxford and Cambridge. Consequently, in the early years students at Aberystwyth were drawn from other quarters, such as theological colleges, private schools and elementary schools. In addition, mature adults, especially farmers, came to study elementary agriculture. In its early years women were allowed to attend only courses in music, rather than study for external degrees of the University of London. Even this concession from a male-dominated academic hierarchy was made only with much gnashing of teeth and attempts to keep male and female students apart, and was withdrawn in 1878.

The college was also beset by acute financial difficulties which inhibited academic developments. A movement to establish it had begun as far back as 1854 but only raised £5,000 by 1867 when a decision was taken to purchase the Castle Hotel, Aberystwyth as a base. Before it opened, the quarry workers of Blaenau Festiniog, Dinorwic and Deiniolen had sub-scribed funds to establish scholarships for local boys, but little systematic attempt had been made to elicit support from local people. This changed when the indefatigable Hugh Owen retired from the civil service to channel his considerable energies into fund-raising. He travelled the length and breadth of Wales, cajoling and organizing house-to-house canvasses and chapel collections. He soon raised £7,000, mostly in small sums, and the debt on the college building had been cleared by 1874. The high esteem in which the college was held in the affection of the people of Wales is reflected in the fact that of the 100,000 individual donations by the end of the century, 91,000 were of half a crown or less. Sadly, this generosity did not characterize landowners and wealthy industrialists. The former were largely indifferent as, with few exceptions, notably the coal owner David Davies of Llandinam, were the latter.

Plagued by financial difficulties, the college enlisted the support of Welsh Liberal MPs, which led in 1880 to a government-appointed six-man committee under the chairmanship of Henry Austin Bruce, Lord Aberdare, 'to inquire into the state of intermediate and higher education in Wales', intermediate being the term then frequently used to describe what we would now call secondary education. After interviewing 256 witnesses the committee produced a report in 1881 which emphasized 'the great prominence that had been given in the evidence of witnesses to the widespread desire for a better education system in Wales'. The committee recommended that there should be two university colleges in Wales, one in the north and one in the south, each supported by a government grant of £4,000. The committee's proposals were soon implemented following the government's assurance that it would accept the recommendation; in October 1883 the University College of South Wales and Monmouthshire opened in Cardiff, followed a year later by the University College of North Wales at Bangor, delegates having turned down the claims of Aberystwyth. The college there nevertheless survived and, from 1886, received a similar £4,000 annual grant.

The Aberdare Committee also determined that secondary education was grossly inadequate and recommended a network of intermediate schools across Wales, though Aberdare's colleagues were persuaded by Dr Hugo Daniel Harper, principal of Jesus College, Oxford, that Wales warranted no more than six or seven schools of the 'first grade', schools which could provide teaching for boys up to eighteen or nineteen years of age in preparation for entry to Oxford and Cambridge.

It took eight years of parliamentary lobbying before the Aberdare proposals on secondary education, somewhat watered down, were enshrined in legislation as the Welsh Intermediate Education Act of 1889, one of the first pieces of legislation of modern times to apply to Wales alone, and therefore of the first importance in modern-day recognition of the distinctive educational needs of Wales. The Act resulted in a system of publicly funded secondary education in Wales thirteen years before England, a crucial precedent for both education and administration.

The Act created in each county a joint education committee, a quasi-representative body, whose members were nominated by the county council (three) and the Privy Council (two), the county councils being answerable to the Charity Commission. The committees were charged with drawing up schemes of intermediate and technical education, the counties being empowered to levy a rate not exceeding ½d for the support of an intermediate education and the sums raised being matched by the Treasury after satisfactory inspection of the schools.

Following the Act, joint education committees were speedily set up and schemes submitted to the Charity Commission for approval and amendment. By the turn of the century there was a network of nearly a hundred schools throughout Wales with a total population of some 7,000 pupils, comprising almost equal numbers of boys and girls. It was the intention of the Aberdare Committee, as of joint education committees, that the existing grammar schools, together with their endowments, should be incorporated into the new county schemes; in the event, seventeen schools did form part of the network, while stout resistance led to several of the more prestigious schools such as Brecon, Cowbridge (until 1919), Llandovery, Monmouth and Ruthin, as well as the Howell foundations in Denbigh and Llandaff, remaining independent, to form the core of the small independent secondary-school sector which remains in Wales to this day.

Ironically, these were schools identified by Harper as 'first-grade'. To fill the gap, several schools in areas where the population had a higher socio-economic element, such as Cardiff, Penarth and Newport, as well as some of the existing grammar schools, such as those at Bangor, Swansea and Wrexham, were allowed to impose higher fees and be considered schools of the 'first grade'.

Fees in the 'first-grade' schools could be as high as £12 a year, but those for second-grade schools (over 80 per cent) generally ranged from £3 to £6. Beneath them in the pecking order were higher-elementary and higher-grade schools, quasi-secondary schools established by school boards under the elementary code. These did not fall within the framework of the 1889 Act and, following the Education Act of 1902, they were taken over by the new local authorities, later being developed as municipal secondary schools. After 1902 local authorities also found it easier to establish new municipal secondary schools than undergo the intricate process of altering their original intermediate schemes drawn up in the 1890s. Thus, in addition to the intermediate-school system with its subtle distinctions and inequalities of resources, another quite separate sector of secondary education developed. As a result, Wales had a dual system of secondary education which was to persist until 1944 and led to confrontation between the bodies involved in their administration.

The administrative and financial arrangements underpinning the intermediate education schemes, in which much of the onus fell on local districts, resulted in a lack of uniformity. The intention was that the average catchment population of a school should be some 8,000; in practice the figures showed a staggering variation. Whilst several districts in rural areas had numbers below this, industrial areas, especially those in Glamorgan, were badly served: Neath (40,249), Aberdare (51,972) and Merthyr Tydfil (58,080). Worst was Porth in the Rhondda with 88,350, an area in which provision was described by J. R. Webster as simply 'woeful'. Glamorgan's was also the last of the schemes of intermediate education ratified by Parliament. Caernarfonshire had been able to make a start in 1893; the Glamorgan scheme, owing to opposition from 'Church' lobbies objecting to the proposal that endowed schools at Gelligaer and Cowbridge be included in a scheme of non-sectarian schools, was not approved until mid-1896.

The consensus in the Aberdare Committee was that the offspring of the upper classes would continue to go to English public schools, whilst first-grade schools under the Act would serve the needs of professional and other middle-class groups. Pupils would expect to remain in those schools until the age of eighteen or nineteen, the more able being prepared for 'Oxbridge' entry. Second-grade schools would provide an education which would cease at sixteen for the majority. The clientele was conceived to be lower-middle-class children, who hitherto had been denied access to secondary education, together with a small number of the more ambitious and able children from working-class families. To this end it would be essential to charge low fees. No second-grade school in Glamorgan imposed a fee greater than £4, but these sums were still a deterrent to many, given the pockets of poverty throughout Wales and the large size of families. Parents also had to meet the cost of uniform, books and rail travel, as well as wages forgone. This had been anticipated by the Aberdare Committee, so the 1889 Act stipulated that scholarships should be provided for between one-tenth and one-fifth of pupils entering the schools from the public elementary schools after competitive examinations. Scholarships were made available by county authorities, district committees and wealthy patrons, often exceeding the minimum number. In addition, district committees awarded bursaries to 'necessitous parents'. Such initiatives were in advance of anything that had hitherto been in place in English or Welsh education.

Most witnesses to the Aberdare Committee were middle class. The few working-class witnesses stressed that a desire for education was widespread among the working class, but it was middle class needs that dominated thinking among protagonists of an extended system of secondary education. Surely, it was only 'exceptional' working-class children who would take advantage of any new system? However, a strong desire to better themselves, and a willingness to make sacrifices, allied to generous scholarship provision, meant confounded predictions. In some rural areas, and in industrial towns in Glamorgan, the proportion of working-class children in the schools at the turn of the century was as high as one in three, substantial numbers being children of unskilled fathers. The intermediate schools had created a 'ladder' extending from the public elementary schools, on the one hand, to the university colleges on the other. There was now a limited opportunity for children of lower-middle-class and working-class parents to go on to higher education, progressively increasing during the next few decades. For some years, social mobility of working-class children was therefore far in advance of that in England, and by 1914 a ladder had been erected which would take more Welsh children into secondary and higher education than anywhere else in western Europe, save Scotland.

This transformation in Welsh society had been effected not only by favourable legislation and sympathetic interpretation by public bodies, but also by the involvement of all sectors of society in providing assistance through scholarships at schools and colleges. A unique feature was the contribution, literally, of countless workers, whether through eisteddfod and chapel collections, or collections by the quarry workers of north Wales and the miners of south Wales. Another facet of this 'culture of support' was its altruism. There was a pride in the achievement of others, the children of one's neighbours or fellow workers who were enabled to attain more respectable jobs or even migrate to more salubrious parts. It is one of the fascinating aspects of the history of Welsh secondary education that it has not only been accepted but a matter of pride in Welsh communities when those who prospered in the system changed their status and left the community.

The intermediate-school achievement has always been a matter of pride in Wales. The higher elementary schools have received less attention. The Aberdare Committee felt that the academic education envisaged in the intermediate schools would be inappropriate for the great majority of working-class and many lower-middle-class children, most of whom would leave school at fourteen to enter employment; an alternative kind of school was therefore needed to prepare these boys and girls for occupations in industry, commerce and agriculture. Such schools had already been pioneered by school boards in some English cities. The members of the Aberdare Committee had little personal knowledge of them but were impressed by the trenchant advocacy of public-school- and Oxford-educated Dr Harper, who had actually visited higher-grade schools in Bradford. He advocated a dozen academic intermediate schools, the remainder of Wales having to be content with higher-elementary schools.

Fortunately for Welsh children the committee rejected this, but proposed that higher-elementary schools would be more suitable in industrial areas.

Further encouragement to set up higher-elementary schools came from A. J. Mundella, Radical MP for Sheffield and Vice-President of the Education Department. On 10 August 1882 he wrote to those school boards in Wales serving populations in excess of 5,000 pointing out that they could receive financial support from the government for doing so. One of the first to respond to Mundella's Circular 213 was that in Swansea, which converted one of its existing schools, Trinity Place, into a higher-grade school, which opened on 10 September 1883 with 150 boys and 100 girls; in the same year, a similar school was opened at Howard Gardens, Cardiff, capable of accommodating 430 boys on the ground floor and 360 girls on the first floor. The curriculum of the schools included mathematics, science, French, history and geography, the fees being 9d a week. Some pupils were prepared for the London University matriculation examinations while, in the upper forms, pupils studied Science and Art Department subjects, examination passes earning grants for the schools. Eventually, some twenty advanced elementary schools were founded in Wales, mostly in the industrial south, only two being in north Wales.

Meanwhile, the intermediate schools, which had been established with such enthusiasm in the 1890s, experienced difficulties of accommodation, staffing, curriculum and school attendance. The first task was the provision of school buildings. Of eighty schools in 1897 only fifty-six were in permanent buildings, temporary accommodation being mostly in private houses; four years later some fourteen schools out of the total of ninety-four were still in makeshift accommodation.

The Aberdare Committee had found that there was urgent need for improvement in the secondary education of girls but it was difficult to make precise recommendations because 'the unsatisfied requirements are so great and the available resources so meagre'. There were merely three endowed schools, the two Howell foundations at Llandaff and Denbigh and the Dr Williams School in Dolgellau, together with a plethora of fee-paying private schools, many of which were sub-standard. The advance in the education of girls may therefore be judged from the composition of the intermediate-school network: the eighty schools comprised nineteen boys' schools, nineteen girls' schools, six mixed schools and thirty-six dual schools, which had separate entrances and classrooms for boys and girls.

As the popularity of the schools increased, pressure grew to provide separate buildings for boys and girls, but accommodation problems were especially acute in sparsely populated rural areas where schools were small. Social differences were reflected in the level of fees charged and in the proportion of pupils drawn from private schools. Whilst in Wales as a whole only 5 cent of pupils were from private schools, in schools of the first grade, such as those at Cardiff and Swansea, some one-third of boys and girls came from privately run elementary schools.

Initially, intermediate-school head teachers were graduates of English universities, mostly of London University and Oxbridge, many of whom had been educated in the classical traditions of English public schools and grammar schools. They had considerable powers in shaping the ethos of a school, in staff recruitment and in determining the curriculum. The head teachers of the two separate boys' and girls' intermediate schools in Cardiff attempted to develop the schools along the lines of English public schools and successfully overcame resistance to having them entitled 'high schools', as opposed to intermediate schools. Most head teachers adopted the practices of school uniform, prefects, competitive games on Saturdays, and school clubs and societies.

In isolated rural areas getting children to school posed a problem, overcome in some cases only by boarding or lodging. At the same time, keeping children at school was difficult. Some parents could not see the advantages in the kind of education provided, but, as with primary schools, the major factors in premature withdrawal from school were financial. The ready availability of jobs in some areas, especially for boys, was an incentive to leave, whilst the expense involved in keeping children at school, the cost of uniform, books, extras for some lessons and train travel, imposed considerable burdens; the head teacher of Bridgend intermediate school successfully prevailed on the Great Western Railway to allow pupils to travel to school at half price. Girls were sometimes withdrawn to care for younger children, ailing parents or widowed fathers.

In 1890 the joint education committees inaugurated a series of meetings to consider setting up a central body to administer the intermediate schools. It was proposed that the Treasury should accept the inspections and examinations administered by such a body as the necessary authority for the payment of government grants to schools under section 5 of the Act of 1889. This was duly approved by the Education Department on 13 August 1895 and led to the establishment of the Central Welsh Board (CWB). It was hoped that coordination by the board would overcome diversity in standards and efficiency in the intermediate schools by inspecting and examining schools on behalf of the Charity Commission, which would in turn report to the Treasury who would sanction the school's grant. CWB examinations led to the award of certificates. Initially there were junior and senior certificates with an honours certificate being inaugurated in 1900; the junior certificate was considered equivalent to Oxford and Cambridge Local examinations, whilst the senior certificate was of the same standard as university matriculation. These certificates were of enormous significance in the development of intermediate schools and in the career prospects of pupils. There were criticisms that they imposed undue pressure on the curriculum and led to cramming, but they provided a focus for the academic work of a school.

Many witnesses impressed on the Aberdare Committee that Wales not only needed an extended system of secondary schools but that they should break away from the traditional classical grammar schools by providing a broad and modern curriculum. As Stuart Rendel, MP for Montgomeryshire, piloted the successful Bill through the House of Commons in May 1889, supporters linked the proposed intermediate education to improving economic and industrial performance, as well as providing a sound liberal education. In the event, the Act referred to technical education as well as to intermediate education. Later, the Central Welsh Board stressed that all schools under the Act were 'intermediate and technical' schools and were expected to make adequate provision for instruction in literary, scientific and technical subjects. The definition of intermediate education under the Act of 1889 included instruction in Latin, Greek, Welsh and English language and literature, modern languages, mathematics and natural science. Of these, English, Latin, a foreign language and mathematics were to be compulsory, as were vocal music and drill, whereas Greek and Welsh were included in a list of 'optional' subjects which also included mechanics, metallurgy, agriculture, woodwork and metalwork, bookkeeping, shorthand and domestic economy. It was not intended that technical education should include the direct teaching of the practices of any trade or industry; in other words, it was not to be orientated towards any specific future occupations.

Central Welsh Board annual reports detail how the schools implemented the various guidelines. For many years the 'core' curriculum of most schools consisted of English, Latin, mathematics, history, geography and French. Initially, about a third of schools taught Greek, but by 1902 only fourteen presented candidates in that subject for CWB examinations. Welsh, on the other hand, showed a very slow but steady growth so that, by 1902, nearly half of the schools, mostly in the north and west, entered candidates. Spanish was taught in only one school, German in fewer than ten. Of the sciences, chemistry was the most popular, though botany was the premier science in most girls' schools; even so, fewer than one in three schools offered botany, whilst physics languished, not more than one in four schools teaching the subject. One in five also offered bookkeeping, shorthand, domestic economy and needlework, whilst a small number included physiology and hygiene.

Despite the intention of the Act, very few schools offered technical subjects. In 1898 four schools included agriculture but by 1903 it had disappeared from the list of CWB successes, as had geology and metallurgy. Commercial subjects and handicrafts proved more popular; in 1901 there were 186 candidates in woodwork and metalwork from eighteen schools and 547 in cookery from thirty-eight schools. The respective numbers of schools presenting candidates for other subjects were: domestic economy 29, needlework 18, bookkeeping 21 and shorthand 20. In an attempt to encourage pupils to take up technical and commercial subjects, the board introduced specific technical and commercial certificates in 1900, but these had little appeal.

Given the background of head teachers and teachers, and the low esteem in which technical education was held, the failure to promote technical subjects was not surprising. Neither was it unexpected that take-up of the sciences proved disappointing for many years. Thirty years earlier, a Royal Commission under the duke of Devonshire had found that the position of science in the public and grammar schools was highly unsatisfactory. Head teachers were hostile, laboratories expensive and qualified science teachers scarce. The only Welsh school among the returns was Monmouth School, where forty out of the 200 pupils were studying elementary science for two hours a week. A surprising omission was the Welsh Collegiate Institution at Llandovery, founded under the will of Thomas Phillips, a wealthy London doctor, whose aim was to foster a national spirit in Wales through lectures on subjects connected with the language, history and antiquities of Wales, and especially agriculture. According to James Bryce, the assistant commissioner for the Taunton Commission, the founder's intentions with regard to Welsh studies 'do not seem to have been carried out', while it could 'hardly be thought either that the experiment of making science an essential part of the teaching has been fairly tried', despite the appointment of a science teacher to teach all boys one hour a week of elementary science.

Thirty years after the Taunton and Devonshire investigations, Welsh intermediate schools were experiencing similar difficulties to those which had hampered the promotion of science in English schools. In the initial years, examiners repeatedly criticized the standard of teaching in the sciences and the poor provision of equipment and laboratories, the latter being especially acute in physics; a further factor jeopardizing promotion of the subject was the failure of the University of Wales (established in 1893) to recognize the subject for the purposes of university matriculation. Improvements there were, but progress was slow. Despite the growing enthusiasm of science teachers, the chief inspector reported in 1902 that science teaching 'leaves much to be desired'; in particular, the position of physics, still unrecognized by the university, was 'not altogether satisfactory'.

The failure of the intermediate schools to promote technical and commercial subjects was the subject of widespread criticism from outside educational circles as well as from the board and the Charity Commission.

In practice, the majority became academic institutions in which the humanities predominated, and they paid little or no attention to the practical side of the curriculum. In 1899 the Charity Commission complained of the 'urgent need of pressing forward the technical as distinct from the literary or general side of intermediate education'. Such a hope, however, was never fulfilled.

Nonetheless the creation of a network of so many schools under a unified system of organization and control was a remarkable achievement. By 1905, over 10,000 children, mostly from lower-middle-class homes, but also including substantial numbers of working-class pupils in some areas, were benefiting from a secondary education which would, hitherto, have been denied them. This was certainly so in industrial areas: sampling second-grade schools, which included Gowerton, Pengam and Porth, revealed that over half the pupils had fathers who were skilled or unskilled workers. This compared with only 10 per cent at the Cardiff High Schools (first-grade schools) and 5 per cent at Swansea and Cowbridge Grammar Schools. None of the pupils at Cardiff, Swansea and Cowbridge had fathers who were unskilled workers, but over a quarter of those at the second-grade intermediate schools were in this category. The majority of pupils left at the age of sixteen, if not earlier, but a growing minority went on to higher education in training colleges and university colleges. From its beginning, the University College at Aberystwyth had suffered from the poor and variable quality of its entrants; this was also the experience of its sister colleges at Bangor and Cardiff in the 1880s. By 1900 the intermediate schools were providing cadres of well-qualified and suitably prepared students; the schools had become essential 'feeders' to the three colleges. The bias towards humanities, though, was reflected in the colleges, where for some time numbers of students of humanities outstripped those in the sciences.

Students at the three Welsh university colleges originally pursued courses leading to a degree of the University of London. But in 1893 the University of Wales received its charter with 'power to grant degrees in faculties of arts or letters, sciences, technology or applied science, law, music and such other faculties as may from time to time be established'. A federal university along the lines of London University, its function was to monitor and approve courses at the three colleges, courses which could lead to the award of degrees, initially only in arts and sciences.

For many years the Welsh university colleges suffered from serious underfunding, despite annual Treasury grants of £4,000 apiece; even in 1914 the Welsh colleges depended on state aid for over half of their income, compared with 35 per cent for those English colleges in receipt of state aid. Especially acute was the lack of endowments to provide chairs. Whereas manufacturers, merchants and even landowners gave generous support to English civic colleges, in Wales they largely stood aside. Consequently the colleges depended on the good will of the middle and working classes who made up in numbers for the small size of their individual contributions. The majority of these were Nonconformists heavily involved in supporting their chapels and theological colleges, so not well placed to provide the considerable sums required. A lack of financial resources, therefore, hampered academic developments in the early years, especially in the technologies.

Nevertheless, by 1900 the three colleges had established a broad range of departments in the arts and sciences. In all the arts faculties there were departments or staff for Greek, Latin, Hebrew, English, Welsh, French, German and history. Music had been promoted at Aberystwyth and Cardiff, courses being pioneered which later led to a Mus. Bac. degree. Aberystwyth founded a Law School in 1899 and introduced teaching in political economy, whilst Cardiff pioneered political science through appointing (Sir) Sydney Chapman, later Professor of Political Economy at Manchester; he was succeeded at Cardiff by an equally distinguished scholar, Henry Stanley Jevons. The limitation of the study of geography to the college at Aberyswyth was partly a reflection of its lack of popularity in schools at the time. A major success story of the colleges was the elevation of the standing of Welsh studies in the academic world as a result of the work of a small coterie of distinguished scholars, first in Welsh language and literature, later in Welsh history. The Cardiff college appointed a Professor of Celtic in 1884.

As with the arts, a 'core' of science subjects was established in all three colleges – mathematics, physics, chemistry, botany and zoology. Geology was taught at both Aberystwyth and Cardiff, whereas at Bangor an attempt to make an appointment failed to elicit the necessary financial support from wealthy local quarry owners. Until the outbreak of the First World War, technologies did not enjoy the same degree of success. When the Aberdare Committee proposed that higher education in Wales be extended by the addition of at least one further university college it stressed that the colleges 'should be adapted in the course of instruction given to the particular circumstances of the country', and that prominence should be given to the various branches of natural science, 'especially in their practical applications to commerce and manufacture'.

The most positive outcome in this respect was the promotion of agricultural studies at Aberystwyth and Bangor, and the consequent benefits to farmers and the agricultural economy. In 1884 (Sir) J. J. Dobbie, who had been educated at Glasgow, Edinburgh and Leipzig, was appointed Professor of Chemistry in Bangor. His interests in the applications of chemistry to agriculture led four years later to the award of annual grants to Bangor and to the creation of a Department of

Agriculture. His work in agricultural education, especially extension work in the science of dairying to farmers, became a model for several other universities, including Aberystwyth. Bangor, too, had been one of the only two colleges selected by the Board of Agriculture to provide instruction in forestry which led to the creation of a department in that subject. An unusual initiative at Bangor was the pioneering of electrical engineering by the physics department as a result of financial support from the Drapers' Company of London.

The University College of South Wales and Monmouthshire, meanwhile, at the hub of commercial activity and adjacent to the thriving south Wales coalfield, had been intended by the Aberdare Committee to be the 'flagship' of higher technological studies in Wales, but no financial support from the government became available for technology at Cardiff in contrast to the support given to agriculture and forestry at Aberystwyth and Bangor. In the absence of funds from that source the college was dependent for the promotion of expensive technologies on the numerous wealthy landowners and industrial magnates in the region. Unfortunately their help was singularly unforthcoming. Engineering was developed after 1891 only with generous support from the Drapers' Company of London, whilst the paltry sums collected in support of metallurgy and mining held back advances in those areas. In 1907 the new principal, Professor E. H. Griffiths, attempted to enlist the aid of leading coal owners to find £50,000 for a department of mining. Less than £10,000 had been donated when the coal owners broke off negotiations, allegedly over differences over the control and content of courses, and set up their own School of Mines at Treforest in 1913, funded largely through a levy of one tenth of a penny on each ton of coal produced.

One success story at Cardiff, on the other hand, was the promotion of sciences relating to medicine. In 1893 the college established departments of anatomy and physiology which enabled students to complete their pre-clinical studies at Cardiff, before embarking on their medical studies in London and elsewhere. Ultimately this led to the creation of a Welsh National School of Medicine under the University of Wales, which made a special feature of the study of tuberculosis. In the 1900s this disease was responsible for 10 per cent of all deaths in Wales, prompting an anti-TB campaign to which David Davies, grandson of the Llandinam industrialist, contributed £125,000; by 1914 ten specialist hospitals had been opened. Of particular significance to the mining industry, TB and other lung diseases continued to be scourges during the Depression of the 1920s and 1930s. TB also devastated rural areas owing to endemic poverty and inadequate housing. In 1931, a chair in the subject was established at the University College in Cardiff as a result of the generous financial support of the Llandinam family.

The Cardiff college was the first of the university colleges in Wales to become involved in teacher training. In 1888, the Cross Commission recommended setting up day training departments in university colleges and universities. These departments would enable students to obtain their training as non-residents; they would get their general education (BA or B.Sc.) in college classes. In 1890 Cardiff started to train men for elementary-school teaching, following it in 1892 with a separate department to train women for secondary-school teaching; Aberystwyth followed suit in 1892 and Bangor in 1894. For women, in particular this represented a significant extension of their opportunities to acquire higher education.

Dependent on the products of the intermediate schools, the student composition of the colleges reflected the curricula available in the schools and the popularity of individual subjects among pupils. The result was a definite bias to the arts and humanities in the colleges. Between 1897 and 1907, 903 students were awarded degrees in the arts but only 298 in the sciences. At honours level the disparity was even greater – 525 to 81. Whereas in 1913 two out of three students in Wales were studying humanities, in English colleges only one in three was doing so. Furthermore, the proportion of engineering students in English university colleges was three times as great as it was in Wales. There was undoubtedly an inclination in Wales to pursue highly esteemed careers in law, teaching and the ministry; but such figures may also reflect a distaste in Wales for industrial technology and careers in industries, as the destructive and unpleasant features were only too apparent. Furthermore, there was little in the way of a diversified manufacturing industry to create much of a demand for engineers.

The Welsh university colleges differed from their English counterparts in other respects, too. Whereas in Wales all first-degree students were studying full-time, at the English colleges there were some 600 students who were pursuing bachelor degrees either on a part-time day or evening basis. While there were nearly 9,000 evening students at English colleges there were none in Wales. Full-time study, though, was more accessible to students of modest means than was the case in English colleges: at Bangor in the session 1906–7 some 30 per cent were from working-class homes, with possibly a further 37 per cent from lower-middle-class backgrounds; at Aberystwyth in the following session, 22 per cent were from the working class and 33 per cent from lower-middle-class homes. That such high proportions of students were from these backgrounds was due largely to the generous provision of scholarships and bursaries available as a result of contributions from individuals, official bodies, chapels and groups of workers as well as local authorities.

Students entering University College, Cardiff owed much to the support given by local authorities, beginning in 1891, when the newly appointed joint education committee of the county of Glamorgan entered into an agreement to pay the college £1,000 a year from funds available to it under the Technical Instruction Act 1889, in return for which the college would maintain twenty-five 'free studentships' for county students successful in a competitive examination, each receiving a scholarship of £30 a year and an annual 'maintenance' award of £40. There were also 'exhibitions' of lower value. Similar agreements followed with Monmouthshire County Council, the Corporation of Cardiff and the County Borough of Newport. By 1913, 478 students had benefited from studentships, 115 from exhibitions.

In improvements in educational provision in nineteenth-century Wales it was generally the needs of boys that dominated thinking. In the moves to provide elementary schooling in the first half of the century, education was seen as being of lesser importance for girls. The 1846 commissioners noted that there were considerably fewer girls in the public day schools than there were boys; not surprisingly, literacy rates among girls in the 1860s were lower than they were among boys. The establishment view was that the object of education for lower-middle-class and working-class girls was to make them more suitable as domestic servants for middle-class families and later, when married, to be good wives and mothers, even a moral force countering the intemperate example of husbands. Following the Revised Code of 1862 instruction centred on the three Rs, with little attempt to provide any 'female' element until the introduction of 'specific' subjects such as needlework, cookery and domestic economy later in the century.

Education for middle-class girls, meanwhile, was seen in the perspective of the ideal of womanhood as the perfect wife and mother; the three Rs were buttressed by 'accomplishments' such as French, needlework, music and dancing. Academic education was not deemed necessary, some die-hards even arguing that women's brain capacity was smaller, so that overload would create stress and mental-health problems. There was no overriding necessity to provide an education which would lead to career opportunities, as these were severely circumscribed, confined largely to positions as governesses or teachers. Even the latter career was largely limited to posts as uncertificated teachers, for, while there were training colleges for women in England in the 1850s, there was none in Wales until 1872.

A plethora of private schools and academies, both day and boarding, throughout Wales generally concentrated on inculcating the correct modes of social behaviour and the acquisition of 'accomplishments to enhance the marriage prospects of girls'. These were expensive institutions, with fees ranging from twenty to forty guineas and patronized, by and large, by the daughters of merchants, manufacturers, professional men and farmers.

Conservatism, prejudice and tradition characterized attitudes to female education. Not everyone accepted this limited vision. During the second half of the nineteenth century, in particular, activists of both sexes demanded greater opportunities and a more advanced curriculum for women. Among them were: Lady Charlotte Guest and Mrs Rose Crawshay, wives of leading industrialists; Lady Llanover and Frances Elizabeth Hoggan, born in Brecon, educated at Zurich, Vienna and Prague, the second woman to be accepted on the Medical Registry of doctors; the radical Denbigh publisher Thomas Gee; the Revd Evan Jones (Ieuan Gwynedd); and John Gibson, editor of the *Cambrian News* and author of *The Emancipation of Women*. The final quarter of the century, in particular, witnessed remarkable efforts by a few public figures, men and women, to modify a male-dominated society. The education system, as the pioneering study by the late Dr Gareth Evans showed, benefited considerably.

No woman was appointed to the Aberdare Committee, but nine women who testified made a considerable impression on the committee. We have seen that there were three endowed schools for girls in Wales, educating only 263 girls; there were in addition seventy-three private schools, mostly of a low standard, with 1,870 girls. By that time advances had been made in England where the Girls' Public Day School Trust had been active in establishing a number of schools. In Wales, the 1880s were marked by an intensity of effort resulting in the first Girls' Public Day School Trust school being founded in Swansea in 1882 and, four years later, a powerful new body, the Association for the Promotion of Education for Girls in Wales. A non-sectarian training college for women was opened in 1872 in Swansea by the British Society in Dr Evan Davies's former school. When the university college opened in Cardiff in 1883, women were admitted along with men, a practice soon followed by the colleges at Aberystwyth and Bangor; within a few years nearly a third of students at each college were women, for whom halls of residence were quickly established. Career opportunities were further enhanced in the 1890s when the colleges established day training colleges in which both men and women could train to be teachers after graduating in arts or science. In 1892 Cardiff also established a section to train women as secondary-school teachers.

Meanwhile, the introduction of domestic subjects in elementary schools created a need for teachers qualified to teach needlework and cookery in particular, so in 1891 the South Wales and Monmouthshire Training School of Cookery and Domestic Arts was established at Cardiff under the joint aegis of the University College and the school board. By 1897, St Mary's Training College, Bangor, originally known as the North Wales Training College, which had trained men since 1856, converted to training women, while women students were admitted to Bangor Normal College from 1908.

Frances Hoggan had called for 'technical' subjects for girls. As we have seen, the ethos of the intermediate schools was strongly 'liberal', non-technical and non-commercial, so not all schools heeded her advice. Nonetheless the intermediate schools made far greater progress towards providing commercial subjects for girls than for boys; of 93 schools in 1900, 21 were offering bookkeeping, 20 shorthand, 29 domestic economy and 18 needlework. While it is generally acknowledged that the advent of intermediate schools, training colleges and university colleges heralded a new era for middle-class girls, the opportunity they presented to the more aspiring element among working-class girls tends to be overlooked. For instance, in five intermediate schools in Glamorgan between one-third and one-half of the girls entering in the 1900s were from working-class backgrounds, and all came from public elementary schools.

In contrast, career opportunities on leaving were limited, the major career path open to women being schoolteaching, which attracted about 40 per cent. Some took up dressmaking and millinery, others became shop assistants, while only a few went in for nursing or clerical work. Between 10 and 30 per cent were described several years later as being 'at home', many perhaps caring for elderly relatives.

Despite the benefits for Welsh society of the establishment of university colleges and intermediate schools, the majority of children left school at fourteen, or even earlier. (The school-leaving age was raised to twelve for all pupils only in 1899.) Throughout much of the century, evening classes centred on the three Rs had provided opportunities which compensated for the lack of elementary education, but changes to the Elementary Education Act in 1893 extended the curriculum, making a range of commercial and craft subjects available. Evening classes, too, constituted the major provision for anyone wishing to acquire knowledge of scientific or technical subjects, areas largely absent from elementary and secondary education until late in the century. It was the Department of Science and Arts' scheme of examinations and financial support introduced in 1859 which helped to spread classes in science and technical subjects through-out the United Kingdom. Intended primarily for artisans, mechanics and factory operatives, classes in twenty-five subjects appealed also to clerks, teachers and pupil-teachers, among others.

There were weaknesses across the United Kingdom in the department's scheme. Local individuals and bodies had to provide accommodation, find suitable teachers and maintain buildings. Putting the onus on local commun-ities led to a very uneven distribution of classes, with provision in many rural counties being greater than in industrial counties. What is surprising, though, is the extent to which provision of class centres, and numbers of students in relation to population, was much lower in Wales, not only compared with those in England, but also Scotland and Ireland. In 1880 23 students per

10,000 of the population in England were in classes run in conjunction with the department's scheme, 16.2 per 10,000 in Scotland and 15 per 10,000 in Ireland. In Wales there were only 11.2 per 10,000. No English county had fewer students under instruction in relation to population than did Wales as a whole. The disparity continued to the end of the century.

Wales was slow to take advantage of the department's scheme, the first classes not appearing until 1866 at Cardiff. The 1859 minutes of the Literary and Scientific Institution at Ebbw Vale noted the receipt of the Circular Science Form 17 from the department, but it was eighteen years before classes were successfully introduced. Other towns in Wales, too, were slow to respond to visits by representatives of the department to draw attention to the merits of its scheme. By 1875 there were thirty-four centres in Wales, rising to 134 by 1890, by which time classes were well established in the leading centres of population. Swansea led the way with six centres and 1,269 students enrolled. In Cardiff there were three centres, with 930 students; Llanelli had five centres and 240 students; Aberdare, four centres and 216 students; and Merthyr Tydfil, three centres and 335 students. The greater provision (and support for) such education in Scotland is reflected in the fact that there were no fewer than fifty-one centres in Glasgow, attended by over 9,000 students. Of course, Glasgow was a far larger centre of population than any in Wales, but even Aberdeen had fourteen centres, with 2,077 students. Outside the major towns in Wales opportunities were more limited, for other towns and villages often had only one class centre: these included Neath (65 students), Briton Ferry (24), Maesteg (9), Cilfynydd (27), Treherbert (38), Treharris (34), Porth (33), Ynyshir (32), Penygraig (16), Abertillery (13), and Ebbw Vale (65), and in north Wales, Wrexham (33), Welshpool (6) and Newtown (22), though there were 116 attending the higher-grade school at Blaenau Festiniog in the centre of the slate industry.

By 1890 board schools had become the major class venue, accommodating sixty-five class centres, whilst some National, British and private schools were also used. Higher-grade schools proved to be popular venues, those at Cardiff, Swansea and Blaenau Festiniog attracting 554, 675 and 116 students respectively. In Merthyr Tydfil the school board had set up two advanced elementary schools, with 174 and 43 students respectively on roll. In the more rural parts of Wales, endowed grammar schools also served as centres, as did the university colleges and St David's College, Lampeter. The response of local communities to the department's scheme is also reflected in the wide diversity of locations which served as class centres, including assembly rooms, YMCAs, Odd Fellows halls, a young ladies' establishment, and academies and institutes of varying kinds.

Twenty years after the inauguration of the department's scheme, concern over the state of technical education had prompted the livery companies of London to set up the City and Guilds of London Institute, which in 1879 took over the scheme of examinations in technological subjects pioneered by the Royal Society of Arts (RSA). This scheme in technological subjects was analogous to that of the Department of Science and Art, with prizes awarded to students and financial rewards to teachers on a 'payment-by-results' basis. The Guilds examinations, intended for artisans, apprentices, foremen and managers, embraced over seventy subjects, covering trades and manufacturing processes, by 1900. As with the department's scheme, the failure rate was high; only one in four students who achieved average attendance in England and Wales succeeded in passing the examinations. That the provision of classes in Wales was but a fraction of that in England, or even Scotland, was to be expected, but what is surprising is that provision in largely rural Ireland exceeded that in Wales. In 1903 there were only ten class centres in Wales when 148 candidates were examined, only eleven of these candidates coming from outside Glamorgan. Respective figures for other countries were: England 340 and 21,421; Scotland 28 and 874; and Ireland 16 and 824. By 1913 the number of candidates presenting for examinations in Wales had increased to 503 at twenty-six centres.

The Technical Instruction Act of 1889 had enabled county and county borough councils to set up technical instruction committees empowered to spend the proceeds of a penny rate to promote technical instruction, with further money available through the Local Taxation (Customs and Excise) Act of 1890. The passing of the Technical Instruction Act within weeks of the Welsh Intermediate Education Act led in Wales to the establishment in each county of joint education committees with a remit to 'promote both intermediate and technical education'.

The Joint Education Committee for Glamorgan, formed in 1892, quickly took over the administration of all technical classes in the county. Additionally it agreed to give University College, Cardiff £1,000 annually, in return for accommodation for technical classes. The committee viewed the intermediate schools, too, as providers of technical education, so it wanted the schools built quickly. The committee was inundated with applications for financial assistance which it could not meet within its resources. According to the Technical Instruction Act of 1889, all twenty-five subjects included in the scheme of the Department of Science fell within the definition of technical education, the department being made the final arbiter of what else could be promoted and subsidized.

The lack of an agreed definition of technical education was reflected in the diversity of the provision that gradually emerged under the committee's auspices. The Glamorgan Joint Education Committee successfully negotiated the award of grants for classes in a broad range of technical, craft, commercial and other subjects. The programme of classes included dairywork, cheesemaking, ambulance work, home nursing, domestic economy, hygiene, dressmaking, cookery, weaving, poultry farming and even music. The committee also established a butter school, gave £2,000 for the setting up of a department of public health at the University College in Cardiff and provided scholarships for cookery students to attend the Cardiff School of Cookery and for dairy students to attend the British Dairy Institute.

By the turn of the century its programme had expanded to such an extent that there were over 200 classes in forty-two towns and villages throughout Glamorgan. Large numbers of students often enrolled, but as was common with evening classes, attendances quickly dropped off. The numbers of students enrolled for the most popular subjects with average attendances in parenthesis were: ambulance work, 1,163 (873); principles of mining, 703 (392); shorthand, 561 (389); mathematics, 506 (280); music, 385 (215); physiography, 343 (213); and French, 348 (201).

The Cardiff technical instruction committee was similarly successful in expanding its programme of evening classes, additionally giving £600 annually to the University College to promote technical education. County councils were active throughout Wales, though, because of the smaller populations involved, not to the same extent. However, expansion in the number of classes and students was not the whole story. Critics pinpointed weaknesses. Classes in Cardiff and Swansea, as elsewhere, were held in a variety of centres, many of which were unsuitable. Technical education was characterized by haphazard and unconnected classes, most held in the evenings. Teachers had no guarantee of a fixed income, facing a severe drop in attendance in the first few weeks following enrolment. One of the features of technical education in England and Scotland in the last years of the century, contrasting with Wales, was the emergence of purpose-built technical colleges in several towns and cities. Their absence in Wales was due partly to the failure of the mechanics'-institute movement in Wales to make the kind of impact it had made in England and Scotland, for mechanics' institutes were the precursors of flourishing technical colleges at Manchester, Bradford, Salford and Keighley, to take a few examples. But local committees also failed to pursue energetically the aim of establishing a technical college through utilizing the funds at their disposal and successfully enlisting the support of manufacturers and merchants.

In Cardiff, the technical instruction committee resolved in its first year to make in Cardiff 'a Technological department that shall more than rival even the famous continental schools'. As we have seen, the University College struggled to establish such disciplines as engineering, mining and metallurgy. Housed in the temporary premises of the Old Infirmary until 1909, the college was in no position to provide a proper base for other technical and commercial education. Not until 1914 were purpose-built premises meriting the designation 'technical college' constructed, and it was 1916 before classes could be transferred there. Meanwhile, one of the first actions of the technical instruction committee at Swansea was to make the Free Grammar School an intermediate and technical school under the terms of the Welsh Intermediate Education Act of 1889, with Dr George Sherbrooke Turpin as joint principal. Given that technical education had a subordinate and inferior position, this was an unsatisfactory arrangement, and Turpin soon argued for separate institutions. It was his intention to work towards such a separation and 'to make Swansea the seat of a National Metallurgical School, occupying the same relative position to the industries of England and Wales as did Freiberg and Clausthal in Germany'. However, Turpin resigned in 1901, the committee in the following year changing the title of the technical side of the school to the Swansea Municipal Technical College. In essence this was a change in name only, for the institution remained a secondary school with an appendage of technical classes, mostly evening. It was not until 1909 that a distinct separation between secondary and technical education was achieved.

Paradoxically, then, for a country whose economy was so geared to heavy industry, technical education in Wales lagged behind that in England and Scotland at every stage of development. Wales, of course, shared with England the same central direction and administration of technical education; in consequence it suffered from the general deficiencies of a haphazard, under-resourced system based largely on night schools, intended mainly for artisans and workers, rather than for future managers and leaders of industry, and superimposed on systems of elementary and secondary education which failed to provide a grounding in basic sciences. That technical education in Wales, therefore, should be as backward as that in England was to be expected, but the evidence suggests that it developed more slowly and was less extensive than in either England or Scotland.

Perhaps for cultural reasons no 'lobby' of prominent industrialists and scientists emerged in Wales to press for technical education, as happened in England. Indeed, the evidence of the Haldane Commission on University Education (1916–18) indicates that there was little demand for educated manpower from industrial leaders, indifference in some cases amounting to a marked hostility to 'college-educated' personnel.

Wales entered the Edwardian 'high noon' in buoyant and confident mood, politically, socially and culturally, with a sense of nationhood exemplified in a new 'national' university, soon to be followed by a national museum and a national library. Central to this was the creation of an educational system from elementary to higher education which served the needs of ordinary people to a greater extent than was the case in England, providing the possibility of economic and social mobility and producing cadres of social, intellectual and cultural leaders. There remained a dissonance between the education system overall and the immediate needs of the Welsh economy, rural and industrial; the system was not tailored to these needs, partly because of the nature of the economy, partly because those directing it made no great demands on the education system.

CHAPTER FIVE

✄

Defiance and Depression, 1902–1939

It is, quite rightly, inappropriate to see the history of education either as that of formal education only, or as the story of state education. Such orthodoxies were exploded by American writing in the 1950s and have remained unfashionable. Nevertheless, there is no gainsaying the impact that state intervention has had on Welsh educational history. In the broader context, it has necessitated historians of education, as much as anyone, making informed comment on the political relationship between the two nations of Wales and England. The state, of course, continued to be that of the inelegantly titled 'England and Wales' in a context in which it was accepted that the two other nations of the United Kingdom as then constituted, Scotland and Ireland, had differently structured education systems. These systems, of course, reflected far more recent unification, different educational histories and disparate social characteristics.

By the start of the twentieth century the state systems of education in Wales and England coalesced. In both countries there had already been thirty years of state elementary education, which was now both compulsory and free. Remarkably, 1902 was to see England come in line with Wales in terms of provision of secondary education, following the pioneering 1889 Welsh Intermediate Education Act. There was greater convergence in the wider society. Following the massive in-migration of the last quarter of the nineteenth century, particularly into industrial south Wales, the English language had made greater inroads than ever before. Throughout the nineteenth century, although literacy rates measured by the ability to write one's name had always been substantially lower than in England, the ability to read the Welsh language had been widespread and had sustained a thriving religious and politically orientated Welsh-language newspaper and periodical press. By the end of the century, with almost all the population able to read English, the grip of the popular English-language daily and weekly newspapers was loosening that of the Welsh-language press.

But Wales differed from England. The religious denominational divisions of the nineteenth century continued into the twentieth. Welsh rural society remained relatively poverty-stricken. Industrialization, on the other hand, produced a Welsh economy substantially out of kilter with that of England, at least from the later nineteenth century until the outbreak of the First World War, an economy concentrated very substantially on the thriving coal communities of south-east Wales, packed with people with money to spend in good times, characterized by a seemingly neverending expansion of productivity and absorbing population from outside Wales at an unprecedented rate. Despite this, a majority of this exploding population remained Welsh-speaking, if increasingly bilingual, into the twentieth century. There was, too, an expanding middle class as numbers entering the professions burgeoned, as did the bureaucratic infrastructure of industry and transport, but it was small-scale compared with that of the great conurbations of England. Indeed, this continued to be a source of disquiet among serious Welsh commentators who measured the stability and economic status of the Welsh population in the aspirational terms of Victorian achievement. There was a mixture of Welsh self-confidence and a sense of inferiority. Formal education was instrumental in both reflecting society and moulding it. As the state increasingly assumed responsibility, the tensions in the political structure were inevitably reflected in policy debates. The history of education is, therefore, a reflection of the story of nationhood.

We have seen that, with the one remarkable exception of the Welsh Intermediate Education Act of 1889, the parameters of formal schooling were established by central-government legislation. The sea change in mass education had been the system of payment by results inaugurated in 1862 and the 1870 Education Act, which brought the board schools into existence. By the end of the nineteenth century, elementary schooling from age five to the end of their school lives for the majority of boys and girls, was the responsibility of locally elected school boards. Nevertheless, there remained at least 300 school districts in Wales in which the only elementary education was provided by voluntary Church of England schools. The demand for change in the system set up in 1870 did not come from Wales but pursuing that change resulted in confrontation between the Westminster government and a socially distinctive, increasingly politically confident Wales.

By the end of the nineteenth century, government, particularly a Unionist government, was faced with fundamental problems over the administration of elementary education which was now dependent on state money. In social terms, there was the traditional fear that so much state finance was being used to educate a working-class population beyond its station. This was accentuated by the progressive policies of many school boards, some in Wales, in using their resources, coupled with grants from the Science and Art Department, to foster higher elementary work which further encroached on the preserve of the middle classes. The religious denominations, whose stake in the provision of elementary education was so much greater in England than in Wales, were struggling to match state investment, with the result that the fabric of Church schools in Wales was often deplorable.

By the turn of the century, administrative structures had developed in England and Wales which allowed for radical change. Potential central government control had been strengthened with the establishment of the Board of Education in 1899. The creation of county and county borough councils in 1889 provided a local administration alternative to school boards. A government Bill of 1896 had already attempted to legislate the school boards out of existence but had failed to become law. Attempts to undermine the boards continued, and the re-election of a Unionist government in 1900 sealed their fate. Sir John Gorst and Robert Morant engineered the Cockerton judgement in 1899 which found that the London School Board had been acting illegally in providing secondary education in its higher-grade schools. The result was the 1902 Education Act.

The Act made the councils of counties and county boroughs the local education authorities. Their responsibility under part 2 of the Act was to 'take such steps as seemed to them desirable . . . to supply or aid the supply of education other than elementary, and to promote the general co-ordination of all forms of education'. County boroughs with over 10,000 population and urban districts with over 20,000 population were, according to part 3 of the Act, to be responsible for elementary education only. These authorities, therefore, were taking over the responsibilities of the school boards and the technical instruction committees. They were also to assume responsibility for maintaining voluntary schools and paying their teachers, although the managers of these schools had to provide the building and keep the school in good repair.

Applying the Act in Wales ensured conflict on two grounds. First, and most serious politically, was the confrontation between the local authorities and the government over the maintenance of voluntary schools. Significant in its administrative repercussions, and of some educational importance, was the implication of local authorities being able, under part 2 of the Act, to establish municipal secondary schools separate from the network already established under the Welsh Intermediate Education Act.

Elementary schools were to be financed by a combination of state subvention and local rate aid. In effect, this meant that the voluntary schools were handed a financial lifeline. It also meant that specific areas would be paying towards local schools. While perfectly acceptable where religious affiliation and educational provision meshed, predominantly Nonconformist opinion was outraged because the voluntary Church of England and Roman Catholic schools would be helped by local authority ratepayers' money, could offer denominational religious instruction, and could effectively control school policy according to the principles of a majority of school managers of the relevant denominational persuasion. In many of the staunchest Nonconformist areas, particularly in rural Wales, children of Nonconformist parents had to go to the only available school, the Anglican school. Although Nonconformist parents had the right to withdraw their children from direct denominational instruction, this was totally unacceptable at a time of intense denominational affiliation and, indeed in 1904–5, of the heightened sensitivities of religious revival.

Nonconformist areas in England opposed the legislation. Wales, in the throes of a national cultural revival, and having experienced attempts to foster political independence through Cymru Fydd, was the perfect ground for opposition to be translated into direct action. Majority Nonconformist affiliation had, for the moment, become the touchstone of nationality.

At the end of 1902 the Education Bill became law. A national convention in Cardiff in June of the following year urged all local education authorities in Wales to refuse to administer the Act. If they wished to do so, all that was necessary was for the authorities to withhold rate aid from non-provided schools, the new nomenclature for the voluntary or denominational sector, since they, along with the provided, or former board schools, were now to be dependent on a combination of government and local-authority rate money. By the end of 1903 only two Welsh counties, Radnorshire and Breconshire, were administering the new system according to the law; in the others there were varying degrees of defiance of central government, grounded in an element of moral authority by the 1904 county-council elections in which all the Welsh counties returned a majority opposed to implementing the legislation. In retaliation, central government passed the Education (Local Authority Default) Act in 1904 which, in effect, allowed the Board of Education to deal directly with the non-provided schools and bypass local education authorities. Little wonder this became known as the 'Coercion of Wales Act'. In response, an alliance of local authorities and Nonconformity determined at the end of 1904 to refuse to administer any elementary education when the Default Act was applied. Five authorities were eventually deemed to be defaulting, their response and tactics varying considerably, but there was no disguising the seriousness of this confrontation between local and central government.

As the struggle dragged on it was, of course, the children who were the casualties. By the end of 1903 some of the worst-affected schools were complaining of insufficient funds to pay teachers, purchase stationery and ink, and buy coal for classroom fires. Increasingly, lack of repairs to the fabric of non-provided schools, generally in a far worse state than the former board schools, meant that they were totally inadequate for their purpose. Ultimately, central government and its Board of Education were not to be defied. Robert Morant and the board devised some skilful means to deal directly with non-provided schools and deduct money from the local authorities. The schools stayed open. The policy employed by some of the Welsh authorities of giving individual schools only the central-government element of grant had failed, circumvented by the provisions of the Default Act. Nonconformists were bitter.

There was ample demonstration of the power of central government. Even in Montgomeryshire, which was prepared to go to the ultimate lengths of making it impossible to fund all schools, including 'council schools' so that the voluntary sector should be denied, found that the government was prepared to go to extraordinary lengths to ensure compliance with the law. Even the seizure of an element of county-council funds was considered. The children in the schools were slowly relegated to being pawns in a propaganda war which used unpaid teaching salaries, fireplaces empty of coal and lack of food as weapons. Confronted by the harsh implications of refusing any funding for elementary education, the authority recoiled. In 1905/6 the situation was resolved by the election of a Liberal government far more in tune with Welsh priorities and the 'Welsh Revolt' petered out.

Aside from its wider political significance, the passing of the 1902 Education Act and the subsequent widespread revolt of the Welsh local authorities were crucial for the future of education. The essential policy in the Education Act of dismembering the school boards arose from England's priorities, particularly those of protecting the position of Church of England schools. In Wales, the school boards had successfully provided democratic sanction for elementary education and a flexibility which allowed some development of higher elementary and evening education. But replacing the authority of the boards with that of county and urban councils merely created other agencies which would want to place their distinctive stamp on educational provision. When the political and social imperatives of powerful local authorities got out of kilter with central government, as happened after 1902, possibilities for confrontation remained. In the distinctive society of Wales this was even more likely. This was not the last confrontation between local government in Wales and central government in Westminster over education.

In the meantime, the victory of the Liberal Party in the 1905 election meant that policies recognizing the uniqueness of Wales were on the agenda. Birrell's Education Bill of 1906 had included provision for a national council for education in Wales, not the first time such an idea had been mooted. It did not materialize, but in 1907 came a major devolutionary measure with the creation of the Welsh Department of the Board of Education, although it was to be located in London.

This department was to be responsible for the administration and inspection of school education. Its major appointments were of a Liverpool solicitor, A. T. Davies, as permanent secretary, an acerbic character concerned far less with the quality of education than extending the power and responsibilities of his department, which brought him into regular conflict with the parent body, the Board of Education. The chief inspector was a man of very different character, both personally and professionally. O. M. Edwards was a historian who had previously taught at the University of Oxford but whose mission in life was to try to educate the Welsh people in the culture and language of Wales. Until 1907 he did this through publishing works of history and travel and, particularly, by means of magazines such as *Cymru* and *Cymru'r Plant*. From 1907 until his death in 1920 he occupied one of the most powerful positions in Welsh education, allowing him to attempt to influence the curriculum and examination system directly. This brought him into conflict with the Central Welsh Board, set up to inspect and examine the intermediate schools, to the detriment of the unity of Welsh education, but it opened up debates central to the relationship between education and the Welsh nation.

Edwards, therefore, was the personification of a particular brand of Welshness and one of the very few renowned educationists that Wales has produced. What was significant was that he was a pragmatist rather than a theoretician and, as chief inspector, able to exert some influence, although nothing like as much as he would wish, on contemporary practice. Some of these ideas were well ahead of his time, at least in Wales. For example, he advocated direct-method Welsh-language teaching. He vehemently opposed a staple method of teaching used particularly in the secondary schools, that of dictated notes, especially in his own subject, history, and in geography. Much influenced by his elementary-school experience in which he was forced to speak only English despite having been brought up in a totally Welsh-speaking home, he used his own progress from the poverty of a small north Wales tenant farm to the academic milieu of Oxford as a template of what was possible for his idealized ordinary people of Wales, the *gwerin*. For Edwards, this cultured, gifted population deserved the best education, in the Welsh language, to bring out their creative gift.

In some ways, as historians of industrial Wales have pointed out, this was a blinkered vision because it was essentially biased towards what he regarded as the true Wales of serious, cultured farmers and craftsmen. For Edwards, much influenced by John Ruskin, industrial Wales had produced grime and ugliness, and was devoted to the exploitation of workers in the quest for maximum returns for capitalists whose last concern was for any creative spark in the mass of humanity. Nevertheless, the practical implications for Edwards were that education and Welsh society were inextricably linked and schools were crucial to developing a healthy and creative country. To this end, any curriculum should include a combination of academic and craft subjects, schools should not be governed by an 'English' scrabbling after qualifications, and rote learning, dictation of notes and the notion of treating the child merely as a repository for the storage of facts were anathema because they quenched the creative spirit.

This education was also to be distinctively Welsh. In those areas where Welsh was the language of the hearth it should also be the language of the early years in school, and should be taught throughout the secondary school. In the secondary school, also, some subjects, particularly history, should be taught through the medium of Welsh, while the language, literature and history of Wales should be prominent in all syllabuses.

Edwards must be regarded as the educationist with the highest profile in twentieth-century Wales. His philosophy of education was embraced so firmly that he was determined to use his official position, one without any parameters of precedent, to practical effect. His moral authority in Wales, deriving from his academic reputation and, above all, his ubiquitous Welsh-language publishing, reinforced that position. He was certainly not prepared to play the quiet administrator.

In terms of his educational philosophy, the elementary schools for the mass of the population posed the least problem. It was not that the education there was particularly enlightened – far from it. Edwards was a stern critic of the inadequate buildings, rote learning and restricted curriculum. Nevertheless, he regarded elementary-school teachers as crucial to the well-being of Welsh society and took every opportunity to praise their efforts, pressing for their improved status at a time when, unlike their secondary counterparts, they were not held in high regard. But it was in the secondary sector that attitudes towards schooling which were anathema to Edwards were institutionalized. These schools were far more difficult to steer in different directions because they were highly regarded as agents of upward social mobility, with an examination system geared to this end, and they had a powerful national agency, the Central Welsh Board, with its local-government democratic sanction, which jealously regarded itself as their custodian. The administrative duality consequent on the setting-up of the Welsh Department in 1907 was a recipe for confrontation. If the national council for education proposed in 1906 had come about this would have been avoided. The idea of unified control of the Welsh system continued to emerge sporadically, as in the draft of a 1908 Bill which included provision for an education council for Wales. Some MPs canvassed for a similar body to be included in Fisher's Bill preliminary to the 1918 Act. But there was powerful opposition, particularly in the Board of Education. Duality of control remained entrenched.

The essentials of elementary education remained unchanged as a result of the 1902 Education Act. It was cemented even more firmly as the education of the mass of the population, carefully demarcated by curriculum and status from secondary schools, despite running in parallel to those schools from the age of ten or so upwards. Attendance was now compulsory, in theory, up to the age of fourteen, although, across England and Wales, nearly 40 per cent of pupils were leaving before that age. Many pupils left at the age of twelve, having reached the required leaving standard, until this practice was dispensed with under the Education Act of 1918. It was extremely difficult to enforce attendance. At times when child labour was particularly useful on farms, particularly at harvest time, absentee rates soared. But, as in the previous century, there were more sinister reasons for absenteeism. School log-books provide ample evidence of school attendance being decimated, even school closures, as a result of epidemics of influenza, whooping cough, chicken-pox and a host of other contagious diseases. This was a society in which the mass of children came from economically poor homes, evidenced most distressingly in the prevalence of the killer disease, tuberculosis. A survey by the Board of Education in 1913 found that, of all elementary-school children in England and Wales, 10 per cent had serious vision problems, 5 per cent had hearing difficulties, 50 per cent had decayed teeth and 10 per cent had 'uncleanliness of the body'.

This was despite the enlightened legislation of the pre-war Liberal government. Across England and Wales there were reforms directly affecting the poorest children. Between 1906 and 1910 a raft of legislation amounted to the so-called Children's Charter. There was to be free school milk. In 1906 local authorities were allowed, although not compelled, to provide school meals out of the rates, while in 1907 they were required to appoint school medical officers and start medical examination of school-children. A medical department of the Board of Education was also set up. Later, in 1918, the government passed a Maternity and Child Welfare Act. These changes were complemented during the war years by enforcing the provision of education for mentally and physically handicapped children.

These reforms, together with old-age pensions and health and unemployment insurance, owing much to Lloyd George's reforming zeal, benefited not only children but also a whole range of people in need. Among much else, the Education Act of 1918 provided for the setting-up of nursery schools, but these, like continuation schools, came to nothing in the post-war economic crisis. These reforms were particularly significant for Wales because, despite the wealth generated particularly by the coal industry of south-east Wales in the years up to the First World War, Wales was still a poor society relative to England. Working conditions in the coal-mining, metallurgical and quarrying industries were dangerous, both in the short and the long terms. Housing was primitive by modern standards, with no indoor bathrooms or lavatories for the vast majority. However meticulous housewives might be, hygiene was difficult. Although infant mortality rates were decreasing, without antibiotics contagious diseases spread easily and were extremely difficult to combat. Rural areas of Wales were poorest, with standards of housing and nutrition even worse than in the towns, reflected in appalling figures for deaths from tuberculosis. Going to school often did not help. With children often inadequately clothed, there are examples of their walking miles in the rural areas to get to the nearest school. In bad weather they got soaked.

Once in school, they had to dry off, as far as possible, near a stove or an open coal fire in the classroom. The school-board era had seen an extensive building programme of elementary schools, particularly in towns, although conditions in the older voluntary schools were often cramped and inadequate. In the most recently built larger schools, classrooms gave off to a central hall. Division of children into standards was roughly associated with age. Class sizes were enormous by today's measure – classes of sixty children being common. Classrooms were often tiered, furnished with long wooden desks, and discipline was harsh. Teachers used the cane regularly, often with excessive physical force. Although payment by results was phased out in the 1890s, the curriculum remained concentrated on reading, writing and arithmetic, if nothing else in order to give pupils some chance of gaining a scholarship to a secondary school.

The social purpose of the schools was made quite explicit, even in official documentation. Fortunate scholarship winners apart, these were the schools for the 'hewers of wood and the drawers of water'. They were expected to impart a modicum of literacy and numeracy, after which pupils would leave for manual occupations either on the land or in local industry. Indeed, this was explicitly stated in the 1904 code for elementary schools, with this type of education providing 'training in followership rather than leadership training, suited to the working classes'. Such attitudes were prevalent among employers, particularly industrialists. In time-honoured fashion they were particularly opposed to the proposal in the 1918 Education Act that juvenile employees should be released for eight hours a week of education after the statutory school-leaving age. This reflected a more general anxiety among the prosperous that elementary-school pupils, as in the eighteenth and nineteenth centuries, should not be educated beyond their station in life, tinged with the view that they were incapable of benefiting from extended education anyway.

The mass of Welsh elementary-school pupils had the opportunity to sit a scholarship examination more than a decade before their English counterparts because of the intermediate-school system which took almost all its entry from the elementary schools. In Caernarfonshire, for example, the examination started in 1897 and dominated the curriculum of the elementary schools. In view of its influence, it is interesting that the original examination was wide-ranging, consisting of English grammar, English composition, arithmetic, needlework or drawing, geography and two optional subjects taken from algebra, history, Welsh and domestic economy. In this intensely Welsh county, the examination was conducted in the English language! In 1915, it was modified to a one-day examination in arithmetic and language, sometimes supplemented by an oral examination. Thus, the concentration of elementary-school work was narrowed, because success was measured by the number of pupils who jumped the crucial scholarship hurdle into the secondary school.

Although the pupil-teacher system was phased out early in the century, many pupil-teachers continued in the system for generations, particularly in rural areas. Morant's not dissimilar student-teacher system lasted until 1937. In 1920/1 there were 170,000 elementary-school teachers in England and Wales. Fewer than half had been trained. More than three-quarters were women. During the inter-war years the normal path into elementary-school teaching in Wales saw pupils transfer to intermediate or, additionally after the 1902 Act, municipal secondary schools where, after 1907, they could continue their education to the age of seventeen or eighteen. Some took a place in an elementary school as a student teacher before attending college. Others took the direct route to a two-year course at a training college. To the existing colleges in Carmarthen, Bangor and Swansea were added local-authority colleges after the 1902 Education Act – in Barry, for women, opening in 1914, and Caerleon for men. For girls, the majority of trainees, subjected to the tightest supervision in their social as well as their academic life, the regime in training colleges was highly structured, but represented a welcome extension to the restricted training facilities for women teachers and became the most frequently trodden route to a professional career for women.

The elementary code lasted until the 1944 Education Act. Teaching methods, curriculum and resources gradually improved during these decades. In larger schools, in particular, geography, history and nature study became more general and educational visits were officially encouraged. Practice changed very slowly, but there were more enlightened ideas, particularly relating to teaching method, in circulation. The most influential proponent of more child-centred approaches was the American John Dewey, whose ideas were taken up in a particularly enlightened Hadow Committee report of 1931, significantly entitled *The Primary School*. The crucial phrase in the report was that the content of education should be considered 'in terms of activity and experience rather than of knowledge to be acquired and facts to be stored'. In the light of later controversies it is significant that this Hadow report recommended teaching younger children through project work rather than discrete subjects, an approach usually associated more with the 1960s. There was, for example, an increased emphasis on oral work in English, but practical changes in teaching approaches in elementary education between the wars were limited. As in previous centuries, there was a marked discrepancy between progressive educational ideas and what went on in the classroom. While notions of learning by doing and the centrality of activity to true education, associated with Dewey and Maria Montessori, had a practical impact on a few educational foundations in England, and influential opinion among the inspectorate and progressive educationalists increasingly took their ideas on board, combining them with increased interest in Piagetian and other notions of children's mental development, the object of elementary education in Wales, as in the majority of elementary schools in England, remained the passing-on of facts.

In parts of Wales which were predominantly Welsh-speaking, the situation was complicated by attitudes to the native language. While views of the Welsh language were far more enlightened than in the second half of the nineteenth century, and Welsh was accepted as a subject for study, teaching took place as far as possible through the medium of English, and parental attitudes encouraged the search for fluency in English. It was in the field of secondary education, however, that the major confrontations emerged over the nature and purpose of schools, educationally, socially and nationally. This was as true of England as of Wales, but in Wales the parameters within which these conflicts were fought out were different.

By the time the 1902 Education Act was passed, Wales had already got its secondary schools, twenty-two for boys, twenty-one for girls, forty-three catering for both boys and girls in dual schools and seven in mixed schools. This system constituted a remarkable initiative both in democratizing education and in making it available in unprecedented numbers to girls as well as boys, so that by 1900 numbers were made up of 3,513 girls and 3,877 boys. Indeed, with continued expansion before the First World War, numbers of girls soon exceeded those of boys.

Given their original remit of a blend of academic and practical subjects, the majority of these schools were, as we have seen, intended to be second-grade schools (in the Taunton classification), with a leaving age of sixteen. Nevertheless, because of their select intake, the aspirations of head teachers often drawn from English grammar schools and, particularly, the Board of Education regulations of 1904 which were specifically drawn up to preserve, as far as possible, this tier of education for the middle classes, the Welsh intermediate schools came to be modelled on academic English grammar schools. They were also demarcated by the fact that they were fee-paying schools, although scholarships were available.

Organizational waters muddied early in the new century. First, the 1902 Education Act, while dispensing with the school boards, allowed local authorities to open municipal secondary schools. In industrial Wales, because of social prejudice which questioned the appropriateness of secondary education for the unskilled working class, there was dramatic under-provision of intermediate-school places. In such areas as Glamorgan and Monmouthshire particularly, school boards had developed higher-grade education of precisely the kind which Morant wished to head off, and a number of these opened as municipal secondary schools which, unlike their intermediate counterparts, were usually free for pupils and financed by local authorities. In Cardiff, Howard Gardens Higher Grade School became a municipal secondary school, as did that in Pentre in the Rhondda valley. Once the Welsh Department of the Board of Education had been established in 1907 it strongly encouraged local authorities to open municipal secondary schools as a way of circumventing the influence of the Central Welsh Board. Six opened in Cardiff, Merthyr, Swansea and Maesteg between 1907 and 1910, a number which doubled in the next four years. Like the intermediate schools, they educated more girls than boys by 1914.

There were, therefore, two separate kinds of secondary schools in Wales, founded under separate legislation. Complications ensued. First, the inspecting and examining function for the intermediate schools was carried out by the Central Welsh Board, established in 1896, but the CWB's writ did not run in the municipal secondary sector. Second, after 1907, the inspection function for the local authority secondary schools was vested in the Welsh Department of the Board of Education. However, because the intermediate schools were in receipt of government money, they were also subject to inspection by the Welsh Department. Third, the Welsh Department had at its helm two very strong-minded individuals, A. T. Davies and O. M. Edwards.

Davies opposed the Central Welsh Board immediately because it wished to take over the inspection of all Welsh secondary schools, intermediate and municipal. Although Davies's arguments were prejudiced, there was a genuine problem over the dual inspection of the Welsh intermediate schools since it imposed an undesirable and burdensome measure of accountability. From 1907, the two bodies with such a significant influence over Welsh secondary education were at each other's throats. A compromise over the frequency of inspections was worked out, but it perpetuated the system of dual inspection in the intermediate schools. It was not until 1925, after Davies had been replaced as permanent secretary by Percy Watkins, that a concordat to rationalize school inspection was finally agreed. These were not the only disputes as the Central Welsh Board found it difficult to match the Welsh Department's administrative efficiency and devolved power. The Welsh Department refused, for example, to discuss the curriculum, syllabus and timetables of the intermediate schools.

The centralization of authority in the Board of Education and its Welsh Department grew ever more extensive. In 1907 the department laid down the approved syllabus for secondary education: 'the course should provide instruction in the English language and literature, at least one language other than English, geography, history, mathematics, science and drawing. Where Welsh is spoken, the language, or one of the languages, other than English should be Welsh.' It is easy to see the influence of O. M. Edwards in the addendum to this regulation, agreed in 1909: 'any of the subjects of the curriculum may (whenever local circumstances make it desirable) be taught partly or wholly in Welsh.' Numbers of hours per week for each subject were also stipulated. The emphasis here was rather different from that envisaged when the intermediate schools were created, but the trend towards an academic curriculum was inevitable once Board of Education officials decided that elementary and secondary education should be strictly demarcated by curriculum.

Davies's attempts at empire building had limited success. The Board of Education was not happy at the fledgeling body's attempt to assume responsibility for technical education and the education of children with mental and physical handicaps. In 1914 Davies made an unsuccessful bid to take over in Wales those powers exercised over the university by the Board of Education.

O. M. Edwards was more successful in organizing the inspectorate along distinctively Welsh lines, and his battles were more central to Welsh education and, indeed, questions of Welsh nationhood. His attempts to encourage technical education in, for example, the municipal school at Cyfarthfa and the county/intermediate school in the Amman valley met with mixed success. As we have seen, Edwards had the strongest views on what an enlightened Welsh education should amount to. Particularly, his view that schools should foster the Welsh language and literature, and that they should interact with the strengths and the needs of the local community, meant opposition to the rote learning of an academic curriculum which, he felt, was particularly encouraged by the examination system imposed by the CWB. This system originally involved four examinations. The Junior Certificate (phased out after the First World War), was taken in the secondary school after two years of study, the Senior Certificate (renamed the School Certificate in 1923), after four years. Pupils who, at one attempt, passed in five specified subjects at Credit level earned matriculation to the University – a crucially significant qualification. There were also Higher and Honours Certificates (the latter disappeared during the First World War), taken two years after the Senior Certificate for the few who stayed on beyond the age of sixteen, the normal age of completion of the standard four-year course. Significantly, as we have seen, the commercial and technical certificates, also available, attracted hardly any takers.

Even this plethora of examinations represented a rationalization of the random system which operated previously, under which many institutions ran their own examinations. From 1908, the CWB Senior Certificate was recognized by a whole range of such institutions from the army to the Institute of Chartered Accountants, as well as for entry to training colleges and to the University of Wales. However overloaded, a more rational system had evolved in Wales than in England, and the Board of Education was prompted to a full-scale review which, after 1917, resulted in the secondary-school examination pattern being a Senior Certificate examination at about the age of sixteen and a second school examination at about the age of eighteen.

The wholly different priorities of the Welsh Department and the CWB were made public when Edwards used his annual reports to blame the board for fostering an overly literary curriculum and poor teaching. There was almost immediate acrimonious confrontation. The 1909 report famously argued that

> the minds of the children seem to be very mechanical, their memory is overburdened where the reasoning power should have been developed . . . the Central Welsh Board should now consider to what extent their rigid examination system may be the cause of the wooden and unintelligent type of mind of which the examiners complain.

This was a typical Edwards gloss on increasing concern in the Board of Education over the stereotyping of secondary education. In particular, technical education was sorely neglected, developing only in the newly emerging central schools such as the four in Caernarfonshire which opened before the First World War and concentrated on practical and technical work.

Hardly surprisingly, secondary-school head teachers reacted much as they would today to a hypercritical inspection report. One of the best-known head teachers in Wales, Major Edgar Jones of Barry, riposted that the Welsh schools had been particularly successful in examinations. That was his criterion of success, reasonably, and indicated that Edwards and the head teachers were basing their arguments on entirely different measures of effectiveness. Given Board of Education regulations, the use of school examinations for university entrance and the underlying social engineering of using secondary education to try to preserve the exclusivity of middle-class education, it was Edwards, however exalted his position in the official hierarchy, who was out of step. Nevertheless, in terms of contemporary Welsh society there was an alternative vision, even if doomed to failure. Edwards deprecated the fact that the Welsh secondary schools had no courses in navigation, agricultural training, or slate working in the quarrying districts, or any adequate training for local trades. Nor were they to get any. In the immediate context of the running of Welsh education, the public confrontation between Edwards and Jones was serious, even leading to questions in the Commons. The effectiveness of secondary education in Wales was not helped when the two major national controlling bodies were at loggerheads. Ultimately, ironically, Edwards was fighting Welsh parents. Increasing numbers of skilled and unskilled working-class parents were prepared to make sacrifices to secure a secondary education for their children on the grounds that they were provided with 'an escape route', and if they acquired 'a safe, clean job by hard work and good academic training the school has done its duty'.

In one respect, Edwards, among others, did make his influence felt. Teaching methods in Welsh improved, and the Board of Education cooperated with the Welsh Language Society to run a holiday course in Welsh and provide grants for evening classes in Welsh and Welsh literature – between fifty and sixty in south Wales alone. The position of Welsh in the education system nevertheless remained anomalous and continued to cause concern. In 1921, 37 per cent of the population spoke Welsh. There had been a decline in real numbers since 1911. In schools, study of the Welsh language and literature was not a high priority. By the end of the war, Welsh was taught in 92 of the 102 county schools, but fewer than half the pupils in the counties and fewer than 20 per cent in the county boroughs studied the language.

Against this background, and continued requests from the University of Wales and the Central Welsh Board, a departmental committee to investigate the position of Welsh in the education system was eventually conceded in 1925. Its 1927 report, *Welsh in Education and Life*, was an important statement of commitment to the idea that the Welsh language, literature, history and heritage were crucial elements in Welsh culture and should therefore be central to education at all levels. The report diagnosed that the problems started in the elementary schools. In theory, pupils were allowed to answer scholarship/free-place examination questions in Welsh but were almost invariably trained in English and therefore opted for the latter. There were no secondary schools in Wales in which Welsh was the everyday language. Sixty-seven per cent of pupils took School Certificate French in 1926 compared with 39 per cent in Welsh (a few pupils were taught both).

Other, more intractable, problems emerged, including the exodus of the great majority of elementary teachers trained in Wales to English schools, although this was less true with secondary trainees. But it was quite remarkable that in 1924/5, of the students qualifying in that most Welsh of areas, the training college in Bangor, only 21 per cent were able to find jobs in Wales. In school and university, while ample opportunities existed for the study of Welsh as a subject, the conclusion was that there were considerable limitations on the use of Welsh as a medium of instruction at all levels, compounded by a dramatic dearth of Welsh textbooks.

The report was something of a landmark, resulting in an improvement in the quality of Welsh teaching and in the use of Welsh as medium of instruction. Welsh was increasingly used in scholarship examinations in the most Welsh-speaking areas but economic conditions, in particular, made it unlikely that there would be any radical alteration in the status of the language. Indeed, an education in the English language became an even more significant key to a good job in the Wales of the Depression, whether that job turned out to be in Wales or, increasingly likely, in England. Indeed, it is arguable that it was the Edwards family who continued to be the more effective guardians of Welsh history and culture. O. M. Edwards's son, Ifan ab Owen Edwards, founded Urdd Gobaith Cymru (the Welsh League of Youth) in 1922. Five years later there were 5,000 members in eighty branches across Wales, with the avowed aim of fostering a love of Welsh literature, tradition, religion and language. Group-branch activities were supplemented from 1928 by summer camps and, from 1929, by the annual eisteddfod. It had considerably more success than Plaid Cymru, founded in 1925, which had as one of its aims making the Welsh language the medium of education from the elementary school through to university.

Nor should we lose sight of the continuing role of chapels and Sunday schools in the Bible-centred education of adults and children, as well as their social role in the dissemination of popular culture by ubiquitous hymn-singing festivals, prayer meetings, literary and debating societies and the performance of operettas, plays and oratorios. There was a falling-off in attendance in the inter-war years, but the chapels remained powerful instruments of informal education in both languages, particularly in rural Wales, until well after the Second World War.

If the secondary-school system in Wales was partly a prisoner of the class-based segregationist policies instigated by Morant, a rather different social engineering was actually at work in Welsh society. By 1911–12, 2,000 pupils were leaving Welsh secondary schools every year. Over the age of twelve, 15.5 per cent of boys and 14.9 per cent of girls entered higher education, 8.5 per cent of boys and 22.8 per cent of girls became teachers, 42.5 per cent of boys and 8.9 per cent of girls went into some kind of professional, commercial or clerical job, 14.1 per cent of boys and 3.9 per cent of girls took industrial or manual work, while 7.5 per cent of boys and 0.3 per cent of girls went into agriculture or rurally based work. The majority of girls either became teachers or did not work. Those who taught were subject to dismissal immediately they got married. Three-quarters of these girls had taken the Senior Certificates in Latin, 85 per cent in French. This was a highly academically educated section of the community – many argued at the time inappropriately educated. But this fails to take account of the incalculable effect on domestic life and the enlightened and ambitious bringing-up of children. This educational change was feeding on itself.

Inevitably, whatever Edwards and others advocated, Central Welsh Board examinations remained, throughout the period, the touchstone of success for pupils, teachers and schools and involved similar academic subjects across Wales and England – English, French, mathematics, science, geography, history, Latin and sometimes art, with the modification in Wales of Welsh. This curriculum, ostensibly that of Board of Education and the schools, and examined by the Central Welsh Board, was ultimately dictated by the matriculation specifications of the universities, particularly the University of Wales, because the needs of those with some chance of proceeding to university took precedence over all others in this sector.

By 1910/11 there were 13,000 pupils in Welsh intermediate schools, double the number at their inception. They were taught by graduate head teachers, the majority men, and an increasingly graduate force of assistant teachers. These were men and women of authority, wearing, originally, mortar boards and, throughout the period, academic gowns, a uniform which symbolized achievement and demarcated them in the social hierarchy. Their job was to ensure that as many as possible of their pupils obtained the treasured School Certificate. It was this crucial role in the social transformation of individuals and communities which endowed them with status and power. Some outstanding Welsh scholars started their careers teaching in the intermediate schools, where the quality of teaching varied from inspirational to grindingly boring dictation of notes and rote learning. The Welsh secondary sector played a major part in transforming the lives of thousands. Indeed, it transformed the nation. Huw Williams and T. M. Bassett have illustrated this graphically in their history of a north Wales intermediate/county school, Ysgol Brynrefail. Taking the three generations of parents of pupils, pupils themselves and the children of pupils between 1918 and 1939 they discovered that, in terms of social class, numbers of higher professionals went from none to 57, lower professionals from 11 to 224, white-collar workers from 20 to 115 and craftsmen from 187 to 37.

There is a case for linking educational change with war. The medical condition of soldiers recruited for the Boer War helped create the climate for legislation on school meals and milk. The ultimate manifestation of Anglo-German rivalry after 1914 prompted inquests into the merits of the rival education systems, partly in discussions of their abilities to produce people and machines capable of making war. It is not surprising, therefore, that a Board of Education committee was set up in 1916 to consider education after the war, which resulted in the Lewis Report of 1917, and that a major Education Act was passed in the following year.

There was no equivalent initiative within the Welsh Department, nor could there be, but the Central Welsh Board did produce an analysis of problems in the intermediate schools. It made this all-embracing by including the relationship of the secondary sector with elementary, technical and university education, although the concerns were more with the structure and administration of the system than with content and courses. The ultimate aim was the acquisition of that holy grail, a Council for Education for Wales, often mooted, never granted, but the problem of the academic and humanistic bias of the curriculum in schools and universities and the lack of technical and vocational provision was a major theme. However, the attitudes of parents and pupils in the secondary schools were already well entrenched and economic developments in the inter-war period were, if anything, to reinforce them.

At the outbreak of war the Welsh elementary-school sector closely resembled that of England, while the secondary sector – at least in terms of a ladder of opportunity – was considerably more extensive. Ninety-nine schools had been established under the Welsh Intermediate Education Act, while a further eighteen had been opened under the 1902 Act, the latter in industrial areas which had previously been least well provided for. In relative terms, urban Wales still lagged far behind rural Wales in provision of secondary places relative to population. There were significant differences in the way they operated, since, already, six of the municipal schools charged no fees.

The overall pattern of education was disrupted far less during the First World War than in the Second. Of course there were problems. An irritant, though significant for those affected, was that a few schools were given over to billeting soldiers or, as in the case of Howard Gardens Secondary School in Cardiff, used as military hospitals. The major disruption, particularly in the secondary sector, arose from the recruitment of male teachers for the armed forces. For example, by 1916 Greenhill School, Tenby had no male assistant teachers left. This did at least provide the opportunity for married women to return. The inspectorate held discontinuity in pupils' education to have been harmful, although this was not reflected in examination results. A moratorium on school building meant an increase in class sizes, particularly from 1916 onwards in the secondary schools, as numbers of entrants began to increase rapidly in each succeeding year.

The examination system was modified in 1917 with the amalgamation of the higher and honours certificates, although the Central Welsh Board did not institute this change immediately. It was far more significant that so many pupils did not complete the four-year course leading to the senior examination. Just before the war, the average secondary-school life for girls was three years one month, for boys, two years six months. There were other complicating factors in devising a satisfactory education experience for the whole age and ability range of the Welsh secondary schools. The age of entry varied from ten to twelve, with increasing access particularly in the rural schools leading to a mixture of ability, and this with many small schools having fewer than 100 pupils. The CWB wanted a standard eleven-plus age of entry. This could be facilitated in Wales because entry to the county-school sector was mainly from the elementary schools, 88 per cent in 1915, with a far smaller number coming from the private sector than in England.

It was, however, the Board of Education which continued to shape the system and indeed, despite the existence of the Welsh Department, to bring secondary schools in Wales even more into line with those in England. First, in 1917 the Board of Education issued revised regulations which, in slightly modified form, applied also in Wales. They were extremely comprehensive, covering the organization of the school, class sizes, numbers of free places, the teaching of Welsh and subjects to be taught in the Welsh language, and the administration of entrance tests for free-place candidates.

The second initiative of 1917 was the implementation of advanced courses, to be taken beyond Senior/School Certificate level. These were the precursors of Advanced Level (A level) courses, and were significant academic currency because they were held to be the equivalent of the intermediate course at a university. Board of Education officials, always determined to preserve the rigid differentiation between elementary and secondary education, wanted the eventual age of entry to university to be seventeen or eighteen, with the normal route through the Higher Certificate. Grants to schools to run these courses were allocated sparingly and became significant status symbols. The courses were implemented against the wishes of O. M. Edwards, who regarded them as further consolidation of the overly academic bent of Welsh secondary education and believed that the university colleges should look after post-matriculation education. However, the system did take root in Wales and the principle of specific grants for pupils on post-matriculation courses approved by the Board of Education lasted until 1933, when all sixth-form work became eligible for grant. Although all Welsh secondary schools were desperate to acquire the status conferred by advanced work, many were small schools and unable to attract sufficient numbers of pupils to allow the courses to run. O. M. Edwards had a case. There was bitterness when courses were turned down by the Welsh Department. In those schools which succeeded in running courses, increasing in number year by year, narrow academic specialisms were consolidated and became that contentious feature of secondary education in Wales, as in England, which is still being debated. By 1920 there were advanced courses in eighteen Welsh schools, which helped secondary school numbers to increase from 187,647 in 1914 to 336,836 in 1921 (more than half the pupils in Welsh secondary schools left before the age of sixteen years). Increasingly, work leading to matriculation and advanced courses grew to dominate secondary education in Wales, consolidating the academic side, virtually ousting practical courses and influencing the whole ethos of the school. What compromised this system educationally was the high proportion of pupils who entered secondary schools, particularly in rural areas, for whom the rigidly academic was not the most suitable approach.

There was no differentiation between the two countries in the 1918 Education Act, although Wales benefited along with England from such measures as increased grants and the loosening of the purse strings of the local authorities. In prospect, one of the most significant measures was that the Act allowed local education authorities (LEAs) to provide courses of advanced instruction for older or more intelligent pupils in elementary or central schools and classes. As these central schools grew in number, the contentious issue of the class-based nature of differentiation between different types of post-elementary education became a feature of debate, particularly in the Labour Party in Wales, which was not to be resolved until the 1960s.

One of the foremost critics of the demarcation policy generally endorsed by the Labour Party was W. G. Cove, one of the youngest presidents of the National Union of Teachers in 1922, an MP from 1923, who succeeded Ramsay MacDonald in the Aberavon seat in 1929, and a leading Labour spokesman between the wars on education issues and vociferous proponent of the multilateral or comprehensive school: 'The Central School is based upon class distinction. It is a structure which emphasises the predestination . . . as far as the educational system can predestine, the lives of the children to be doomed as slaves in the life and industry of this country.' For much of the inter-war period the debate over secondary education was to be dominated not by the Wales-centred concerns of Edwards, who died in 1920 and whose post effectively disappeared, but by the class-based Labour concerns over equality of opportunity and equity in the education system.

War exacted a terrible human cost from Wales but, if anything, it had increased demand for the products of Welsh staple heavy industry, especially coal and steel. In the inter-war years the Depression exacted a very different but almost equally destructive human cost, not least in terms of missed educational opportunity for countless individuals. The euphoria of the immediate post-war period was reflected, for example, in Glamorgan's plan, required under the 1918 Education Act, completed in

1920, to build thirty-three new schools and provide free secondary education for pupils, with all children leaving elementary school at the age of twelve. It provides a glimpse of what might have been.

There was also promise in official reports which applied specifically to Wales. The first was that of a departmental committee set up by H. A. L. Fisher, President of the Board of Education, in 1919 to 'inquire into the organisation of secondary education in Wales', and to advise on what might be 'consolidated and co-ordinated with other branches of education with a view to the establishment of a national system of public education in Wales . . .'. The problems of post-elementary education, such as the disparity between opportunities in rural and industrial areas, and short school life, were inevitably addressed. But the most significant question to be raised was that of the organization of secondary schooling, given the emphasis on providing mass post-elementary education in some form or another. Cove gave evidence to the committee. Despite the success, for example, of the two central schools which opened in 1918 in Llanelli – so oversubscribed that two more quickly followed – the report recorded that the Labour spokesman rejected the idea of the central school, wanting free, compulsory, full-time education to at least the age of sixteen in secondary schools. The Bruce Committee was not persuaded, and concluded that while there should be a 'large extension' of secondary education in line with the sentiments of the 1918 Education Act, it should take place in a variety of types of school.

The Bruce Committee did conclude that Welsh education should be under the control of a National Council of Education in Wales, an idea which refused to go away, though, like so much of the residual Liberal programme of late-nineteenth-century Wales, it became increasingly irrelevant in the Depression, when survival mattered most. Even the continued bickering between the Central Welsh Board and the Welsh Department of the Board of Education seemed irrelevant.

Slowly, in the wake of the 1889, 1902 and 1918 Acts, the secondary system was assuming the shape which characterized it until 1944 and, in many respects, the 1960s, a structure in all essentials common to both Wales and England. What Edwards believed to be Welsh priorities were subsumed in the wider set-up. The economic realities of the Depression impelled the system in the same direction. The secondary schools, and the University of Wales in particular, now played a very different social role. The agricultural areas of Wales, particularly the extensive hill-farming districts, had always been poor. With the collapse of the post-war boom in 1921, the return to the Gold Standard in 1925 and the aftermath of the 1929 Wall Street crash, the Welsh industrial economy, based on the coal and metallurgical industries which had been the motor of unparalleled Welsh prosperity in the second half of the nineteenth century, faced ruin.

Communities to which it had given rise faced destitution. Post-elementary education (in whatever kind of school), the training colleges and for, the favoured few, the university colleges, provided some chance of escape.

The scale of unemployment in Wales in these 'locust' years, as Kenneth O. Morgan has termed them, is scarcely credible to modern generations – climbing to 38.2 per cent in 1932. The population in every Welsh county other than Denbighshire and Flintshire fell between 1921 and 1951. Against a background of general population increase between 1931 and 1937 in England and Wales, the combined population of Glamorgan and Monmouthshire fell by 9 per cent. With hindsight, it was a blessing in disguise that the curriculum of the secondary schools had not been geared more closely to local industries. Given their collapse, qualifications for white-collar and professional jobs were precisely what were needed. Unfortunately, it was at the expense of denuding Welsh communities of the cream of their talent, as they moved to the more prosperous Midlands and South-East of England, particularly in the 1930s. For those with ability, education offered an even more significant opportunity to escape, particularly into public-sector employment safe from the horrors of hunger alleviated by soup kitchens. The pride of these destroyed committees was never wholly undermined, but the desperation was etched on them for generations. The exodus of many of the most talented of the younger generation out of Wales was facilitated by their education. The school population of Wales fell from 482,000 in 1928 to 415,000 in 1936/7.

The depredations of the Depression demanded even greater sacrifices of parents to provide an education for their children. Education was compulsory between the ages of five and fourteen, but ill health and sheer shortage of adequate clothing, allied with the long walks to school for so many, conspired to make absenteeism a continuing problem. We have seen that the vast majority of pupils who attended Welsh secondary schools came from the elementary schools, and that, from the earliest days, there was a generous system of scholarships. With the 1907 Education Act came the requirement for a minimum of 25 per cent of places in all secondary schools to be free, a number considerably exceeded in Wales. However, as eco-nomic conditions worsened, the pressures of incidental costs for books, pens, school uniform, school dinners and travelling expenses became even more burdensome in a system in which the drop-out rate before the completion of the normal four-year course had always been of worrying proportions.

A number of counties – Anglesey, Flintshire and Cardiganshire, for example – did provide some maintenance allowances but most of this money went on travelling expenses. This highlights a further problem in rural Wales – that distances to school, particularly secondary school, were a considerable deterrent. In 1922, for example, it was reported that some pupils of Barmouth County School had to leave at 5 a.m., not returning home until 7 p.m. So, despite the increasing use of parental agreements that pupils taking up places in secondary schools would complete the four-year course, early leaving remained an intractable problem. Once the statutory school-leaving age of fourteen had been reached, the prospect of that extra family wage was a major incentive to leave school. As rates of unemployment rose across Wales the attraction of a steady job, offered at whatever point in the course, became increasingly magnetic. Paradoxically, in the 1920s, demand for secondary education was increasing while measures to deal with early leaving met with only limited success. The result was that the qualifying examination for secondary education – usually tests in English and arithmetic, even in Welsh-speaking areas – was being used to limit numbers of entrants to avoid the overcrowding now evident in most schools, while at the same time local authorities were attempting more stringent measures to keep pupils in school to Senior/School Certificate level, the accepted school-leaving examination. The Welsh Department also attempted to siphon off some demand into central schools, providing high-level work under the elementary code.

Against a background of increasing economic pressures the Hadow Report of 1926 advocated that the nature of elementary education should change from a system providing all-through education for the majority of pupils from the age of five to the school-leaving age of fourteen, to one in which all pupils should change to a different type of school at the age of eleven. These schools would not, however, be of the same type. Those pupils presently not successful in the increasingly competitive scholar-ship examination would transfer to central schools where they would pursue a more practical and vocational curriculum than in the existing secondary sector. The central schools would continue to operate under the elementary code, thus being rigidly demarcated from existing secondary provision.

In Wales this distinction was to lead to continuing discussion, and occasional serious confrontation, over the shape of provision – for geographical and ideological reasons. Except in the towns, lack of numbers of post-eleven pupils available to transfer made separate central schools hardly feasible. Ideologically, parents were justifiably suspicious, as increasingly were vociferous Labour politicians, that central schools were a second-class and second-rate alternative form of education which would lead neither to the qualifications nor the employment opportunities available to secondary-educated pupils.

The result was that even in the most populous of Welsh counties, Glamorgan, reaction to Hadow was such that only nine central schools had opened by 1936. The Welsh Department tried faithfully to press this alternative form of post-elementary education on reluctant LEAs, but the majority of local politicians were highly suspicious of a quasi-secondary route which, in practice, led to none of the benefits of existing secondary education. In fact, the instincts of Labour politicians in both Glamorgan and Cardiff authorities were correct – that the Conservative Party and Board of Education senior civil servants were determined that existing forms of secondary education, with their controlled entry systems and class connotations particularly in England, should remain entrenched and the resulting anomalies in Wales should not be allowed to interfere with this overall strategy.

With the 1929 Labour government's proposal to raise the school-leaving age to fifteen, the nature of post-eleven school education came increasingly under the microscope and led to a confrontation between the Welsh Department and its parent body which turned out to be as revealing as any of the nature of their relationship. There was no doubting the special circumstances of Wales in 1929. Industrial Wales was under the cosh as a result of the Depression; the development of another tier of secondary education in rural Wales posed impossible logistical problems. Percy Watkins, A. T. Davies's successor as permanent secretary at the Welsh Department, was driven to the conclusion that, for social and economic reasons, the Welsh education system should be developed differently from that in England. His solution for rural Wales was simple. All pupils in a particular neighbourhood should transfer to the local secondary school – as 26 per cent were already doing. These schools would, of course, be what came to be known as bilateral or multilateral schools. Indeed, for the first two years of school life, they would be organized on comprehensive-school lines, with a common curriculum. Thereafter there would be a bilateral organization within the school.

There would then be the question of fees, because the majority of those who transferred from the elementary schools would be entitled to free education. This made anomalous the position of existing fee-paying arrangements which had come in with the 1889 Act. Watkins had the temerity to suggest that all post-elementary school education in Wales should be free or, at worst, fees charged only for those pupils whose education extended beyond the first two years of secondary school. Such proposals on curriculum and, especially, on fees cut right across traditional Board of Education thinking which endorsed a rigid demarcation between the elementary and secondary codes by a substantial element of fee paying, with the higher the fees the more prestigious the school. This had been enshrined in post-elementary education from the beginning and was an essential plank in the thinking of both the Board's civil servants and most ministers, who saw fee paying as essential to preserving the distinction between working-class and middle-class provision.

The Welsh Department's proposals for industrial Wales, against a background of economic disaster, were equally radical. While rural Wales was relatively well endowed with secondary-school places, there had, from the beginning, been far less generous provision in such counties as Glamorgan, Monmouthshire and east Carmarthenshire. Only 16 per cent of pupils in these areas went to secondary schools. A full reorganization would require 90,000 places for children over the age of eleven. The complement in 1929 was 15,000 secondary-school and 6,000 central-school places. Watkins argued that the councils concerned would not agree to provide central-school places because they regarded them as inferior and 'dead-end'. He therefore suggested that a concurrent programme of secondary- and central-school building should be allowed, with some of the new schools being comprehensive or bilateral schools. By implication, therefore, Watkins was pressing, in all but three counties and the Welsh county boroughs, for a substantial element of common secondary education, not only educationally revolutionary in the context of official thinking in the 1920s and 1930s, but also, in effect, a system peculiar to Wales.

Not surprisingly, his proposal created a furore in the parent government department. Detail alarmed the Board. Teachers in secondary schools had always been academically and socially superior, as reflected in their substantially higher pay. The new arrangements would require a common salary structure. Despite an initially favourable reaction from the Labour President of the Board of Education, Watkins's proposals were doomed, partly on the grounds that they were 'bound to have repercussions in England' and devalue secondary education. The crux of the matter was put devastatingly by one civil servant: it was not the Board of Education's job to 'satisfy aspirations, however praiseworthy, but to recognise facts and take account of real needs . . . the hard facts . . . are that a majority of the pupils over 11 will leave school at 15+ and get their further education in contact with life.' Watkins had to be content merely with allowing some shared facilities between different types of school. The division between the secondary and elementary/central sectors remained almost as rigid in Wales as in England.

Government policies to cut back on public spending were particularly hard on those areas, like most of Wales, worst affected by the Depression. There were economies in grants for elementary education, and cuts in teacher salaries. Hadow reorganization (and the building of central schools) was drastically curtailed. However, the fall in the school population meant that opportunities for a secondary education widened so that, for example in 1931, 19.33 per cent of elementary-school pupils in Wales aged between eleven and twelve went on to secondary school, compared with 9.58 per cent in England. Sixty-one per cent of these pupils had free places, compared with just over 44 per cent in England.

It was the government's determination in 1932 to economize on these free places by replacing them with means-tested special places that provoked yet another highly significant confrontation in Wales, this time with the largest local authorities. The Board of Education acknowledged that there were twenty-six 'free' secondary schools in Wales and that fees, where they were charged, were low. But, despite protests from across Wales, the board, and its compliant Welsh Department, would not be moved. The likely fee income under the new regime in Wales was £30,000 out of a total secondary-school cost of just over £1 million per year. For this sum, the government was prepared to antagonize most sections of educational opinion in Wales.

Relative to population there were more protests from Wales than from any region of England. They were couched not only in terms of social justice but also in the belief that Wales had gone a different way from England in its secondary-education provision which ought to be reflected in its treatment over the fee issue. The government was adamant. Each local authority had to negotiate separately with the Welsh Department over the level of fees to be charged and numbers of special places. All were forced to charge fees but most managed to extract a very high number of special places out of the Welsh Department. In some counties, Breconshire for example, all secondary-school places were to be special places, subject to the new sliding scale of parental income. In Flintshire, the number of special places over the previously available free places nearly doubled. In Monmouthshire, Glamorgan, Cardiff, Merthyr and Swansea all secondary school places were now to be special places.

It was ironic that, because of the scale of poverty in Wales, and the number of family incomes which did not even reach the level required for the payment of minimum fees, the majority of the new special places turned out, in practice, to be free. In 1932 the figure was 67.5 per cent, but even by 1938 it had fallen only to 64.2 per cent. In terms of access to secondary education, therefore, the Welsh system was now even more egalitarian than that in England – in 1936, seventy-six of the 266 non-fee-paying secondary schools in England and Wales were located in Wales.

The Depression did not only prompt the government to economy measures. Such was the effect on Wales that fundamental issues about the relationship between the education system and the Welsh economy were raised at last, particularly in a government report on the educational problems of the south Wales coalfield, published in 1931, concerned mainly with the education of adolescents and older people in that area. It provided some useful correctives to traditional interpretations of the role of education, particularly secondary schooling, in moulding Welsh society. It demonstrated that because of Welsh reliance on the primary industries of coal and steel, and the lack of development in heavy and light engineering, the opportunities for technical jobs had been particularly limited so that 'there has . . . been little incentive to most of these boys to enter industry at all, and they have been compelled to find careers either in commerce or in the professions'. This was despite improved careers guidance and even the existence of secondary-school appointments committees in north and south Wales. There was no answer to the problem of the brightest and best youngsters leaving their area of birth to find employment. Where industrial employment was available, employers regarded the elementary schools as their natural recruiting ground, wanting pupils preferably at the age of fourteen.

Whenever industrial blight descends on any part of the United Kingdom the education system is held to bear substantial blame. Inevitably the 1930s prompted an inquest into educational provision in industrial Wales. We have seen that elementary education ended at age fourteen, had a restricted curriculum and supplied what market there now was for manual labour in industry. Central schools attempted to provide a more practical and technically orientated curriculum and, in Flintshire, provided evening technical education. There were only twelve junior technical schools in Wales, clustered almost wholly in Glamorgan and Monmouthshire. North Wales was particularly short of this kind of education; for example, the Wrexham junior technical school opened only in 1934, while there were few facilities in Caernarfonshire and Merioneth.

The deficiencies of existing technical education were regularly highlighted, and resulted in 1934 in the formation of the Advisory Council for Technical Education in South Wales. One motive was to ensure that not only the few junior technical schools, but also the secondary schools, should reflect the needs of local industry in their curriculum. But it was partly the threat to extend designated junior technical schools, with their age of admission of thirteen, to other areas of Wales, and the increased competition for pupils which that would imply, that prompted the secondary-school head teachers to press for the extension of technical education within existing secondary schools. The Welsh Secondary Schools Association pressed this argument on Sir William Spens's consultative committee which eventually reported in 1938. More significantly, this kind of thinking impelled secondary-school head teachers to press for a brand of multilateralism.

The Spens Report of 1938, which cast such a long shadow over the future pattern of secondary education, was only marginally influenced by the evidence submitted to it from Wales. However, the wider impact of recent economic travails could not be ignored. The Spens solution was not to be bilateralism or multilateralism on lines which logic implied to be the necessary pattern in Wales, but increasing numbers of technical high schools, of equal esteem to the secondary grammar schools and working towards a leaving examination equivalent to School Certificate. The secondary-grammar-school sector should continue in existence, and secondary modern schools take all other pupils from the age of eleven. Multilateral schools were rejected as the template for all but a very few areas, one of which should be rural Wales. There should, however, be a common curriculum to age thirteen and, in a phrase made famous in post-war education, parity of esteem. Many Welsh voices, those of Labour politicians, trade unionists and educational professionals in particular, had already condemned the idea that pupils should be channelled into different types of education as the result of an examination taken at the age of eleven. In any case, the government shelved Spens's proposals on grounds of cost.

At the outbreak of the Second World War in 1939 the fundamentals of Welsh schooling had changed relatively little since the beginning of the century. There was an elementary education for the majority, technical education for the few, and increased opportunities for a post-elementary education in central schools in urban areas. Substantially increased numbers were accommodated in the secondary schools proper (the grammar schools of the post-Second World War period) as a result particularly of the expansion of the municipal secondary sector after the 1902 Act, and the exodus of population during the Depression. The thrust of the education on offer had changed little. In those schools which were the main agents of social, economic and status change, there were marginal differences only in the pattern of provision. In the School Certificate examination of 1938, 47.91 per cent of entries were in arts subjects, 43.19 per cent in pure science subjects, which included geography, and 11.26 per cent in subjects with some practical bent – mechanics, metallurgy, needlework, music, shorthand, bookkeeping, drawing, domestic science, woodwork, metalwork, agriculture, laundry work and dairy work.

The most fruitful development in technical education in the period was the creation of the National Certificate scheme – National Certificates being introduced for part-time, and National Diplomas for full-time, students. Normally, 'Ordinary National' took three years to complete, 'Higher National' a further two. By 1925, courses were available in mechanical and electrical engineering, chemistry and naval architecture. Later, building, textiles, commerce and civil and production engineering were added. Certificates and diplomas were joint awards of the Board of Education and the professional bodies concerned, with examinations being set and marked by schools and colleges. The scheme brought formal education into closer relationship with industry as industrialists provided gifts of equipment and machinery, and served on local and national consultative and advisory committees.

The impact of the scheme must not be exaggerated. Growth in numbers in this period was slow, especially in Wales. The technical education continued to be the Cinderella sector – a Board of Education pamphlet of 1926 severely criticized the quality of college buildings and facilities. Industrialists in Wales were reluctant to give apprentices time for day-release and other studies, and failed to bring pressure to bear for the expansion of technical education. The Second World War revealed all too clearly the shortcomings in technical and technological education, a situation endorsed officially in a report produced by the Percy Committee in 1945.

Throughout the inter-war years the University of Wales was criticized for dominating, and in the view of many distorting, the secondary-school curriculum in an overly academic direction, so minimizing the status of technical subjects. It was universities which decided which subjects at School Certificate level merited approval for matriculation. Inevitably, the university was concerned with its own criteria of scholarship and these had to be international standards of teaching and research. To this end, all teaching in the constituent colleges was through the medium of English, although there was a degree scheme in Welsh. This resulted in constant criticism from committed cultural and political nationalists similar to that levelled at the Welsh secondary schools, that the university was endorsing English values along with the English language and making very little contribution to specifically Welsh matters.

Although the university never achieved its once-cherished ambition of controlling secondary education in Wales, it came of age in this period. In 1909 superb new buildings in Cardiff were opened at a cost of £290,000. In the same year, the Treasury grant to the three colleges of the university nearly doubled. In 1911, an impressive purpose-built arts block opened in the Bangor college. The University College of South Wales and Monmouthshire in Cardiff was particularly keen to foster engineering, mining and metallurgy, while the University College of North Wales, Bangor had a department of agriculture, although here, as elsewhere within the University of Wales, the teaching of science was sorely restricted by inadequate resources of buildings and cash. While agriculture at Aberystwyth and Bangor had profited from generous government subsidies, technologies at the Cardiff college suffered from lack of similar support. As the Haldane Commission made clear in 1918, local industrialists and businessman had signally failed to give adequate help. Believing in the virtues of apprenticeship and the notion of the 'practical man', they were generally against formal education, and their meagre financial contributions reflected this. Engineering at the college had been promoted only with the help of the Drapers' Company of London, while metallurgy languished.

Most anachronistic, given the Cardiff college's location near the largest coalfield in Britain, was the case of mining education. Attitudes in south Wales were little short of bizarre. Coal had propelled the area to the forefront of the world economy. By the outbreak of the First World War there were nearly a quarter of a million men employed in the area's mines. The south Wales economy depended on coal and steel. Ever since the Paris Exhibition of 1855 there had been growing worries in Britain over increased competition from Europe and America, with the McKinley tariff demonstrating how the country's share of trade in a world industry, tinplate, could be undermined. But contemporary opinion indicated that tariffs were only a small part of the problem. While the notion that Britain's relative industrial decline was due to an outdated educational system has been substantially undermined, there is no gainsaying that the increasingly sophisticated machinery which could now be deployed in the coal industry, for example, required skilled operators and management. Miners were becoming convinced of the benefits of machinery. Germany demonstrated how coal's by-products could be used to establish new industries, a development completely ignored in south Wales. Very few chemists, for example, were employed to exploit by-products. In human terms, a much higher price had to be paid for official tardiness in exploiting scientific and technical theory and experiment. Far more could have been done far earlier to lessen the incidence and extent of colliery accidents. Germany and France, both with considerably smaller coal industries, had famous schools of mines, with one German school training more full-time students than the whole of United Kingdom.

Professor E. H. Griffiths, principal of the University College of South Wales and Monmouthshire, was one of those prepared to blame both educationalists and industrialists, arguing that pure scientists were too aloof to involve themselves in the nitty-gritty of industrial practicalities, while industrialists were suspicious of pure scientists. There were similar rivalries and suspicions across the whole range of technical education, with a divorce between its providers and local industrial practice. This was amply demonstrated when Griffiths attempted to found a school of mines in his college. In 1907, with only fifteen students of mining and annual expenditure only £250, Griffiths launched a £50,000 appeal fund to establish a school of mining. He, and William Walker Hood of the Glamorgan Coal Company, went round the coalfield seeking support and obtained promises of £35,000. By 1910 only £9,000 had materialized, the coal owners broke off negotiations with the college and set up their own school of mines. It opened in 1913 at Treforest, funded, in essence, by a levy of a tenth of a penny on each ton of coal produced by eleven, later thirty, coal companies. It had a disastrous impact on the development of mining education at the University College. The focus now was on the new school which also established part-time courses at Crumlin. During the Depression of the 1920s the coal owners discontinued their support and the school was taken over by Glamorgan County Council.

Principal Griffiths, along with a wide representation of industrialists, was equally unsuccessful in establishing a University Faculty of Technology, to be centred on the Cardiff college and involving technical colleges and institutes all over Wales. They put this proposal to the Haldane Commission in 1917, but the industrialists' case was unsophisticated and the commission, in turn, was suspicious of an emphasis on vocational training which would, in its opinion, devalue the concept of a university education. At a time in the early twentieth century when international awareness of the link between successful industry and a sophisticated scientific and technological education was growing, neither the limited base of Welsh industry nor the vision of the educational and industrial establishment propelled Welsh education along this path. But perhaps the abiding impression is of leaders of industry wilfully ignorant of the actual and potential contribution of the university colleges of Wales to native industries and an even greater reluctance to back the colleges financially.

By modern standards, student numbers in the University of Wales were tiny – 277 in Bangor in 1900; 628 in Cardiff. Only the University College of Wales, Aberystwyth drew a substantial number of students from outside its immediate catchment area. In Aberystwyth, also, there were more women students than men by 1908. Academic staff were paranoiac about protecting the reputation of women students by taking draconian action against the slightest breach of rigid rules governing contact between the sexes. The majority were carefully chaperoned in purpose-built halls of residence such as Alexandra Hall in Aberystwyth and Aberdare Hall in Cardiff. Men were regarded as being able to look after themselves and generally lived in college-approved lodgings. Residential training colleges for teachers avoided this problem by being open only to members of one sex. Despite such puritanism, the social and sporting life of the university and training colleges was extremely rich, involving staff and students in corporate activity unrecognizable in modern days of student mass production. St David's College, Lampeter, although outside the University of Wales, was a significant part of the university sporting scene.

The First World War inevitably affected university education drastically because so many students volunteered. One hundred and six students and former students of Aberystwyth, for example, lost their lives. With the war at its height, a Royal Commission chaired by Viscount Haldane in 1916 began its inquiry into the University of Wales. His report resulted in a far greater measure of teaching independence for constituent colleges, as well as the vital participation of the university in adult education through the creation of a University Extension Board which provided leisure-time classes for adults.

Another result of the Haldane Commission was the founding of a fourth University College at Swansea. In 1901 Swansea County Borough Council had established a technical college, and it had always been an ambition that the borough should become the seat of a national metallurgical and mining school to rival the great continental schools. This was, after all, a world centre of metallurgical industries, and Swansea had bid to be the site of the University College of South Wales and Monmouthshire, but lost out to Cardiff. It therefore proposed to Haldane that the technical college be incorporated as a constituent college of the University of Wales to serve as such a school. Imbued with the prevailing ethos of 'liberal education' the members of the commission turned down the proposal but accepted that a broadly based arts and science college be established as part of the University of Wales. In 1920 the University College of Swansea was opened in Singleton Abbey, former home of the Vivian family. Of the first six appointments, five were in science and technology, among them the first chair of metallurgy in Wales, and the college quickly established a reputation in several of these disciplines. Among its outstanding alumni was a physicist, Evan Williams, son of a stonemason from Llanybydder. After leaving Swansea he studied under Bragg at Manchester, Rutherford at Cambridge and Niels Bohr in Copenhagen and in the Second World War made a decisive contribution to the campaign against the U-boat. Not only did Swansea pioneer new technologies but it also helped boost the output of scientists produced by the University of Wales, helping to bring about a transformation in the role of science in Welsh education compared with the nineteenth century so that, while graduate numbers had doubled since 1913, numbers of science graduates had multiplied fourfold.

The creation of the University of Wales Press and the Board of Celtic Studies by 1922 added crucial dimensions to disseminating research. The latter had three committees, covering Welsh language and literature, history and law, and archaeology and art, with the aim of fostering research and publication in these areas. The Haldane Commission also recommended setting up a national medical school for Wales separate from the University College in Cardiff. This came to fruition in 1931 with the creation of a Welsh National School of Medicine.

Both the university colleges and the training colleges, operating under severe financial restraints in the inter-war years, continued to provide an opportunity for talented working-class students. Nevertheless, the financial depredations of the Depression years made it impossible for many of the most able of the population to attend either institution. In these desperate years the university colleges and local authorities tried to provide some hope for the future. There were some coveted scholarships and a small supply of student loans, but countless talented individuals lost out. The proportion of women students in the university colleges declined sharply as many opted instead for the considerably less costly training-college courses. The university colleges remained tiny by modern standards. In the 1938/9 session there were 663 students in Aberystwyth, 485 in Bangor, 970 in Cardiff, 488 in Swansea and 173 in the medical school. Over 90 per cent of these students were born in Wales.

Other avenues of higher education did exist for some of the most talented, particularly, perhaps, young members of the Labour Party fired by political ambition. These were the years when the Workers' Educational Association (WEA) continued in the tradition of liberal self-help to provide classes which were intended to encourage discussion of contemporary social ills but without any revolutionary overtones. The South Wales District was formed in 1906, with the burgeoning town of Barry establishing the first branch in that year.

The district got off to a shaky start. University influence tended to dominate and the movement found extreme difficulty in attracting the working class with a message of collaboration and cooperation which seemed to offer a far less effective route to social justice than class conflict. Many working-class leaders regarded the WEA as an instrument for purveying capitalist propaganda, an outmoded endorsement of social harmony based on a similarly outdated vision of Welsh values.

From 1924, when the WEA became an approved association, the government provided some financial support so that by 1933 there were more than 4,000 students in over 200 classes. WEA philosophy remained essentially conciliatory, based on a belief in the necessity to reconcile the seemingly impossibly conflicting interests of capital and labour. Its concern was to provide opportunities for the working class to 'better themselves' *en route* to responsible citizenship in a democratic society, its emphasis on the integration of society according to the theories of the nineteenth-century Idealists. From this viewpoint, the rise of socialism, with its connotations of class conflict, was a fundamental threat. What was required, according to the leading lights of the WEA, was increased state intervention which would satisfy the ambitions of organized labour within a market economy. The perceived danger was an increasingly strident endorsement of full-blooded socialism among some in the Labour movement.

A similar philosophy lay behind the establishment in 1927 of Coleg Harlech, brainchild of Thomas Jones, former cabinet secretary and closely linked to the Idealist movement through his university teacher, Sir Henry Jones, staunch supporter and early district treasurer of the WEA. At Harlech, working-class students could pursue courses in, for example, history and philosophy in the collegiate atmosphere otherwise denied them.

Other, more radical strands in working–class education were concerned less with conciliation than a belief that only a revolutionary transformation of society would result in social justice. From 1906 the South Wales Miners' Federation provided scholarships at Ruskin College, Oxford, set up in 1899 to cater for trade-union and working students. Its influence spread to south Wales, not only through its residential students but also the correspondence courses sponsored by the college, whose students met together to discuss their courses, largely in social science, politics and history. Even with scholarships, Welsh students were only able to take full-time courses at Ruskin College at great personal or family sacrifice. Nevertheless, by 1907, thirteen of the fifty-three residential students were south Wales miners.

The Ruskin experience was not always congenial intellectually or socially for working-class students in a town of pretentious undergraduates. Students returning to south Wales became increasingly militant in their outlook, advocating more direct challenges to capitalism than orthodox trade unionism offered. South Wales students also played a significant part in the so-called Ruskin College strike of 1909. Out of disputes at the college grew a movement for a more radical working-class college, with a crucial south Wales involvement. The outcome was that the South Wales Miners' Federation withdrew its support for Ruskin College and backed a new, wholly independent, Central Labour College in 1909. It had an intermittent existence until 1929, but fed back into the coalfield a consuming interest in Marxist interpretations of current economic ills and convinced some of the need for revolution. The Labour College also spawned numerous local classes under the auspices of the National Council of Labour Colleges. Initially far more successful than the WEA, the rivalry between the organizations intensified as the WEA increased its appeal to trade unionists during the inter-war years and was able to draw on state funding. Both traditions were intent on educating the mass of the working class, rather than producing leaders, but many products of the Labour College endowed with intellect and ambition – for example, Aneurin Bevan and James Griffiths – did assume positions of leadership within organized labour. The Depression years also spawned less formal attempts to compensate Welsh communities for the trauma of unemployment, impoverishment and the indignities of means testing. A whole range of clubs and activities provided opportunities for handicrafts and music, for example.

Neither Depression nor its educational palliatives would last. The coal miners who sought solace and inspiration in the burgeoning miners' institutes and their libraries stocked with classics of English literature and countless commentaries on the revolutionary implications of Marxism, and the students in the more grandiose settings of impressive arcades of former industrialists' mansions, were alike to have their lives transformed by another world war.

CHAPTER SIX

✄

War and Relative Peace, 1939–1965

With the declaration of war in 1939, the government implemented its pre-planned programme of evacuation of children from the major cities to designated areas of safety. Evacuees did not remain long, drifting back gradually during the 'phoney war' only to return once more when the Blitz began in earnest in late 1940. Some children from the East End of London, which had suffered so much deprivation in the inter-war years, and other inner city areas of England caused consternation among rural hosts because of their small, ragged, unruly and often filthy condition. Homesickness could be overwhelming. On the other hand, many evacuees developed close relations with their foster parents. Ruth Inglis records the story of Johnny from Stoke Newington who, at the age of three, was evacuated to Bargoed with his five-year-old sister. After a year the family visited Bargoed. His father made to put his arms round Johnny only for the child to turn his face to his foster-father's shoulder in an attempt to hide. When Johnny and his sister returned home after five years, he was, according to his elder sister Kathleen, 'very stroppy, I think he missed his Welsh dad'.

As part of the evacuation programme Wales received some 200,000 children from London, Liverpool and the West Midlands. Bomb damage took enormous toll of school buildings in English cities, whereas in Wales only Swansea and Cardiff suffered badly. Nevertheless, the influx of large numbers of children caused extreme overcrowding. Local authorities, schools and teachers were forced to improvise; the solution often included the use of village halls and, in schools, the operation of a double-shift system. Difficulties were compounded by a halt to pre-war plans for new buildings, extensions and improvements, and acute staff shortages on account of teachers being drafted into the armed services and other war work.

The war, while causing enormous social dislocation, also imposed great burdens and stress on local authorities, schools, teachers and pupils, not least on the evacuees. In rural Wales, apprehension among staunch supporters of the Welsh language over its possible dilution acted as a spur to the idea of Welsh-language schools. The drafting of men teachers into war work and the armed services gave women opportunities to fill the gaps, especially with the removal of the ban on married women teachers in 1944.

The more favourable position of women in the workforce persisted in the post-war years. They filled a whole range of jobs in light engineering, textiles and clothing, and by 1948 constituted 37 per cent of employees in government factories. There was a big rise, too, in the number of women employed in the professional and service sectors. Moreover, by 1961 50 per cent of women workers were married.

The war caused unparalleled dislocation for men and women, but it was the latter who bore the brunt of the stress involved in coping with shopping and catering for the family, especially hard on those who worked long hours in armaments factories or other war work. Ironically, while there were severe shortages of food, children's health was better than it had been before the war when malnutrition had been rampant among the poor, with one in four undernourished and a majority having bone disorders, enlarged or septic tonsils and malformed or decaying teeth. Rationing of ham, bacon and sugar began in January 1940, other food-stuffs gradually being added so that eventually there was very little that was not rationed. In February 1941, white bread was replaced by the national loaf which, despite its unpopularity because of its grey colour and gritty texture, was more nourishing because it contained most of the grain. Milk was rationed, but pregnant women and children under five were given a daily pint. The new-born received cod liver oil and orange and rose hip syrup.

Free milk was provided in schools, while the numbers taking advantage of school dinners in England and Wales escalated from a quarter of a million to nearly two million. In country areas, home of many evacuees, there were farm products, fruit and vegetables – often spurned initially by city evacuees who hankered after their usual fare of sausages, fish and chips and bread and scrape. Despite the hardships, wartime children generally enjoyed better health.

The focus of the new wartime thrust towards a more just post-war world centred on education and social reconstruction, for while better housing, full employment and improved social security would help to eradicate poverty, disease and ignorance, it was accepted that education should play a crucial part. The government appointed a committee under (Sir) William Beveridge, economist and social reformer, to review social insurance schemes. Its report (1942), known as the Beveridge Report, proposed a comprehensive national insurance scheme that formed the basis of post-war welfare legislation. Meanwhile, in June 1941 the Board of Education had circulated a document to educational organizations seeking their views on proposals for reform. Although marked 'confidential', the document, which became known as the Green Book, was distributed in 'a blaze of secrecy' and became the subject of wide debate outside educational circles. A month later, R. A. Butler was appointed President of the Board of Education, and it fell to him to sift through the memoranda that had poured in, and to meet the many deputations from LEAs, teachers' organizations, churches and other interested bodies.

In Wales, the CWB called for a National Council for Education and a Secretary of State for Wales, as did the Federation of Education Committees. The latter urged a free, compulsory and universal system in which the school-leaving age would be raised to sixteen, with part-time compulsory education to eighteen for those not in full-time schooling. This would follow a common schooling to age eleven, with children being allocated 'to the type of education judged best suited to their capacities and needs', which should be available in modern, grammar and technical schools, while in the sparsely populated parts of Wales there should be multilateral schools.

The government's response to the mountain of advice was to publish in July 1943 a White Paper on Educational Reconstruction founded on two principles: education should be a continuous process from five to eighteen, while the secondary-school system should reflect diversity as well as equality of opportunity. It proposed that the school-leaving age should be raised to fifteen, with no exceptions, and extended to sixteen as soon as circumstances permitted. The term 'elementary' should be abolished, education between the ages of five and eleven being termed 'primary'; from age eleven, children should go to schools of diversified types but of equal standing. From age fifteen all children should attend a school full-time or a young people's college part-time. Coincidentally with the publication of *Educational Reconstruction*, a committee under Sir Cyril Norwood, president of St John's College, Oxford, produced a report in which he endorsed the White Paper's scheme of diversity of schools and, reviving echoes of the Taunton Commission Report of 1868, a quasi-psychological justification that there were three types of child for which there was an appropriate school, termed respectively, grammar, technical and modern.

The Norwood Report and the White Paper were widely welcomed on all political sides, so it was no surprise that a Bill presented in December 1943 passed into law in August 1944, though it did not specify the tripartitism inherent in the Norwood Report. There was almost another year of war to endure before implementation could begin. During that time, opinion crystallized that there should be no return to Conservatism and the mass unemployment of the 1930s. As a result, the general election of 1945 saw a Labour government come to power, with, for the first time, a commanding majority in Parliament. Committed to reforms in economics, social and welfare issues and education, the scene appeared set fair for a massive reconstruction of British life. The expectations of radical reform stemming from the 1944 Act were, in the event, only partly realized, in Wales as in England, when conservative policies implementing a tripartite secondary-school system were pursued.

Nevertheless, despite the serious difficulties of the post-war years, fundamental changes in welfare and the economy led to improved social conditions, health care, falling unemployment, rising incomes and increased equality of opportunity in education. In the immediate aftermath of the war Wales experienced increasing prosperity and economic growth, south Wales especially benefiting from its status as a development area under the Board of Trade, which offered loans and tax concessions to industries. The wartime ordnance factories (which employed many women, unusual in Welsh industry) were converted into trading estates, and some 112 government-sponsored initiatives brought a diverse range of light-engineering companies; later there were car-component factories, while the oil industry developed at Milford Haven. Meanwhile, the inauguration of the National Coal Board in 1947 prompted optimism in that industry, while the steel industry benefited both from huge investment in modernization and from a vast new steelworks at Margam in 1951, though both industries were to experience major difficulties later.

In rural Wales, the increasing mechanization of agriculture led to a fall in demand for labourers and craftsmen such as blacksmiths and saddlers, so young men, especially, drifted away from the land. The Beeching cuts in the railway network from 1962 accentuated the decline in rural and village life. The availability of cheap houses for those seeking to purchase second or holiday homes led to an influx of English-speaking immigrants which, in turn, weakened the grip of the Welsh language and culture in areas where Welsh cultural activities had been a dominant feature, the bitterness created being a factor in the fight to preserve the Welsh language reflected in the formation of a new movement, Cymdeithas yr Iaith Gymraeg (Welsh Language Society) in 1962. Influential opinion looked to the education system to bolster the position of the Welsh language, which would have considerable implications for the shape of the system in Wales.

It was not only sea changes in industry and the economy which carried major implications for education and training. They were accompanied by decline in Church and chapel influence and the weakening of trade unionism as the old industries decayed. A transformed education system interacted with these wider changes. There was a substantial increase in qualified manpower, part of which was absorbed within Wales itself, in industry and commerce, the service industries, public service, local government, the health service and teaching. But Wales could not accommodate all the products of the new educational structure; the result was a 'brain drain' to England and abroad. Among the professional classes, teachers, always prominent, had become the dominant group, found throughout the schools of England. The impact of education and the resultant burgeoning of the middle class, especially of the professional classes, may be illustrated by reference to the general elections of 1945 and 1979. In 1945, Wales politically was fairly solidly Labour and was to remain so until the mid-1970s. In the election of 1945, only two Conservatives were returned, the remaining MPs consisting of seven Liberals and twenty-five Labour. Of the Labour members no fewer than eight had received an elementary education only, with a further nine going on from elementary school, not to a secondary school, but to the Central Labour College in London, Coleg Harlech or Ruskin College, Oxford. Seven only had received a secondary education, with a similar number having studied at university, some after a period at night school rather than secondary school. Among the group were a barrister, three university lecturers and two teachers. In contrast there were fourteen miners, two steelworkers and one railwayman. Of the miners, seven had served as miners' agents and three had been at work by the age of twelve. Never again in the following fifty years was such a pattern of education and occupations to be found among Wales's representatives at Westminster. In 1979, eleven Conservatives were elected along with one Liberal and two Plaid Cymru candidates. Of the Labour members who were Welsh-born, all but three were educated in one of the former intermediate/grammar schools (now comprehensive schools); two were public-school educated and there was only one whose school education had been limited to an elementary school, prior to going to Ruskin College, Oxford. Eighteen were university-educated, most subsequently pursuing professional careers: lecturers and teachers (8); barristers and solicitors (6); and doctors (2).

Any examination of the profound changes to Welsh education between 1939 and 1965 which were instrumental in this social transformation must begin with the provisions of the Education Act of 1944 and their implications. The Act abolished the term 'elementary education' and declared that 'in following the principle of education for all to eighteen years of age' there should be three stages, primary, secondary and further. All school fees in the state system were to be abolished on 1 April 1945. The school-leaving age was raised to fifteen. Beyond that age, education would continue, either full-time in school or part-time in continuing education classes. To meet the latter requirement, the provisions of the Fisher Act (1918) regarding day continuation schools were to be revised and implemented. LEAs were to establish, within three years after operation of part 2 of the Act (1945), 'county colleges' which would, in working hours, provide part-time education of 330 hours a year up to age eighteen. A new Ministry of Education with greater powers to direct and control education replaced the Board of Education, while part 3 local education authorities (such as Merthyr Tydfil in Wales) were abolished amidst a storm of protest; this reduced the number of LEAs from 315 to 146 in England and Wales, and to seventeen in Wales alone. The Act stipulated that it was their duty 'so far as their powers extend, to contribute towards the spiritual, moral, mental and physical development of the community by securing that efficient education ought not to cease when the child has left school'. Further, all LEAs were required to submit their plans giving effect to the Act's proposals to the ministry by 1 April 1945. Putting this into effect, though, proved difficult, for the LEAs were beset by problems.

There were many casualties of the Act. The school-leaving age was not raised to fifteen until 1947, and a further rise to sixteen was indefinitely postponed. County colleges were scheduled to open by 1950, but problems of providing buildings, teachers and finance delayed their appearance. Thus, there was no compulsory part-time education for those between fifteen and eighteen, all-age schools continued and nursery-school provision did not materialize.

The Butler Act said nothing about the types of secondary schools which had so much concerned the Spens and Norwood committees; they had envisaged separation at age eleven-plus into three distinct types of secondary school (grammar, technical and modern), with 'parity of status' between them. It was this tripartite system that most LEAs adopted, with children selected according to 'age, aptitude and ability'. Selection procedures, however, were controversial, most LEAs relying on standardized intelligence tests and attainment tests in English and arithmetic, checked against reports by head teachers or school records. Borderline cases were decided following interviews between teachers and parents. In accordance with a Norwood Report recommendation, LEAs permitted 'late developers' to transfer from a modern school or technical school at thirteen to a grammar school, but differences in curricula made transfer difficult; it was the eleven-plus examination alone which decided the fate of most children. Although about one in twenty children on average in England and Wales attended a grammar school, the proportion varied greatly. Constraints of finance and building materials meant that LEAs found it difficult to build new secondary modern schools, many being housed in unsuitable former elementary schools, while all-age schools continued in existence in some areas.

Parity in buildings and facilities was not achieved. Parity of esteem proved unattainable also, with the secondary modern school seen as an 'also ran', and all too few technical schools opened. Some LEAs experimented with 'bilateral' schools, a combination of two out of the three types, while a small minority wanted 'multilateral schools' which combined all three forms of secondary education under the same head teacher. They shared facilities, often on the same campus, contributing players to the same school teams and orchestras. This policy initiative had a particular impact on Wales.

With the Butler Act the distinctive Welsh system of secondary education coalesced with that of England. The pattern of school education for Wales as for England was laid down by legislation applicable to Wales and England. There were ways in which Wales could try to influence both the passing of the Act and its implementation, but Welsh input into policy and its practice was limited. Butler had to deal with a number of peculiarly Welsh difficulties; the delegations which visited him, however, were often more concerned with the problems of the old Wales. In particular, the Church in Wales and the Roman Catholic Church were apprehensive about the financial implications of reorganization, with secularization of schools and with their loss of influence. Butler's uniform solution was to devise two new categories of school, voluntary-aided and voluntary-controlled. As a result, the intermediate schools established by the Act of 1889, and funded partly through a ½d rate, were in a legally anomalous position. Under the 1944 Act they were voluntary schools but few had the necessary endowments to thrive as such, most being absorbed into the new system and the ½d rate abolished. The Central Welsh Board, the nearest institution Wales had until then to a national representative body in education, was disbanded, its inspections of former intermediate schools and its examinations remit being taken over in 1948 by a newly constituted Welsh Joint Education Committee which attained a unique place in the examination structure of the United Kingdom. The WJEC was an all-embracing body reflecting all aspects of education in Wales; in 1956, Sir David Eccles, when Minister of Education, described it as 'a unique instrument in the administration of education in Britain', and, misleadingly, 'a representative education Parliament in Wales'.

The requirements of the 1944 Act that local authorities should submit their plans for secondary reorganization by April 1945 posed all kinds of difficulties, most significantly the inadequate state of existing school buildings, compounded by the raising of the school-leaving age to fifteen in 1947. Government policy of implementing a tripartite system spelled out in the White Paper, but significantly omitted from the Act, ensured that pressures in Wales for the more radical development of multilateral systems, dictated variously by the internal logic of the situation or by proponents of a more egalitarian philosophy, were kept under the firmest control by the Welsh Department acting in concert with the Ministry of Education.

Pressures on the rural counties of Wales were different from those in urban areas such as Swansea. Most rural county councils were dominated by Independents and Liberals who were more conservative in outlook than their industrial counterparts and prone to eschew radical innovations favoured by Labour-dominated councils in some urban areas. In rural areas, freedom to plan was circumscribed by problems of scattered population, together with the relative lack of buildings and finance. Therefore, in counties like Radnorshire and Montgomeryshire, for example, existing resources dictated possible patterns of provision. Duplication of facilities in different types of secondary schools was a luxury they could not afford.

In rural Wales a high percentage of the relevant age group had always received a secondary education, a far larger percentage than in the English counties, so that in the country grammar schools the ability range was already far greater than was the case in England or urban Wales. In the plans submitted by rural counties, concern was expressed by the ministry and by the Welsh Department in those cases where they believed adequate provision had not been made for the grammar-school pupil element. Mostly the plans were conservative. Where they were not, as in the case of Merionethshire which proposed multilateral 11–18 schools throughout the county, proposals were overruled by the Welsh Department in collaboration with the ministry. It was only in Anglesey, which had its plans for reorganization approved early, that multilateral 11–18 schools catered for the whole county from the mid-1950s. All the rural authorities were forced by geography to propose some form of bilateral structure, sometimes with a common curriculum for the first two years of secondary schooling. Although the Welsh Department was determined to safeguard the interests of the 'grammar school' type of child, it was forced to accept that a wholly bipartite system was in practice impossible; hence some bilateral grammar/secondary modern schools were an inevitable feature of education in rural Wales.

In urban areas there was no uniformity in the responses of local authorities to the requirements of the 1944 Education Act. In several of them, notably Cardiff and the Anglicized county of Flintshire, proposals were conservative and conventional, reflecting the attitude of directors of education and of the local authorities concerned. Plans were largely based on two types of school, namely, grammar and secondary modern. Swansea and Glamorgan, however, both with staunchly Labour councils, submitted contentious plans for multilateral schools catering for all secondary-age pupils. The proposals were not well received. The result was delay and confrontation with the ministry and its Welsh Department of Education. It was not until the late 1950s that plans for these two authorities were finally approved by the ministry, with multilateralism based on 11–18 schools being allowed only in areas of new council-estate housing. This reflected ingrained class assumptions in the top echelons of the civil service, largely accepted by the Welsh Department and many of Her Majesty's Inspectors (HMI), that working-class education allowed of experiment while education of the middle class in grammar schools must be safeguarded.

Local authorities also fought strenuously against moves by the Church of England and Roman Catholic communities to have their own schools within the secondary educational system and, despite pressure from the ministry, only in one or two authorities were such schools established. By 1951, pupils in Welsh secondary schools were evenly divided between secondary modern (47.5 per cent) and grammar (45 per cent), with only 4.5 per cent in bilateral or multilateral schools and 3 per cent in technical schools. There was a wide divide between grammar schools and secondary modern schools in curriculum, ethos and social values, as well as in buildings and resources.

From the inception of the intermediate schools in the 1890s the tendency, under the influence of English-educated head teachers, was for them to adopt the ethos and practices of the public schools and endowed grammar schools. We have seen that this was best exemplified in Cardiff where the respective head teachers, Dr J. J. Findlay at the boys' school and Mary Collin at the girls' school, modelled their schools on the English public school and successfully fought to have their titles changed from 'intermediate' to 'high' school. Throughout Wales, the intermediate schools adopted the emblems and trappings of school songs, colours, badges, uniforms, prefects and house systems, while competitive games were encouraged. These features continued in the Welsh grammar schools in the post-war years. Deidre Beddoe has provided a vivid description of how this was presented in a girls' grammar school. It was a 'world of gowned mistresses, prefects, house systems, rules, school uniforms – box-pleated gymslips, house girdles, shirts and ties, Burberries and school hats, hockey, lacrosse and netball, and strict discipline, enforced by detention and lines'. Ceremonial prize days were big occasions which recognized pupils who had been successful in examinations by the presentation of prizes and certificates. Paradoxically, speakers on these occasions often decried the importance and significance of examinations, claiming that the *raison d'être* of the school was to provide a 'liberal' education. Despite ritual denunciations of examinations, for governors, teachers and head teachers, parents and pupils alike, it was achievement in examinations which was the hallmark of a good school. In the profusion of school histories that appeared in the centenary years of the 1990s, past examination successes were proudly proclaimed.

The grammar schools were restricted to the privileged minority – larger in number in Wales than in England – who had passed the dreaded eleven-plus; especially fortunate were the select group sufficiently successful in the school certificate examination to be allowed to proceed to the sixth form and thence to higher education. For the majority of children, however, considered pejoratively by some as the 'also-rans', opportunity was confined to the secondary modern school, intended for children of modest intellectual ability. As a newcomer to the education system the secondary modern school lacked 'tradition', if anything inheriting the mantle of the former elementary school. The curriculum was much less academic than that of the grammar school, concentrating, especially with the less able pupils, on English, mathematics and handicrafts. Pupils who progressed sufficiently could, in theory, transfer to a grammar school at thirteen, though differences in curriculum created difficulties. After the introduction of the General Certificate of Education (GCE) in 1951 head teachers had discretion to enter pupils for the 'Ordinary' Level examinations. By 1963, for example, 58,000 candidates from nearly half the secondary modern schools across England and Wales were entered.

Some LEAs also instituted their own leaving examinations; of a lower standard than GCE, they consolidated work in the upper forms of secondary modern schools. For example in 1956 the Cardiff authority introduced certificates of merit as well as certificates in typing, commerce, engineering and technical studies. Some employers were sceptical, but increasing concentration on certification meant that the number of pupils staying on beyond the statutory leaving age trebled from the early 1950s to the early 1960s.

Apart from the academic differences between grammar and secondary modern schools, there were wide disparities in the quality of buildings, staffing, equipment and amenities, with between two and three times as much per pupil being spent on the former as on the latter. It is hardly surprising that parents were anxious to obtain a grammar-school place for their offspring, given the disparity in life chances for products of the two types of school.

School experience for girls was rather different from that for boys, as Deirdre Beddoe records. The 1944 Act and the Norwood Report, she points out, made no distinction on grounds of sex in the education offered to 'able' pupils. But in some areas of Wales there were more places available for boys than girls. Furthermore, girls' grammar schools had inferior facilities to boys' schools, in particular, fewer and less well equipped laboratories; not all girls' schools were able to offer physics, a marked disadvantage for those wishing to pursue a medical career. While girls did as well as boys at the Ordinary Level of the GCE in 1969–70, they lagged behind at Advanced Level. Fewer went on to the sixth form where they studied a smaller range of subjects. Whereas the Norwood Report saw boys of lesser ability as the future breadwinners, girls continued to be seen as future wives and mothers, such 'gender stereotyping' being characteristic of subsequent reports such as those of Crowther (1959) and Newsom (1963). Girls in secondary modern schools were given little careers advice, and vocational training centred on domestic subjects and typing, so that half the girls entering further education studied shorthand, typing and hairdressing.

The division of secondary education in Wales into grammar and secondary modern schools resulted largely from the educational orthodoxies embraced in the Ministry of Education and its Welsh Department. Nevertheless, the Norwood endorsement of the notion that it was possible to differentiate between three types of mind at the age of eleven had always been under attack, and eleven-plus selection had quickly become a political as well as an educational issue. Research in the 1950s cast doubt on the validity of intelligence tests, and identified a range of about 10 per cent of misallocation. On academic grounds on the one hand, and social and political concern over inequity on the other, there was growing criticism of the tripartite system and endorsement of the all-inclusive 'comprehensive' school, defined by the Ministry of Education as 'intended to provide for all secondary education of all the children in a given area without an organisation on all sides' (modern, grammar and technical). The terms 'multilateral' and 'comprehensive' were used loosely after the war, the ideal multilateral school being on one site which educated three types of pupils separately but allowed social mixing, and the ideal comprehensive school involving full integration. In practice, because of division of pupils into ability 'streams', the early comprehensive schools did not fit that definition. After the war the term 'comprehensive school' was used generally in Wales as in England, with London, for instance, first publishing plans for comprehensive schools in 1945.

Gradually, in the face of mounting research evidence of the detrimental effects of the eleven-plus examination, criticism of the highly favoured status accorded the 'grammar-school child', the failure to achieve parity of status between the various kinds of school and of an incomplete tripartite system lacking technical schools, the notion of a comprehensive system widened its appeal. When a Labour government came to power in 1964 after thirteen years in opposition, there were only 195 comprehensive schools in England and Wales out of a total of 5,894 maintained secondary schools, and a further sixty-nine multilateral and bilateral schools. The government soon issued Circular 10/65, *The Organisation of Secondary Education*, which requested local authorities to submit to the Secretary of State their plans for reorganization along comprehensive lines. By that time the move to comprehensivization had advanced more rapidly in Wales than in England: there were forty-one comprehensive schools in Wales, more than in any English region outside London and Middlesex. Another distinctive feature of Welsh secondary education was the small number of independent and direct-grant schools.

A particular defect of the Welsh system, on the other hand, was the dearth of technical schools: in 1951 the secondary-school population in reorganized schools divided almost evenly between modern schools and grammar schools, but there were only 3 per cent of the age range in technical schools. The distinguishing feature of a secondary technical school according to the Ministry of Education in 1947 'is the relationship to a particular industry or occupation or group of industries and occupations – [it] caters for a minority of able children who are likely to make the best response when the curriculum is strongly coloured by industrial or commercial interests'. The secondary technical schools comprised those previously known as junior technical schools, junior art and junior commercial schools. National policy was that they should recruit from the same intellectual levels as the grammar schools; by the mid-1960s the schools were preparing pupils for GCE and for other more specialized external examinations. They were always few in number, in England decreasing from over 3,000 in 1947 to 186 in 1964, in spite of the national need for more technologists, technicians and craftsmen. Why were they not more successful and popular? Not everyone thought such schools were needed; they had to contend with the social prestige of the grammar schools; and they were handicapped by a feeling that a technical-school education was a 'second best', only of value if one had failed to gain a grammar-school place. These handicaps were perpetuated by the fact that for years after 1944 many secondary technical schools continued to receive their pupils at age twelve or thirteen instead of at eleven. Although in theory children at eleven-plus were supposed to be sent to an appropriate school on the basis of aptitude and ability, technical schools failed to achieve parity of esteem. Many did not have their own separate buildings and were housed in technical colleges, using accommodation and equipment intended for adults.

While technical schools in England were never numerous, the position in Wales was much worse. In 1951, 3 per cent of secondary-school pupils were in twenty technical schools; by 1965 the number of schools had dwindled to six, though there were, in addition, technical streams in some grammar and secondary modern schools. The lowly position of secondary technical schools in Wales reflected the historic low esteem in which technical education was held compared with an 'academic' education, an inferior status stemming from the pervasiveness of the ideal of a 'liberal' education, that fundamental ethos of the public schools and grammar schools of the nineteenth century and carried over into the Welsh inter-mediate schools at the end of the century. An education related to a trade or vocation was considered to be more of an 'instruction' in the acquisition of skills and knowledge than a training of the mind, and thus inherently inferior.

Technical schools generated no enthusiasm among influential politicians, the Ministry of Education or the Welsh Department. Some of the local authorities thought that technical work rightly belonged to the technical colleges. Welsh local authorities had never wholeheartedly embraced junior technical schools before the war, so there were only thirteen in Wales in 1935. In cases where LEAs proposed 'technical sides' attached to grammar schools they were unfavourably received by the ministry, so they were usually attached to the secondary modern schools. Even if this was not the case, it was more common for the former higher elementary and municipal schools to take on board technical education than it was for the former intermediate schools. One example was the Bargoed Technical Grammar School which began life in 1910 as a higher elementary school.

The indifference associated with technical education is epitomized in Cardiff. In 1950 the newly appointed director of education, Robert Presswood, wanted to set up two technical schools. He did not succeed in acquiring dedicated or purpose-built accommodation. The best he could manage was a school, sharing premises with primary and secondary modern schools, which opened in 1951 and transferred in 1953 to the vacated Howard Gardens school which had been built in 1885, had been bombed in the war, and now was dilapidated. That school, Fitzalan Technical High School for Boys, remained there for ten years before new premises were built. Even this level of commitment was entirely dependent on the director, who received no encouragement from local government, teachers' organizations or parents. It was an indifference widely shared with England, with 40 per cent of local authorities providing no technical schools.

During the 1920s and 1930s widespread poverty in Wales, in conjunction with liberal interpretation of the rules by the LEAs, had resulted in more 'free' and 'special' places in grammar schools than were generally available in England. In 1945, therefore, the Welsh situation was distinctive in that a high proportion of pupils at age eleven were already going to secondary grammar schools. There was, too, a higher proportion than in England of children staying on at school beyond the age of fifteen – 34.4 per cent in 1953. By 1961, when the proportion had increased further to 42.9 per cent, several areas of England had overtaken Wales. The legacy of advantage had been slowly eroded.

This points to increased synchronicity of school systems in Wales and England from the 1950s. The social pattern in England, where grammar-school pupils went on to higher education and entered the professions, civil service and other administrative positions, while secondary modern pupils generally entered mining, manufacturing or agriculture, was also evident in Wales. The English and Welsh systems tended to converge partly because of the influence of government policies on Welsh LEAs and, to a lesser extent, because some English regions came to reflect the best pre-war features of the historic Welsh system such as selection by merit and greater numbers of special places in the secondary schools. After 1945, Welsh secondary education was marked by a more egalitarian structure of a system which, in other respects, was similar to that in England, rather than a celebration of a different system. In 1950 between 35 and 45 per cent of the age group went to grammar school, compared with some 18 per cent in England.

In 1961, 52 per cent of secondary-school pupils in Wales were in secondary modern schools, 34 per cent in grammar schools and 11 per cent in comprehensive schools, with some 3 per cent of senior pupils still in all-age schools. The continuing grip of the tripartite system sat oddly with the 1947 recommendation of the Central Advisory Council (Wales) that Welsh secondary schools should be either multilateral or bilateral. The retention of the tripartite system and the relatively slow take-up of comprehensivization reflect the subtle influence of the Ministry of Education, conservative forces among civil servants and attitudes in the Welsh Department of the ministry. Section 1 of the 1944 Education Act accorded the Minister of Education virtual dictatorial powers over LEAs, which were put under the 'control and direction' of the minister, but no minister until 1965 attempted to use these powers overtly, generally relying on consultation and negotiation. Even so, negotiations over the Swansea and Glamorgan development plans demonstrated how subtly effective central control could be. The civil service, particularly with sympathetic ministers, always seemed to make compromises work in their direction. Welsh local authorities were not allowed to step out of line; some, notably Swansea, wished to establish secondary schools catering for all abilities in a single building but were not permitted to do so. With few exceptions, Welsh secondary education was set in a bipartite mould reflecting political and class priorities in central bureaucracy.

Not all the proposals of the 1944 Education Act were put into effect, a notable casualty being nursery schools. Nursery education was the first of a three-stage system of primary education: nursery education (2–5); infant (5–7 plus); and junior (7-plus to 11-plus). Section 8 of the 1944 Act instructed LEAs to have particular regard to the 'need for securing that provision is made for pupils who have not attained the age of five years by the provision of nursery schools, or, where the authority consider the provision of such schools to be inexpedient, by the provision of nursery classes in other schools'. However, partly because of the enormous post-war growth in school population, local authorities were preoccupied with providing accommodation for children of compulsory school age, so this clause remained largely inoperative.

Although there was a fourfold increase in grant-aided nursery schools in England and Wales between 1939 and 1964, accommodating 24,000 pupils, the scale of expansion anticipated in the Act did not occur; there were only some forty nursery schools in Wales in 1964. Similarly, the number of children in nursery classes in primary schools was disappointingly small, fewer in 1964 than in 1939.

According to the 1944 Act, and the amending Act of 1948, compulsory primary education should begin not later than a child's fifth birthday and could conclude as early as ten years and six months but not later than the twelfth birthday. Infant children could be taught in separate schools or departments or in a combined infant and junior school; with rare exceptions, infant schools were co-educational. In the first year, the 'reception class', children were usually occupied with activities similar to those in a nursery school, but were also taught to acquire the rudiments of reading and number, learned to draw and paint and to measure and weigh, while music, dance and movement also played important parts. Teaching methods with the older children varied: some teachers relied on formal instruction, others on informal individual and group activities. Between the ages of seven and eight, children proceeded to a junior department, sometimes moving to another school, or transferring to another part of the same building. Whereas some junior schools were single-sex, the majority were co-educational. More formal class teaching characterized junior education, though this was largely centred on English and arithmetic, while in other subjects such as history, geography, nature study and art there might be individual or group project work. In mathematics, science and French new practical and direct methods were pioneered in the 1960s – resulting, for example, from the science project funded by the Nuffield Foundation.

Most junior schools 'streamed' their pupils into classes of children of roughly equal ability, though the incidence of unstreamed classes increased. The object of streaming was partly to ease the task of teachers, and partly to suit the content and pace of the instruction to the varied ability of the children. In particular, it was designed to give the abler children a better chance in selection tests for secondary education.

The character of junior schools had been influenced by a report of the Consultative Committee of the Board of Education (the Hadow Report) published in 1931, which advocated that the curriculum offered in schools should 'be thought of in terms of activity and experience rather than of knowledge to be acquired and facts to be stored'. In the liberating educational ambience of the 1960s, pushed by college of education lecturers and encouraged by inspectors, 'activity and experience' tended to become a mantra which eventually brought the approach into disrepute, particularly with politicians having an axe to grind, and generated bitter controversy. However, HMI reports indicate that this approach was considerably less widespread in Wales.

The Hadow Committee had also stressed that a major objective of primary education was to produce healthy and happy children. These aims were partly vitiated by the need to prepare pupils to sit the scholarship examination for secondary school, teachers coming under pressure, especially from parents, to ensure that as many pupils as possible succeeded. After 1944 such parental pressure persisted, its objective now to get children into grammar schools, with the result that the school curriculum tended to be distorted by an overemphasis on examination subjects. In many schools, opportunities for subjects such as art, nature study and physical training were severely restricted.

Among the beneficial aspects of the 1944 Act was the improvement it brought about in the education of handicapped children. Concern for children suffering from disability of mind or body led to the Act's laying down that LEAs had a duty to provide special schools or special educational treatment, that is, education by special methods appropriate for persons suffering from disability. It became national policy that handicapped children should be educated as far as possible along with ordinary children so that they would be able to participate in the normal life of society but, where necessary, to provide a special school, preferably on a day basis, boarding special schools and boarding homes for handicapped pupils to be 'reserved for those where there is no satisfactory alternative'.

In Wales, the Order of 1948 setting up the Welsh Joint Education Committee (WJEC) provided that the LEAs should refer to the joint committee 'the co-ordination of provision of special education treatment for pupils who suffer from any disability of mind or body'. The WJEC itself undertook a number of surveys of handicapped children – on physical handicap, spina bifida and partial hearing difficulties – in response to which it recommended to the Ministry of Education (by then the Department of Education and Science), that residential schools for the physically handicapped should be set up at Cardiff and Swansea, and itself was responsible for establishing a residential school for the deaf at Llandrindod Wells.

The period of prosperity which began in the late 1950s induced a mood of optimism, reflected in a growing belief that an improved education system could change society and solve many of its problems. The result was an unprecedented increase in expenditure on education and a welter of reports and blueprints for action, provoked by educational research in the 1950s and 1960s which produced a range of data indicating the need for curriculum reform, innovation and compensatory programmes. There were, at the same time, a number of persistent problems such as teacher shortages, the devising of appropriate examinations within a policy of 'secondary education for all' and a continuing failure to persuade more pupils to stay on beyond the school-leaving age.

Fundamental changes occurred in the external examination systems of secondary schools. In 1951, a General Certificate of Education examination replaced the School Certificate and Higher Certificate examinations. The new examination had three levels, Ordinary, Advanced and Scholarship, the first intended to be approximately equivalent to the old School Certificate. Unlike its predecessor, however, which required simultaneous passes in a group of subjects, a certificate could be awarded in one subject. Furthermore, the grading system, of pass, credit and distinction, was replaced by a simple pass, the certificate merely recording each success. Hitherto, state scholarships had been awarded on the results of the Higher School Certificate examination whereas, under the new system, candidates for state scholarships took special 'scholarship' papers. Such candidates were deemed to give promise of gaining a first or upper-second-class honours university degree, while others who did not seem to possess such exceptional ability, but nevertheless showed promise of being able to benefit from a university education, were eligible for LEA awards. While state scholarships, introduced in 1921 (they were abolished in 1963), had played an important but necessarily limited role (in view of their small numbers) in assisting able pupils to proceed to university, LEA awards brought the opportunity of higher education to a far greater number. This was especially true in Wales where several LEAs interpreted the ruling generously. In Wales, the WJEC became the examining and certification body for almost all schools and worked in close collaboration with the university, the inspectorate and the teachers over the Advanced Level of the GCE.

In 1955 an autumn supplementary examination was introduced in certain subjects at Ordinary Level (O Level), candidates being able to offer those subjects they had failed in the summer examinations. New subjects were introduced from time to time to meet the needs of technical schools and institutions of further education, while there were changes, too, in the arrangements for examinations in Welsh. In 1953 an additional Ordinary Level examination was introduced for candidates who had gained their knowledge of Welsh by studying it at school, followed in 1961 by an Advanced Level examination for the same pupils. By 1969 Welsh-language papers were provided in history, geography, music, scripture, art, French, Latin, metalwork, cookery, dressmaking and domestic subjects.

When introduced in 1951, entry to GCE O Level examinations was limited to candidates who were at least sixteen years of age in the September of that year and beyond the school leaving age, in an attempt to preserve the elitism of the sixth form. A year later this regulation was removed, candidates below the age of sixteen being allowed to sit but exceptionally, and only at the discretion of the head teacher. Nevertheless, some secondary modern schools entered their ablest pupils for the examination. It was, however, an academic examination unsuitable for the great majority of pupils in these schools. Following the report of the Beloe Committee (*Secondary School Examinations other than G.C.E.*, 1960), the Minister of Education in July 1961 accepted the proposal of the Secondary Schools Council for the introduction of a new school examination designed for pupils of a lower level of ability than those for whom the GCE examinations were considered suitable, and which should be largely under the control of teachers. In Wales, the WJEC became the examination body for the Certificate of Secondary Education (CSE), and set up a CSE Committee which had a majority of serving teachers. The first examinations, with assessment of course work playing an integral part in several subjects, were held in 1965, numbers of candidates multiplying rapidly.

Throughout the post-war years, growth and the reorganization in education were bedevilled by an acute shortage of teachers. The war had massively disrupted training and supply, especially of men, and an emergency scheme was proposed in 1943 whereby suitable candidates could be recruited from the armed services to undergo a one-year intensive course of training in 'emergency colleges' established by the LEAs acting as agents for the government; of some fifty colleges three were in Wales, at Cardiff, Llandrindod Wells and Wrexham. In addition, the Board of Education launched a Further Education and Training Scheme (FE and T) which remained in existence after the war, ending in 1951, by which time it had produced 35,000 teachers across Wales and England.

The teacher-supply problem was accentuated by the 'bulge' in the school population resulting from the increase in the birth rate in the 1940s and again in the late 1950s. The result was a continued failure to reduce class sizes; as late as 1963 there were 19,893 primary and secondary pupils in England and Wales in classes of forty and over, and 42,643 secondary pupils in classes over thirty. For a brief period the situation was made worse when the academic profile of the training colleges was raised, they were renamed colleges of education and two-year training courses were extended to three years. Eventually, a four-year degree course was introduced in the colleges in alliance with their local university. The teacher-supply problem was less acute in Wales, many products of the Welsh training colleges going to populate school classrooms in England.

The continuing teacher shortage and constant upward revision of Ministry of Education figures affected the Welsh training colleges as they attempted to meet the targets assigned to them. The McNair Report of 1944 had recommended that Area Training Organizations be set up, with universities playing a central role; in Wales the federal University of Wales was seen as the proper body to assume responsibility for the education and professional training of teachers. Eventually, in 1948, a University School of Education was established, with the training colleges being constituent members of that body and the colleges of the university as focal points.

The first problem was the fate of the emergency training colleges. In the event, two, at Cardiff and Wrexham, were to remain and share in the enormous expansion of the 1950s and 1960s. Between 1958 and 1963 the number of students in Welsh training colleges doubled, but in July 1965 the ministry was once more forced to appeal to the training colleges to meet a further substantial need for teachers caused by the still rising population. In response it was proposed to double the number of students in Wales from the 2,909 of 1963. Along with the expansion went a change from single-sex colleges to co-education, a movement which was radically to affect the character of the colleges. It was a development that had been recommended by the McNair Committee, the first moves coming from Trinity College, Carmarthen a few years later, though it was not until 1957 that the first women were accepted by the college. The huge expansion in teacher training required in the 1960s necessitated this transformation to a co-educational college; of the nine colleges in Wales in 1965 seven were mixed.

The McNair Report had stressed in 1944 that a two-year training period for teachers was inadequate and should be extended to three years, followed by a probationary first year of teaching. Not until the 1960s was this implemented, when the School of Education planned a suitable course. While there were courses common to all colleges, there was also a degree of specialization, advanced courses in arts and crafts being available only at Cardiff and Swansea, handicrafts at Caerleon and Trinity College, Carmarthen, needlework at Barry, Bangor and Carmarthen, and physical education (PE) at Cardiff (men) and Barry (women), the former becoming renowned for its sporting products.

There remained little integration between colleges of education and the departments of education at the university colleges. Each had its own awards, college of education students obtaining a Teaching Certificate awarded by the University School of Education, students in the university departments a postgraduate Diploma in Education. The university maintained a paternalistic attitude towards the training colleges. The university colleges, believing themselves to be the only guarantors of standards, kept a close eye on training-college courses, examinations and awards, including, eventually, degrees. Following a recommendation in the report of a committee under Lord Robbins (1963) the University of Wales introduced a four-year course leading to the award of a Bachelor of Education degree (B.Ed.). The differentiating title of the degree was significant.

The McNair Report had devoted a chapter specifically to the needs of Wales. After referring to the high esteem in which education was held, it claimed that the system of training would have to produce teachers 'with a sense of responsibility towards their country and its cultural heritage'. Teachers would, in many cases, be required to speak the Welsh language, teach through the medium of Welsh and be expected 'to give due prominence to the language, literature, history and traditional culture of the country'. The training colleges, of course, offered Welsh as a subject of study already, with Welsh history being studied in history syllabuses. In 1951, a paragraph in the regulations noted that 'a course in Bilingual Method will be provided for those candidates who have included Welsh in their scheme of study, and who seek endorsement for proficiency in Bilingualism'. In the same year a supplementary course in Bilingual Studies was established at the University College of Wales, Aberystwyth.

The 1953 report, *The Place of Welsh and English in the Schools of Wales*, emanating from the Central Advisory Council for Education (Wales), was highly significant in emphasizing that 'as many students in the training colleges of Wales as desire it should themselves receive the greater part of their training in Welsh', which could best be achieved by 'establishing a training college in Wales to be devoted exclusively to the training of teachers through the medium of Welsh'. The University Faculty of Education rejected the idea of a Welsh-medium college but at the same time suggested that complete courses of training through the medium of Welsh should be provided at Bangor Normal College and Trinity College, Carmarthen. Eventually, in January 1956, the Ministry of Education approved the appointment of additional lecturers at the two colleges to fulfil this purpose. By 1965 over a third of students in both places were pursuing courses through the medium of Welsh, 10 per cent of students in all Welsh colleges.

Breakneck expansion in the colleges of education was duplicated in other higher-education establishments, especially in science and techno-logy, the product of expenditure on a scale unimaginable in earlier years. It was driven by, for example, the demands of rearmament and defence in response to the Cold War, the desire to remain a great power in the face of the loss of empire, the emergence of the USA and USSR as superpowers and the remarkable economic recovery of Germany following the Marshall Plan, resulting in a German industrial challenge which, as in the nine-teenth century, caused concern. Against this background the assumed link between national prestige, power and prosperity on the one hand, and scientific expertise on the other, was a constant refrain, with repeated comparisons drawn between expenditure on education and training and the production of skilled personnel in Britain with that in Germany and the USA.

The scene had already been set in the closing years of the war with the publication of a report, *Higher Technological Education*, produced by a committee under Lord Eustace Percy, a former President of the Board of

Education. A seminal document, it stressed that the position of Great Britain as a leading industrial nation was endangered by a failure to secure the fullest application of science to industry, a failure related to deficiencies in the education system. The committee urged the setting-up of a number of regional advisory councils to coordinate technological studies in universities and technical colleges, together with a similar body at national level. By 1947 Regional Advisory Councils had been set up, one being the Council for Wales and Monmouthshire. Meanwhile, a committee under Sir Alan Barlow had called for a doubling of the annual output of qualified scientists on the grounds that Britain would need 70,000 by 1950 and 90,000 by 1955.

Although the numbers of scientists and technologists produced annually continued to rise, a parliamentary committee claimed in 1954 that the number of technologists per head of population was three times as great in the USA as it was in Great Britain. In the following year the Conservative government introduced a long-awaited White Paper, *Technical Education*. In his introduction, the Prime Minister, Sir Anthony Eden, warned that 'prizes will not go to the countries with the largest populations. Those with the best systems of education will win.'

Among its proposals the White Paper recommended a 50 per cent increase in advanced courses, with a doubling in numbers of day-release students. The paper listed twenty-two colleges in England and two in Wales which provided courses eligible for the 75 per cent grant for advanced work; early in the following year eight colleges were designated colleges of advanced technology, among them the City of Cardiff Technical College which became the Welsh College of Advanced Technology, while two more were added later at Bristol and Brunel respectively. They were to be the apex of a hierarchical structure of technological education embracing local, area and regional colleges.

Meanwhile, there had been an enormous expansion in numbers of full-time British university students (an 80 per cent increase between 1938–9 and 1956–7). The overriding urgency to produce more scientists and technologists is reflected in the breakdown of the percentage increases by faculty: arts and social sciences (73); medicine (9); pure science (160); and technology (136). A similar pattern is apparent in the 20 per cent increase between 1956–7 and 1961–2: arts and social science (20); medicine (0); pure science (32); and technology (37). The expansion had resulted largely from ever-increasing capital and recurrent grants from government through the University Grants Committee, Exchequer grants as a proportion of total income doubling in the 1950s. The University of Wales shared in this expansion, profiting more than most from the extension of state funding because its endowment income was so small. However, the push towards science had less effect in Wales. In the expansion in student numbers of the late 1950s and early 1960s the proportion of students reading arts actually increased, while the proportion of science students remained stubbornly static. In the later 1960s and early 1970s, proportions of arts and science students were roughly equal. For those students who wished to remain in Wales the lack of high-level science posts, particularly in research, was a deterrent.

Following recommendations in the Robbins Report, the Ministry of Education was reorganized in 1964, becoming the Department of Education and Science (DES) under a Secretary of State. For the first time, a central government agency existed with responsibility for the oversight of the whole formal provision of education in England and Wales, even the University Grants Committee (UGC) coming under its purview. With regard to higher education, the Robbins Report enunciated the principle that 'courses should be available for all those who are qualified by ability and attainment to pursue them and who wish to do so'. The Robbins Committee estimated that by 1967–8 there would be a need for 328,000 full-time places, of which 197,000 would be in universities; by 1973–4 the respective numbers would need to be 390,000 and 219,000. As Wales had no autonomy in running its own higher-education system, this being a matter of central government policy, it is necessary to look at the general picture before looking specifically at Wales.

Until the early 1960s, expansion of the university system was mainly centred on increasing the student populations of the existing single and federal universities, but by the end of the 1960s eight new universities had been founded, while a number of colleges of advanced technology were granted university status, including the College of Advanced Technology (CAT) at Cardiff which became the University of Wales Institute of Science and Technology. Expansion in higher education was not without its many critics. Among them was Kingsley Amis, a young lecturer at the University College of Swansea, where he wrote *Lucky Jim*. In an article in *Encounter* (July 1960) he fulminated against the increase in student numbers ('more means worse'). Others, too, claimed it would lower standards and dilute talent in the university population, going so far as to argue that higher education was 'scraping the barrel'.

In reality, entry to higher education was still highly selective in England and Wales; only 14.5 per cent of the age group qualified for entry in 1962, and only 4 per cent actually went to university, a much lower proportion than in other countries. Protagonists of expansion argued that there were hidden reserves of talent. Many sixth-formers qualified for entry to higher education but failed to gain a place, while the Robbins Report pointed out that only one in four was a woman (in Wales one in three). It was not only sixth-form talent which was not cultivated; there were, too, the eleven-plus failures and the 'drop-outs' from secondary schools, with research showing that substantial numbers of children failed to fulfil their true potential in school. This was a situation which no advanced society could afford, whether on grounds of equity or efficiency. At another point in the scale, increasing numbers of mature students would seek entry to higher education in the post-Robbins era, by no means all of whom would be absorbed by the Open University, established in 1969.

A feature of the expansion was that the increase in numbers of scientists in Britain was far greater than the increase in the number of technologists; the proportion of scientists among scientists and technologists was 42 per cent in Britain, compared with 30 per cent in the USA. Mathematicians and physicists comprised 42 per cent of scientists in Britain, compared with only 24 per cent in the USA. A report by the University of Oxford Department of Education in the mid-1960s found that nowhere in Europe was the preference for pure science among the intellectual elite as strong as in Great Britain. It concluded: 'nowhere does technology fail to attract the best brains to anything approaching the same degree as in this country.' The expansion in higher education was swept along by the need for more scientific manpower at the expense of humanities and social sciences. It put higher-education institutions under strain in terms of providing the essential buildings, staff and facilities to support the ever-increasing number of students. Consequently, poorer working conditions such as inadequate laboratories and support staff, in conjunction with higher salaries abroad, led to an exodus of highly qualified scientists and technologists, especially to the USA.

Informed opinion in Wales, epitomized in a report by the Central Advisory Council for Education (Wales) in 1965, held that science laboured under even greater handicaps in Wales. According to the council's report, Welsh-speaking students had to take Welsh as an additional subject and were usually pressured by tradition into studying French, and even Latin, as well. The allied difficulty was that Welsh was not the language of science. The council was also convinced that there was also an inherent Welsh bias towards the humanities, allied with a suspicion of, even hostility towards, technical education.

Against this background, how did the Welsh university colleges fare? Fortunately, they suffered little bomb damage during the war, but much-needed expansion had to be set aside, and maintenance work was of low priority. The colleges suffered in other respects, too, with acute staffing problems resulting from the drafting of staff into the armed forces and other war work, and difficulties compounded by having to share accommodation and facilities with other universities and research institutes. At Swansea, for instance, the Department of Explosives Research of Woolwich Arsenal took over a major part of the chemistry and physics facilities, while Aberystwyth had to cope with students from University

College, London. During the war years, student numbers declined, especially postgraduates, with the proportion of women students doubling and a consequent increase in the proportion of students studying arts. At the end of the war the colleges received hosts of ex-servicemen and others who had been engaged on war work so that student numbers increased rapidly at a time when buildings and facilities were ill-equipped to cope. Numbers continued to rise until 1950–1, the session marking the point at which most ex-servicemen had completed their studies. A decline then set in which lasted until 1953–4, when numbers began to rise again; they continued to rise thereafter as the colleges responded to urges from the UGC and government-provided finance for expansion through ever greater recurrent grants and generous assistance for capital projects. The eventual consequence of the Robbins policy for Wales was that the number of students in the University of Wales rose from 8,279 in 1963–4 to 13,945 in 1969–70, then 14,678 in 1970–1.

The great majority of Welsh students in 1938–9 lived at home or in lodgings, but in the post-war years the pattern changed, only 16 per cent living at home by 1960–1. Whereas in 1938–9 the overwhelming majority of students in the University of Wales came from Wales, by 1954–5 the proportion had fallen to 80 per cent, and to 63 per cent by 1960–1. In that session, 31 per cent came from England, 6 per cent from abroad. This trend was to continue, so the student body became markedly less Welsh, as indeed did the staff; correspondingly, of course, far more Welsh students were going to the English universities.

The problem of accommodating these numbers of students proved a major headache. The colleges responded by buying and converting old houses and other properties such as Clyne Castle at Swansea and the Lion Royal Hotel at Aberystwyth, and by erecting splendid, purpose-built residential hostels. During these years student life changed out of all recognition; the colleges provided Student Union buildings with excellent amenities, purchased new sports fields and established sports complexes with equipment to cater for all sports.

Academic buildings, which had been neglected during the war, were not capable of coping with the existing student body in 1946, let alone with the great increase in numbers that was predicted. With the cooperation of the UGC and its non-recurrent grants for capital projects, the colleges drew up ambitious plans, bought land and embarked on extensive building programmes. At Aberystwyth, a radical expansion was accommodated in the new 'college on the hill' on the Penglais estate. It was highly subsidized by the UGC, but at the same time the college was expected to contribute its share, launching an appeal. Eventually this raised £270,000, the college relying on its traditional supporters such as the Davies family of Llandinam. The loyalty of its students and former students – a special feature of this oldest of the Welsh colleges – was reflected in the multitude of sums it received from them in the rerun of the events of the 1860s and 1870s. At Bangor several sites were purchased; one on the Menai straits to develop a marine biology centre; another for the construction of a 'Science Park'; and a third on the Deiniol Road site for ambitious blocks housing botany, forestry, and extensions to zoology and physics departments. Developments at Aberystwyth, Bangor and Cardiff were rather scattered. Swansea came closest to developing a cohesive 'campus', based in Singleton Park; indeed, the college used that Americanism to describe its extensive building project. The greatest single development undertaken by the University of Wales, however, was in medical education in Cardiff, where at the Heath, an open area of small allotments, the University Hospital of Wales was gradually developed, a vast complex comprising teaching hospital, medical school, dental hospital and dental school.

Expansion went hand in hand with the development of new curricular initiatives in response to the changing social and industrial needs of society. The University College at Swansea was especially strong in the applied sciences, developments there reflecting major changes taking place in south Wales industry; there were new chairs in chemical engineering and physical metallurgy, the latter due to an endowment of £100,000 from Richard Thomas and Baldwin and the Steel Company of Wales. Exciting new initiatives were not confined to applied sciences, though, for the college became a centre for Russian and East European Studies, and promoted the social sciences. A remarkable community project involving the University College of Swansea was the Lower Swansea Valley Project, a cooperative effort between the college, the Nuffield Foundation, the Ministry of Housing and the borough council to remove slag heaps and reclaim heavily polluted land. At Aberystwyth a chair in agricultural biochemistry was added to supplement its strength in agriculture. Another strength in Aberystwyth was Welsh language and literature, while Celtic studies were promoted by appointing specialists in Breton, Cornish and Irish.

As the colleges expanded, they changed from being small, intimate groups of buildings to extensive campuses of far-flung departments, bringing a danger that departments might become insular and inward-looking. Furthermore, increasing specialization due to the vast explosion of knowledge brought increased breakdown in communication. An experiment to overcome early specialization attempted under A. D. Lindsay at Keele was based on a four-year degree course, with a foundation course in the first year. John S. Fulton, who was appointed principal at Swansea in 1947, had come under Lindsay's influence at Balliol College, Oxford. Motivated by a strong desire to 'liberalize' the education of under-graduates, and committed to broadening students' cultural awareness,

Fulton introduced a 'freshers' essay' scheme across disciplines and a programme of weekly lectures of general academic interest. Not everyone was convinced, however, for the rapid expansion of knowledge led inevitably to specialization. C. P. Snow's polarization of 'two cultures' was perhaps an oversimplification, for, as knowledge expanded, experimental scientists were themselves finding it increasingly difficult to communicate to other scientists outside their own narrow field.

Unlike English colleges outside London, the Welsh colleges were part of a federal structure, the relationship between individual colleges and parent body often proving rancorous. But the University of Wales had responsibilities going beyond that relationship and was involved in initiatives of its own. One such, as we have seen, was its coordinating role in teacher training, another was the duty of the university to supervise, check and validate the work of the theological colleges. One signal service rendered to the intellectual life of Wales was the establishment of a Press Board. The Press was subsidized to publish works on Wales and Welsh studies, but special publication subsidies were also given to academic staff to help them publish on non-Welsh subjects. Between 1955 and 1963 the Press produced 132 books (49 in Welsh, 67 in English, 16 in both languages); most were in the fields of Welsh history, Welsh language and Welsh studies, but also there were works on music, economics, geology, biblical studies and philosophy. Journals published by the Press also broke new ground; in 1961 *The Welsh History Review* (edited originally by Glanmor Williams, subsequently by Kenneth O. Morgan and Ralph Griffiths) first appeared, followed a year later by *Y Gwyddonydd* (edited by Glyn O. Phillips) which published scientific research in Welsh.

Prior to the Act of 1944 the areas of education that fell within the purview of LEAs included vocational and 'other adult' education, secondary education and teacher training. However, according to section 41 of the Act, the term ' further education' did not include secondary schools or teacher training. It was defined as (a) full-time and part-time education for persons over compulsory school age and (b) leisure-time occupation in such organized cultural, training and recreative activities as are suited to their requirements, for any persons over compulsory school age who are able and willing to profit by the facilities provided for that purpose. Further education, according to this definition, was both an extensive and highly diverse field. No person above compulsory school age in Wales was required to participate in further education or, indeed, in any educational activity at all. The Education Act of 1944, like those of 1918 and 1921, legislated for a system of part-time education in 'county colleges' for all young people beyond compulsory school age who had not attained the age of eighteen, and who were not undertaking other recognized forms of full or part-time education. Up to 1965 the relevant section of the 1944 Act had not been implemented. Nevertheless, numbers attending day or evening part-time courses increased very considerably.

By far the greatest number of students in LEA establishments of further education took vocational courses leading to qualifications related to professional, clerical, commercial and industrial occupations, either on a purely voluntary basis, or as one of the conditions of their apprenticeship. Prior to 1956, further education establishments, many of which were technical colleges, offered courses at many different levels. Following the White Paper of that year, a four-tier pyramidal structure was introduced at the apex of which were ten colleges of advanced technology (including Cardiff Technical College). CATs were entirely devoted to advanced studies while the next stratum, regional colleges of technology, also had substantial amounts of full-time and sandwich advanced work. Area colleges were intended to deal with intermediate work – mainly at Ordinary National Certificate (ONC) and City and Guilds level – leaving the more elementary studies to district colleges. We have seen that, in Wales, Treforest, Newport and Swansea each had its college of technology, while below these in the pecking order were eleven technical colleges, two technical institutes and sixteen colleges of further education, as well as more specialized vocational institutions.

Further vocational education, most of which was provided by LEAs, did an impressive range of work by 1965. Across England and Wales it involved over 8,000 establishments and 17,000 full-time, 18,000 sandwich and 616,000 part-time day students, as well as many evening students. In Wales by 1965, 65,946 students enrolled in fifty colleges. A characteristic feature of technical education in the post-war years was the shift away from evening study to full-time and day-release courses, and the remarkable growth in the number of National Certificates and National Diploma awards.

Impressive numbers could not disguise serious defects in technical education: a high wastage rate; inadequate apprenticeship facilities; and a lack of cooperation between industry and further education. Apprenticeship training was a matter of particular concern in Wales. England and Wales had been split up into regions, in each of which there was an advisory council to oversee the promotion of further education. We have seen that, in Wales that function was delegated to the WJEC, which proceeded to establish a technical-education subcommittee and advisory panels for technical, agricultural and art education respectively. In 1961 the technical panel of the Advisory Council for Wales published a report which called for a reform of apprenticeship training, proposing a national craft apprenticeship scheme supervised by the Ministry of Education and working through representative bodies. A feature of the scheme would be a network of apprentice-training centres, to which, at sixteen, recruits would be admitted for a three-year full-time training. No immediate action was taken on the committee's proposals but, in 1962, a White Paper on industrial training paved the way for the adoption of first-year full-time courses of training for apprentices in England and Wales under the supervision of industrial training boards.

In Wales, as in England, there was a rapid expansion in technical education in the post-war years, with a doubling in numbers of vocational students by 1965 and a fivefold increase in technical teachers. The development of technical education, both in terms of the growth in student numbers and in the range and level of courses provided, reflected changes in existing industries and the establishment of new industries, as well as the ever-increasing demands of industry for trained craftsmen, technicians and technologists. As in England, there was a shift to full-time, block-release and day-release courses as industry increasingly recognized the value of education and training. Cooperation with industry increased as the WJEC acted in collaboration with the Industrial Association of Wales and Monmouthshire.

Further education also comprised non-vocational education for adults and subsumed leisure-time educational, cultural and recreational activities. The 1944 Education Act enjoined LEAs to play a more proactive role in promoting this area of further education. They were given the responsibility for ensuring 'adequate and efficient facilities' for such activities and urged to collaborate closely with all other bodies in so doing. Since the beginning of the century, formal instruction had been provided by a variety of bodies which came under three categories: the LEAs; the 'responsible bodies', that is bodies recognized for grant by the Department of Education as being 'responsible for the provision of liberal education for adults'; and voluntary bodies other than 'responsible bodies'.

The LEAs provided non-vocational adult education in evening institutes, colleges of further education and special adult education 'centres', while the majority of 'responsible body' work was provided either by the universities through their extra-mural departments or by the WEA. 'Other voluntary bodies' providing liberal adult education comprised a vast array of organizations such as learned societies, arts associations, the trade unions, youth organizations and the churches. There were, too, those bodies which provided 'education' through talks, theatre and museum visits and other such activities; they included, *inter alia*, the Townswomen's Guilds, the Women's Institutes, Soroptomists, Probus and Rotary groups, not forgetting, of course, the splendid work of the broadcasting authorities with their mass audiences. All played their part in contributing to a 'learning' society.

In the post-war years, radio and television were crucial elements in adult education. Apart from education programmes proper, which aimed at systematic and progressive study, there were talks, discussions and feature programmes which had an educative aspect because they awakened interest and imparted knowledge. Initially in Wales, little of this was given a Welsh slant, the Englishness of the BBC offending Welsh-language supporters. However, following the publication of the Pilkington Report in 1962, BBC Wales was established and given responsibility for preparing twelve hours of television programmes a week, about half of them in Welsh. Welsh-language programmes were also broadcast by commercial stations TWW and Granada.

The range of provision from these myriad bodies defies classification. At the more intellectual end, provided mainly by the universities and WEA, came different levels of courses in most university subjects, with local studies centred on history, archaeology and geology being especially popular. The LEAs, though, were by far the major providers, catering for over 1.5 million students in England and Wales. By 1965, in Wales alone, there were over 102,000 students attending adult education centres. The LEAs provided programmes which had much in common, ranging over domestic arts and crafts; painting and the plastic arts; music, drama and movement; speech and creative writing; office skills; physical skills and games; languages; and general education.

Too few full-time staff and too little adequate accommodation were available. Recognizing that adults needed comfortable, suitably equipped and appropriate settings, LEAs developed some special adult education centres in redundant schools or converted houses; lack of money meant that all too few were established. LEA plans to develop short-term residential centres were similarly hampered, though some twenty of these were in fact established in England and in Wales, including 'The Hill' at Abergavenny and, later, 'Duffryn' in Glamorgan, the former home of the coal owner John Cory.

In the post-war years, university extra-mural departments in Wales as in England, recognizing the higher general education level of the public, tended to move increasingly towards providing education for the 'educated', as opposed to offering opportunities for those who had been deprived of education. Long three-year tutorial classes gave way to short, sessional or one-term courses. At the same time, numbers of courses in visual arts, foreign languages, literature and culture, and local studies of various kinds multiplied at the expense of economics, politics and international affairs. Extra-mural departments also took on work for professional groups using the expertise of internal staff to provide refresher and training courses for teachers, social workers, lawyers and other professional groups. The major demand for such courses came from the servants of the new welfare state – child-care officers, health workers, probation officers and voluntary social workers.

Some in 'responsible body' circles were troubled by these trends, but it remained true that the bulk of the work of the extra-mural departments and the WEA still lay in the realm of 'liberal' adult education, that is, learning for its own sake, and not from professional or vocational motives. It is significant that such a tradition remained strong in Welsh adult education. Whereas overall in England and Wales the LEAs provided some 80–90 per cent of all adult education and catered for over three-quarters of all students, 'responsible body' work in Wales, as a proportion of the whole, was twice as great as that in England, and the number of people who attended such classes in Wales was appreciably higher proportionally than it was in England.

Another remarkable feature of adult education in Wales was the continuing success of Coleg Harlech. Founded in the confrontational days of 1927 to foster cooperation between the classes, it continued to thrive in times when state-financed opportunities for the education of the working class were available on an unprecedented scale. It was estimated that, by 1960, about 1,000 full-time and 1,000 part-time students had attended courses. By the late 1960s, the University of Wales was awarding Diplomas of the University at the college, although this development was not to the liking of some critics, who argued that the tradition of non-examination courses should continue. Nevertheless, by the 1970s, Harlech was teaching about 130 full-time students from all sections of society, significant numbers of whom proceeded to the University of Wales to read for degrees.

Despite improvements in formal school provision and increasing prosperity in the 1950s and 1960s, juvenile crime, adolescent rebellion and the diminishing deference to authority were continuing causes of concern to the establishment and focused thinking on the lot of school leavers. County colleges that would have accommodated many fifteen- to eighteen-year-olds remained in abeyance. A committee under Sir Geoffrey Crowther posited solutions to some of the problems. Its report, *15 to 18*, published in December 1959, stated that raising the school-leaving age to sixteen and establishing county colleges providing compulsory part-time education to eighteen 'should be re-affirmed as objectives of material policy'. Three months later, a committee chaired by the countess of Albermarle published a report that expressed unease at the neglect of the youth service and proposed a service for young people aged fourteen to twenty under full-time leaders and part-time paid voluntary workers. The government accepted the committee's recommendations, setting up a Youth Service Development Council for England and Wales.

Following the Albermarle Report, the WJEC strengthened the representation of youth organizations on its further education committee. The link between schools and the youth service had always been close in Wales, an inquiry in 1957 revealing that over half the part-time youth leaders were teachers. In 1962, after widespread consultation between the joint committee and relevant organizations, eight training agencies were established in Wales, and, as a result, between 1963 and 1965 over 500 part-time leaders received basic training involving courses lasting six months. A centre was established in Snowdonia to train teachers and leaders, while Pembrokeshire provided a sailing centre. Action by the WJEC also led to the setting-up of a Welsh Sports Council in 1966, and the committee maintained and supported the National Youth Orchestra of Wales, which gave concerts at the Edinburgh Festival and undertook concert tours abroad.

The 1920s and 1930s had been traumatic, with few parts of Britain experiencing greater deprivation than Wales. The post-war transformation was such that Wales enjoyed a level of affluence and prosperity never previously approached, notwithstanding the fact that unemployment in Wales was still generally higher than the average for England and incomes always lower than average incomes in most regions of England.

Prosperity engendered a feeling of pride and new-found confidence leading to demands for the recognition of the Welsh language and of Welsh culture, and to a burgeoning of national consciousness which saw Cardiff being elevated to the status of a capital city and James Griffiths being appointed the first Secretary of State for Wales.

The immense expansion of the education system brought immeasurable benefits to Welsh society. While the numbers of English students seeking to study in Wales gradually increased, it was nonetheless the case, even in 1965, that a large majority of students in the university colleges, training colleges and technical colleges were Welsh. The production of educated youngsters was such that the Welsh economy could not cope with the huge increase in numbers, the result being a 'creaming-off' of talent to England and elsewhere as young people sought career opportunities outside Wales. Of the traditionally dominant professions of teaching and the ministry, teaching retained its popularity whereas, with the increasing secularization of society, the importance of the ministry declined dramatically. The greatest change, however, came with the increasing diversification of Welsh industry which demanded a greater range of skills, so that for the first time the sciences and technologies became significant career pathways for young Welsh men and women.

In the post-war years, the education system of Wales, as in England, was shaped to meet the urgent economic, political and social needs of Great Britain, and most sectors of Welsh education became indistinguishable from their counterparts in England. Despite the formal setting-up of specific Welsh bodies, the structures of the education system in Wales reflected few differences from those in England. There was only limited Welsh administrative input from the 1944 Act onwards, despite a Welsh Department based in Cardiff and the creation both of an Advisory Council for Wales and of the WJEC. Local authorities, too, had little autonomy in matters of basic policy. However, notwithstanding the general convergence of the systems in Wales and England, traces of the Welsh radical Nonconformist heritage of the nineteenth century remained in the more meritocratic structure of secondary education, the differing social composition of students in higher education and the continuing emphasis on a liberal, non-vocational ethos in adult education.

In 1964 came a development of immediate symbolic and longer-term practical significance. A Secretary of State for Wales was appointed. This changed the parameters within which education policy operated. By 1970 the Secretary of State was responsible for primary and secondary educa-tion in Wales. From that time there was an incremental administrative devolution which continued until the creation of the National Assembly in 1999 changed the process of policy-making yet again.

CHAPTER SEVEN

✕

Comprehensive Change, 1965–1979

The prosperity and concomitant confidence to which post-war generations had grown accustomed persisted into the early 1970s, the Middle East crisis of 1973 bringing a downturn in the British economy which presaged more difficult times ahead for Wales. Meanwhile, the factors which had been responsible for the metamorphosis of Welsh society continued to operate well into the 1970s. Government policies and financial incentives introduced diverse new industries which helped in the process of diminishing reliance on a few staples. Higher levels of employment and rising incomes led to better health and housing, a boom in consumer durables and changes in the pattern of holidays and entertainment. Improved educational opportunities were available to an ever wider sector of society. Women enjoyed greater freedom, both economically and socially, with the feminist movement emerging in Wales in the 1970s as a powerful political and social force, action groups lobbying for equal pay, equal opportunities in education, free contraception and abortion on demand, twenty-four-hour nurseries and refuges for battered women.

Culturally, too, Wales flourished as never before. The International Eisteddfod at Llangollen attracted contestants worldwide, and the Welsh National Opera achieved international status. The following for classical orchestral music increased as the imposing new concert hall, St David's Hall, opened in Cardiff in 1982. Much-needed support for the arts generally came from the Welsh Arts Council established in 1967.

There were less welcome changes – a general weakening of community life with the advent of television, the increasing use of cars and the closure of churches and chapels as religious observance declined. The oil crisis of the mid-1970s compounded some of the problems experienced by the staple industries of coal and steel in particular; throughout the 1960s and 1970s pit closures proceeded relentlessly, so that by 1979 only some 30,000 were employed in an industry which had once employed 233,000, while in the same year the situation reached crisis point in the steel industry with the announcement of 6,000 job losses at Shotton in Flintshire and 11,000 at Port Talbot and Llanwern.

The impact of the gradual demise of the coal, steel and slate industries was not offset by the introduction of new industries, welcome as these were. Oil, nuclear power, car-component plants and light engineering industries became an increasingly important sector of the Welsh economy, while further diversification brought in government departments such as the Royal Mint at Llantrisant and the Driver and Vehicle Licensing Centre (DVLC) at Swansea. What emerged following the decline of traditional industries and the geographical location of new industries was a divide between, on the one hand, the prosperous south-east and north Wales coastlines and, on the other, the high unemployment and stagnation of the industrial Valleys of south Wales and of many rural parts of Wales. Economic development and increasing migration had their political consequences in the unprecedented success of the Conservatives in winning eight seats in each of the elections of 1974 and 1979. The Anglicization of rural areas contributed to an alarming decline in the Welsh language and triggered the emergence of Cymdeithas Yr Iaith Gymraeg (The Welsh Language Society) which was more militant than the established Welsh Nationalist Party (Plaid Cymru). It was particularly successful in attracting the support of the young, especially students, and achieved dramatic results by adopting direct action techniques of sit-ins and mass demonstrations by which it waged a relentless campaign to pressurize the government and other agencies to give the Welsh language equal status in their literature and documentation.

Heightened awareness of the fate of the language resulted in the Welsh Language Act of 1967 according to which 'Welsh should enjoy equal validity with English for official, governmental and legal purposes'; another outcome was a fully-fledged Welsh TV channel, S4C, which came into operation in 1982. Perhaps the greatest success of the movement for the perpetuation of the language was the dramatic change it wrought in the position of Welsh in the education system.

Changes in education in England and Wales during this period were punctuated by conflict: progressive teaching methods as against traditional; comprehensive schools versus grammar schools; the struggle for the control of the curriculum. Conflict came to be accentuated by economic circumstances which split the period into two; the expansion and buoyancy of earlier times continued into the early 1970s, whereas fiscal problems, rising inflation and world recession following the oil crisis of 1973 brought contraction and expenditure cutbacks. From 1974, instead of coping with the strains engendered by rapidly increasing numbers, the system was having to accommodate severe financial stringencies and falling numbers. At the same time, the increasing unemployment of school-leavers was a matter of concern to successive governments, attempts to alleviate the problem leading to radical changes in the post-school sector.

During the 1960s and 1970s there had been a gradual devolution of powers to Wales, largely administrative, with over 2,200 civil servants employed at the Welsh Office headquarters in Cathays Park, Cardiff by 1984. However, it did not follow that control over educational develop-ment passed to Welsh agencies, as central government increased its grip on educational policy. The Welsh had no power to legislate, nor was there democratic accountability (other than that of local authorities) within Wales. Nonetheless, as the hold of central government tightened, the existence of a Welsh Office Education Department, with its own civil servants and an associated Welsh inspectorate, provided more avenues than had previously been available for pressure groups to influence the process, a notable development being the Welsh schools movement.

In 1974, the counties of Wales, which had remained largely unchanged since Tudor times, were radically reorganized. Thirteen counties and four county boroughs (Cardiff, Newport, Swansea and Merthyr Tydfil) were replaced by eight large authorities and thirty-seven district councils, the former being designated by the historic regions of Wales: Clwyd, Dyfed, Glamorgan (West, Mid and South), Gwent, Gwynedd and Powys. These changes resulted from the Redcliffe-Maud Commission Report of 1969 which affected England and Wales similarly, the number of local education authorities being reduced from 146 to 104. Reorganization in 1974 came after a steady decline in the powers of local education authorities as central government assumed ever greater control. The traditional relationship between them, based on consensus and partnership, was significantly under-mined, and, under the influence of the radical right, power was to move still further to the centre in the late 1970s. As Roy Lowe has remarked, local government shifted towards delivering policies devised elsewhere and 'in this sense LEAs were becoming increasingly part of a bureaucratic system'.

In the 1950s, the curriculum of the primary schools in England and Wales was largely dictated by the needs of the eleven-plus examination; it imposed a stranglehold on the schools which were feeders to different types of secondary school. These tests in English and arithmetic, together with intelligence tests, were viewed with trepidation by pupils, their parents and teachers because they were instrumental in determining access to grammar schools, and O Level and A Level examinations which, in turn, governed access to higher education and to secure, well-paid employment. Teachers were under considerable pressure to ensure the success of their pupils in the examination so as to produce the maximum number of children proceeding to the grammar school. In the process, the great majority of schools depended on streaming their pupils according to their ability, as Brian Jackson's 1964 survey, *Streaming: An Education System in Miniature*, revealed. At the same time, he demonstrated that the result was social stratification of pupils, with the majority of those allocated to upper streams being drawn from professional and managerial family backgrounds, while the children of parents in unskilled or semi-skilled occupations were more likely to be found in lower streams. The harmful effects of streaming had been highlighted, too, in a particularly influential longitudinal study, Douglas's *Home and School*, published in 1964.

A key factor affecting primary schools in the 1960s, therefore, was the gradual abandonment of the eleven-plus examination by numbers of local authorities, triggered by increasing doubts as to its validity and fairness, and the shift to comprehensive secondary education. Streaming in the primary school became less essential as the pressure to maximize the number of successes in an examination subsided.

Released from the straitjacket of the eleven-plus, primary schools were freer to explore more innovative approaches to the school curriculum. Innovation was stimulated by the publications of the teacher-dominated Schools Council, formerly the Curriculum Study Group (1962), and by projects in mathematics, science and modern languages sponsored by the Nuffield Foundation in the mid-1960s. The so-called 'progressive' philosophy of the school curriculum reached its apogee in the report of a committee under Lady Plowden in 1967. The report, *Children in Primary Schools*, endorsed curriculum reform and supported child-centred education, accompanied by a shift away from streaming and greater emphasis on the needs of the individual child. Significantly, it advocated more attention being given to the early years of schooling, and urged closer links between schools, homes and communities.

In Wales, the Plowden Committee was paralleled by a committee having a similar remit under Charles Gittins, Professor of Education at University College, Swansea. Its existence is a touchstone of educational devolution in 1966/7. The Gittins Committee was in fact the Advisory Council for Wales which complemented that of England, both having been set up under the terms of the 1944 Education Act. Other than its unwelcome (at least to the Ministry of Education) endorsement of comprehensive schools in a report of 1947 it had made little impact. Its activities were sporadic, prompted not by the specific needs of Wales but by political expediency in the Ministry or Department of Education when circumstances decreed. Nevertheless, the fact that Gittins dealt with Wales while Plowden was in theory (though not in practice) concerned with England was of considerable symbolic significance. Gittins certainly ruffled some feathers with pronouncements on some issues relating specifically to Wales such as the language.

His report, *Primary Education in Wales*, was published early in 1968 (though it bears a 1967 imprint). The 1967 Plowden Report advocated the expansion of nursery education and priority-area designation, that is 'positive discrimination' by which pupils with the greatest need should be given most help. The common thread in the reports was the stress on social deprivation, educational researchers reinforcing the message that attainment was closely correlated with social background. The Gittins Report recommended that universal part-time provision should be made available as soon as practicable from the age of three to entry to the first school, but with provision for an estimated 15 per cent full-time places for children with particular social and emotional needs. In Welsh-speaking areas, nursery assistants and nursery teachers should be trained to meet the needs of those areas, and nursery classes in Welsh should be provided to meet the desires of parents in Anglicized areas.

With regard to primary schools, the committee saw the fundamental problem being the organization of groups in such a way as to meet the needs and capacities of the child. The class should remain the basic social and administrative unit, but teaching groups should vary in size to meet varying conditions. Teachers should be given the material and facilities to organize their teaching approaches, in particular, to develop group and individual work. 'As far as possible, the fixed timetable in the junior school should be replaced by planned but flexible programmes of work.'

In the transition from primary to secondary stage, selection should be abandoned, examinations at this stage abolished or replaced by 'test-free' methods of allocating pupils, and use made of primary-school assessments to guide placement in the secondary school. In the view of the committee, the period from eleven to thirteen should be regarded as transitional; in particular, the first six months at least should be diagnostic, with a common curriculum and with teaching groups shared by a small number of teachers.

In considering the primary-school programme, the committee looked at how children learned and developed, and at the implications which those findings had for primary education. It emphasized the importance of evidence pointing to the need for children to learn through activity, experience and personal understanding, and to work within groups. 'Learning how to learn' was more important than the acquisition of information, while 'subjects' were not relevant to the primary school. In making learning significant to the individual, and in the acquisition of fundamental concepts, the committee argued that the 'discovery approach' was crucial – concrete experience, personal activity and understanding, as well as information from experiment. Education, the committee concluded, was as much concerned with personal relationships and learning to live with others as with academic learning; the teacher had a fundamental part to play in transmitting attitudes and values as well as knowledge.

The child's environment was held to play a particular part in the learning process. In the past, schools had tended to ignore this. Even in the 1960s, work in arithmetic and reading was begun without inquiring what skills and experience the child already possessed which were relevant, yet learning was helped by linking what was done in school with what the child did outside; hence, teaching approaches should be shaped by what the child had acquired from its background. In the field of language, for instance, it was presumed that children could communicate through speech, had acquired the language system of their mother tongue, and had a considerable experience of using spoken language. In practice, children varied greatly in the richness or poverty of their language background, and in the organization of their experience through language: 'We are only now becoming fully aware of the differences created by cultural or class influences and experience in the early years.'

The committee paid particular attention to the teaching of individual subjects, notably history and science. In history, although teachers were free to produce interesting schemes of work, the committee claimed that they often disregarded the history of Wales in favour of English history. Teachers of science should take account of the effects of maturation and experience on children's understanding at different ages. Children's experiences in primary-school science were not only valuable in themselves, but also made them more ready to deal with the systematic approach to science found in the secondary school. As with other subjects, the committee stressed that attitude of mind was more important than mere acquisition of facts. Children whose first language was Welsh should be able to study science in their mother tongue. A vocabulary of scientific terms was now available in Welsh, and interest in science had been fostered by the publication at university level of a periodical such as *Y Gwyddonydd*, while a series of books on primary science had recently been translated into Welsh.

The Gittins Committee was unequivocal over bilingual education: 'The organisation of schools, in terms of their basic medium of instruction, should ensure in general that children are taught through the medium of their mother tongue but given full opportunity to acquire their second language.' Children in Anglicized areas should have the opportunity to be taught through the medium of Welsh if this was their home language or if their parents desired it. For children in Welsh-speaking areas Welsh should be the basic medium of instruction, but consideration should be given to meeting the needs of English-speaking parents who wanted their children to be taught from the outset through the medium of English.

For a time after publication of the Plowden and Gittins Reports there ensued changes to the curriculum and in teaching approaches in many schools. Both the Welsh and English committees had sung from the same hymn sheet. The new orthodoxy, promoted by colleges of education and endorsed by the inspectorate, involved a shift away from streaming, moves to group work, and the adoption of creative approaches and topic work; some LEAs experimented with open-plan classrooms and integrated days. It was not long before a backlash began, headlined in the orchestrated publicity of the first of the 'Black Papers' in 1969. It was alleged that standards in schools were falling because of the abandonment of tried and familiar pedagogic techniques and their replacement with projects, discovery techniques, 'new maths' and 'creative English'. Black Paper authors gave every indication of being unaware of the existence of Wales, nor was there a Welsh contributor.

In practice there was a gulf between popular perception and reality. Only a minority of schools adopted full-blooded modern approaches, though project work became ubiquitous. Grouping of furniture was more in evidence than group work among pupils. In Wales, inspectors' reports indicated that there was no neglect of the core subjects, while a mantra of the Black Papers was greater emphasis on the core curriculum in primary schools, echoing the widely held view that the fundamental role of the primary school was to establish the bases of literacy and numeracy. The ideological and practical debate over the curriculum was polarized between the child-centred 'romantics', together with those who saw the curriculum as an instrument to enhance the cause of social justice, and the 'cultural transmission' conservatives. A report by a committee under Lord Bullock, *A Language for Life* (1975), failed to substantiate claims in the popular press that standards in schools were falling, or the views of industrial leaders who criticized levels of literacy and numeracy among school-leavers entering employment, claiming they were ill-equipped and insufficiently prepared for working life.

The cause of progressivism was dramatically undermined by an acrimonious dispute centred on the William Tyndale School in London. The head teacher of this Lambeth primary school, Terry Ellis, and some other staff, attempted to develop a 'child-centred' curriculum derived from a Marxist-inspired view that the traditional curriculum of knowledge transmission amounted to capitalist indoctrination. This was challenged by the Inner London Education Authority; the ensuing dispute led to an adjudication by the Auld Committee, its report being interpreted by the press as a damning indictment of teachers generally, and a heaven-sent opportunity to press the case for greater teacher and local-authority accountability. This played into the hands of a government increasingly anxious to exert greater control over schools. It had already responded to anxieties by setting up an Assessment of Performance Unit in 1974 to monitor schools, but its continuing concern was encapsulated in a speech given by the Prime Minister, James Callaghan, at Ruskin College, Oxford in October 1976 reflecting both popular misgivings and Department of Education and Science ambitions. There was concern, he stated, over 'methods and aims of informal instruction', and he advocated a core curriculum and monitoring of standards in order to achieve a national standard of performance. He emphasized the need to improve relations between education and industry, stressed that schools should play a fuller part in preparing pupils for working life as a key to economic efficiency, and pressed for a more technological bias in science teaching leading towards practical applications in industry as opposed to academic attainment.

The speech initiated a 'Great Debate' in a series of regional conferences organized by Shirley Williams, Secretary of State for Education and Science, with the object of discussing, *inter alia*, the aims and content of school curriculum, the performance of the school system and its relationship to the demands of working life. A direct result was a government Green Paper, *Education in Schools*, which reflected the government's determination to exercise greater authority over primary education and wrest control from teachers and educationists. Then came Circular 14/77 which required all local authorities to report on the curricula followed in their schools, and a spate of guidelines from DES and HMI seeking to establish a common area of the curriculum and agreed aims and objectives for all stages of schooling. Ironically, among the publications was an HMI survey, *Primary Education In England* (1978), which attacked the myth of falling standards and demonstrated how little primary schools had really progressed beyond traditional didactic methods and a restricted curriculum.

This education debate was going on without any specific reference to Wales. A climate of opinion was being created through the Black Papers and hyped up by the media, which had virtually no Welsh dimension and took no account of differences in practice between Wales and England. This had enormous implications for education in Wales in the 1970s and 1980s. While the broad economic and political contexts of the debate in both countries were similar, there were specifically Welsh aspects. For example, in 1949 the Central Advisory Council (Wales) reported that 'activity should be pervading the quality of school life'. In the 1960s there was little evidence of this; the basics of reading and writing, the alleged shortcomings of which produced so much acrimony in England, did not seem to be reflected in Wales.

The realities of power in education decreed that Westminster politicians and civil servants took no account of such differences as they pursued larger political objectives. By the late 1970s central control over primary education in England and Wales had been reasserted. In the process the Department of Education and Science had become politicized to an unprecedented degree.

Established in 1964, it had originally pressed for curricular reform through the Schools Council which flooded the schools with suggestions as to the organization and content of teaching, and throughout the 1960s and 1970s it worked through its inspectorate to achieve change through consultation. The Assessment of Performance Unit was headed by an HMI, and the Yellow Book of 1976, which precipitated the Ruskin College speech, was in part compiled by HMI. But with the growing dependence of central government on the Downing Street Policy Unit from 1974 and on backroom advisers, the inspectorate was increasingly marginalized. In response, HMI became defenders of professional autonomy. While once there had been complaints that the DES was merely a post-box between local authorities and teachers' unions, the powers of the LEAs were being gradually eroded due to financial stringencies and local-government reorganization.

Ironically, just as government control over education tightened, some increase of influence passed from Whitehall to Wales through devolution, though the impact of this on central thrusts of policy was marginal. Until 1947 the Welsh Department of the Ministry of Education had conducted its work in London, a Cardiff office being opened in that year and, by 1952, much of its work being carried out there. Far more significant, in October 1964 a Secretary of State for Wales was appointed, backed up by a Welsh Office, full responsibility for primary and secondary education being handed over by 1970.

In secondary education, meanwhile, attempts to reform the curriculum affected all subjects. The Schools Council, which had been established by Sir Edward Boyle in 1964 with a strong teacher representation, played a prominent role, as did the Association for Science Education in the sciences. A Schools Council Working Party in 1967 advocated the establishment of teachers' groups to act as forums to plan curriculum development, local authorities responding by establishing some 200 of them by 1968. A crucial issue was devising a suitable curriculum for those pupils who in earlier times would have left school at fifteen years of age, most of whom belonged to lower-ability bands. When the Newsom Committee drew attention to the problems of this group in *Half Our Future* in 1963, there was general acceptance that the school-leaving age would be raised to sixteen, so the late 1960s witnessed a series of research projects and reports focused on the needs of pupils who would remain at school for a further year. The school-leaving age was eventually raised to sixteen in 1972.

Modernization of secondary education came under attack in the Black Papers, with the reform of English teaching drawing the most adverse publicity. By the mid-1960s there had been moves in the teaching of English to give greater emphasis to creativity and personal development, moves which by the early 1970s were being severely criticized. In 1975 the Bullock Report gave rise to a press furore centred on claims that standards of literacy were falling, despite the fact that this had been rebutted by the committee, while the Yellow Book in the following year called for better basic standards of English and mathematics, echoing the complaints of industry and business.

Curricular controversies stemmed from the radical transformation in the structure of secondary education from the 1960s. Of 5,654 schools in England and Wales under local-authority control in 1964, only 264 were comprehensive or bilateral schools, a further 186 being technical schools; the great majority (70 per cent) were secondary modern, while there were 1,298 grammar schools. Nearly 500 secondary schools were either independent or direct-grant schools. Of maintained schools in Wales, 231 were secondary modern, 116 grammar schools, 14 technical schools and 31 were comprehensive or bilateral schools. Increasingly over the next few years, as comprehensive schools were established, technical schools and bilateral schools disappeared, as did most secondary and grammar schools, only a few authorities still retaining selection at eleven-plus by 1980. None of these was in Wales. Meanwhile, the Labour government had abolished direct-grant schools, most of which became independent, the independent sector thus comprising a substantial element of the secondary education system in England. In terms of numbers the independent sector remained relatively insignificant in Wales.

By 1979 Wales was a country of comprehensive schools and they dominated provision in most local authorities in England also. Comprehensivization was a divisive political issue. When Labour came to power in 1964 after thirteen years in the political wilderness there were only 195 comprehensive schools in England and Wales. Then the new government issued Circular 10/65, *The Organisation of Secondary Education*, in October of the following year, which requested local authorities to submit their plans for reorganization of secondary education along comprehensive lines to the Secretary of State. The response of LEAs varied, though most in Wales were broadly sympathetic. For the recalcitrant the government adopted the tactic of withholding approval for those building plans based on segregation. Threats of compulsion were realized when a Bill was introduced in February 1970 by Edward Short, Secretary of State, in response to a 'minority of local authorities and a minority of governors ignoring or openly flouting national policy'. The fall of the Labour government in June of that year meant that such drastic action was not implemented.

When Labour returned to power, the comprehensive-school movement had become deeply entrenched, and under the impact of renewed central government pressure, authorities such as the Conservative-controlled council at Cardiff were reluctantly obliged to move towards a non-selective system. There was indeed a measure of reluctance across Wales to lose the grammar schools, with their proven academic track record and proud traditions. Any scheme which proposed alteration to their status, let alone their demise, inevitably aroused protests from parents and teachers. Conservative and Independent councillors (the latter forming substantial ruling blocs in some parts of Wales) were generally opposed. Many Labour councillors, too, were committed emotionally, personally and politically to the grammar schools (which in Wales were mainly the schools established under the Welsh Intermediate Education Act of 1889), which had done so much to provide educational and career opportunities for generations of able working-class children. Furthermore, the 1944 Education Act had necessitated a major upheaval in secondary education involving changes in the functions of school buildings, and investment in new buildings and resources, especially in secondary modern schools. Naturally there was resistance from a number of education officers, councillors and parents to the further upheaval and the radical changes that would be required by a move to comprehensive schools. Grammar-school teachers wanted to preserve their elitist traditions and superior status, and secondary modern teachers often felt that pupils would be better served by the intimate atmosphere of a small secondary school rather than being lost in the vast, 'soulless' 2,000-pupil comprehensive schools such as had appeared in London. Supporters of the bipartite system in Wales pointed to the high percentage of children who passed into the grammar schools and to the schemes of local authorities to effect transfer beyond the age of eleven. Furthermore, it was claimed that the introduction of GCE courses into secondary modern schools enabled those who had failed narrowly to pass the eleven-plus examination to pursue a 'grammar-school'-type education.

The Ministry of Education's official report of 1965 claimed that none of the Welsh authorities opposed the principle. This bland ministry gloss is misleading. A. G. Geen's research on the county borough of Cardiff's reaction to Circular 10/65 is indicative of where power really lay and, in terms of the future of state policy, some of the battle lines drawn up locally and nationally were to have lasting implications. From 1957 a small, vociferous section of the Labour group in Cardiff became committed to the abolition of the eleven-plus, with the Conservatives equally vehemently opposed and many of the 'old' Labour group being equivocal. Two years before Secretary of State Anthony Crosland's Circular 10/65, in the teeth of Conservative opposition, the Cardiff authority had committed itself to a two-tier 'Leicester' plan which at least did away with the eleven-plus. When Circular 10/65 was received the debate was in full swing, made more acute by the realization that the proposed thirteen-plus selection envisaged by the authority would not be an acceptable long-term solution. On the other hand, the circular did not impose any specific pattern of comprehensive schooling.

There soon came a demonstration that, once again in the history of the Welsh local authorities, it was central government which held the aces. In 1966 the now-controlling Conservative group in the city council was adamant that the grammar schools would be preserved, but in 1967 it accepted that selection must go. The reason was simple. Circular 10/66 made it clear that the DES would not sanction any funding for building or extending selective schools. At a time of increasing pressure of numbers on the system this was the trump card. Cardiff devised a new pattern of 11–16 and 11–18 comprehensive schools. By the time Secretary of State Margaret Thatcher issued Circular 10/70 reversing effective compulsion it was too late.

Even so, local authorities in Wales moved less reluctantly to adopt a comprehensive-school system than those in most areas of England. Already between 1958 and 1965 the number of comprehensive schools in Wales had grown from twenty-five to forty-one and, more significant, the proportion of secondary-school pupils in comprehensive schools from some 10 per cent in 1958 to 28.4 per cent in 1965. Following the issue of Circular 10/65 the majority of councils proceeded with plans to act. In practice, reorganization took a long time but, by 1969, nearly half Welsh secondary pupils attended comprehensive schools; ten years later it was possible to count the number of grammar schools left in Wales on the fingers of one hand. Wales had become a country of large, 11–18 comprehensive schools. The number in Wales quickly increased to 118 by 1969 and to 202 by 1976, the proportions of pupils in such schools increasing to 89 per cent in 1976. Correspondingly, the number of secondary modern schools and grammar schools declined: the former from 231 in 1960 to 32 in 1976, and the latter from 116 in 1960 to only 18 in 1976. In 1961, 52 per cent of Welsh pupils were in secondary modern, 34 per cent in grammar, 11 per cent in comprehensive and 3 per cent in all-age schools. By 1976, 6.8 per cent of children were in secondary modern schools, 4.3 per cent in grammar schools and 89 per cent in comprehensive schools, while technical schools had disappeared. The proportion of pupils in comprehensive schools in Wales was significantly higher than in England (in 1979, 96 per cent of schools in Wales were comprehensive compared with 83 per cent in England), reflecting a more radically inclined and somewhat less class-conscious society than that prevailing in many parts of England. By that time the only grammar schools left in Wales were in Aberystwyth, Gwendraeth Valley, Llandysul, West Monmouth (at Pontypool) and Whitland.

Wales was distinctive, too, in that its system was largely uniform – large 11–18 comprehensive schools, with 14 per cent of schools in 1977/8 having more than 1,500 pupils, compared with 5 per cent in England.

Another special feature of Welsh secondary education was the small part played by direct-grant schools and the independent sector. There were always fewer than half a dozen direct-grant schools, the proportion of pupils in Wales in such schools falling from 11 per cent in 1960 to 3.8 per cent in 1976.

The debate regarding control of schools and of the school curriculum had far-reaching implications for teacher training. The McNair Report of 1944 had recommended that there should be established area training organizations (ATOs) in which the universities would play a central role 'by assuming responsibility for the training and assessment of all students seeking to be recognised by the Board of Education as qualified teachers'. We have seen that, in Wales, the area training organization was a University School of Education comprising two bodies, the University Board of Education and a University Faculty of Education, the former body dealing with administrative matters, the latter with academic issues such as syllabuses, courses and regulations. Membership consisted of representatives of the university, the university colleges, the training colleges and the teaching profession.

In 1965, the school introduced a four-year Bachelor of Education degree which comprised a study of education and two academic subjects. It was envisaged at first that the course would only be available for a small proportion of students who would have qualifications equivalent to matriculation, although provision was made to transfer exceptional students from the certificate course after one year of study. Later, the university sanctioned a B.Ed. degree for serving teachers, requiring one year's full-time or two years' part-time study. The numbers pursuing the degree full-time in the colleges of education rose disappointingly slowly during the late 1960s, the colleges arguing that the course was too academic and especially unsuitable for primary-school teachers, similar complaints to those being voiced by other area training organizations.

Criticism of teacher-training courses mounted. The Plowden and Gittins committees in England and Wales respectively were highly critical, especially of the B.Ed. course, and recommended a thorough review. In 1970, a committee was established under the chairmanship of Lord James of Rusholme, vice-chancellor of the University of York, to conduct an inquiry into teacher training. The committee's one Welsh member was J. R. Webster of Aberystwyth. Its 1972 report stressed that greater priority should be given to in-service education, and recommended the introduction of two new qualifications, a two-year Diploma in Higher Education (Dip. H.E.) and a BA (Ed.). The committee condemned the influence of universities on training courses and proposed the abandonment of the area training organization system, with less influence given to the universities in their new proposed reorganization. Webster demurred, insisting that the university's continuing involvement in Wales was both historically justified and educationally crucial.

In response to the James Report the government published a White Paper in 1972, *Education: A Framework for Expansion.* The White Paper dropped the idea of a BA (Ed.); instead, new three- and four-year B.Ed. degree courses were to be developed, while the Dip. H.E. was to be introduced as a qualification in its own right. On the administrative side, the existing university-based ATOs were to be disbanded and replaced by new regional committees in England. In Wales, thanks to Webster, the University Faculty of Education and collegiate faculties continued a modified existence.

Publication of the James Report heralded contraction, not expansion. Demand for teachers began to decline a few years after the birth rate started to fall in the late 1960s. Circular 7/73 predicted a requirement of 70,000 training places for 1981 across England and Wales compared with 110,00 in 1972, only 4,800 for Wales alone, though the Welsh colleges had always populated staff rooms in England liberally. These figures were revised downwards once more to 46,700 and 2,900 respectively (both including an allocation of 20 per cent for in-service training places). Thus, drastic cuts were to reduce teacher-training places in Wales from 6,300 in 1971 to 2,900 in 1981, a drop of 54 per cent.

The inevitable consequence was wholesale reorganization, a complete redrawing of the map of the fragmented college structure in Wales after 1975 in a frenzy of amalgamation, decided not by the University School of Education but by the DES. The changes gave shape to institutional grouping which remains to the present, though now, in 2002, it is deemed to be 'not an option' for the future. For that reason its detail warrants rehearsing. Wrexham College of Education amalgamated with Denbighshire Technical College and Flintshire College of Technology to create the North-East Wales Institute of Higher Education. Swansea College of Education amalgamated with Swansea College of Technology and Swansea College of Art to form West Glamorgan Institute of Higher Education. Caerleon College of Education joined with Newport and Monmouthshire College of Technology and Newport College of Art. Cardiff College of Education amalgamated with the College of Food Technology and Commerce, the College of Art and Llandaff College of Technology to create South Glamorgan Institute of Education. St Mary's College, Bangor was merged with the University College of North Wales, and Llandaff College of Education (Home Economics) with the University College of South Wales and Monmouthshire. Barry College of Education was merged with the Polytechnic of Glamorgan (later the Polytechnic of Wales). Only Bangor Normal College and Trinity College,

Carmarthen remained free-standing, the latter continuing as a Church-based college.

The restructuring differed from the proposals submitted by both the School of Education and the WJEC, satisfying neither body. It was clear, as usual, that the role of the two bodies was limited to advice and recommendation, final decision-making powers residing with the DES. The University of Wales lost its supervisory and coordinating functions. Its role was now limited to that of examining body, all degrees to be validated by the university with the exception of those at Barry which, as part of the polytechnic, came under the Council for National Academic Awards (CNAA) regulations.

The DES, in time-honoured fashion, was not particularly interested in education in the Welsh language (nor was it antagonistic) despite the beginnings of dramatic changes in attitude and practice. Twenty-eight per cent of the population spoke Welsh in 1951. A decline to 20 per cent in 1971, when it was spoken mainly in the rural west of the country where employment was falling and prospects for the young diminishing, caused great anxiety. Against this background, education was seen as a key battleground for those wishing to preserve the language and safeguard its future. Official support came in a report on the Welsh language published by the Council for Wales and Monmouthshire in 1963, followed four years later by the Gittins Report which advocated that the Welsh language should be a means of expressing the cultural, social and spiritual values of the society which gave it birth. Gittins gave a new stimulus to the Welsh schools movement, already making good progress – by 1970 there were 41 Welsh-medium primary schools with some 5,000 pupils. By 1976 there were 71 forms or sets in secondary schools in which Welsh was taught as a first language, mainly in Dyfed and Gwynedd, and 47 in which Welsh was used for teaching some subjects. By 1980, 52 secondary schools were offering history through the medium of Welsh, while in 34 schools Welsh was used to teach five or more subjects. The first Welsh-medium secondary school, Ysgol Glan Clwyd, opened in Flintshire in 1956 and others soon followed; by 1980 there were eleven secondary schools designated as Ysgolion Cymraeg (Welsh Schools) with 8,000 pupils.

The Welsh school movement to increase numbers of primary and secondary was controversial, but flourished because of a more enlightened attitude in government departments, a greater degree of good will from local authorities and increasing support from English-speaking parents, some of whom sent their children to Welsh-language schools.

It was crucial that the movement was not restricted to the north and west but advanced into the industrial heartland of Glamorgan and Anglicized Cardiff. The capital, with its expanding university colleges, and home of the Welsh Office, BBC, Harlech TV, and later S4C, had become a Mecca for a generation of young Welsh-speakers. Traditionally, the pathway for ambitious youngsters had led to London, but its preeminence had been supplanted by Cardiff, especially for those seeking a career in the media. They demanded a Welsh-language education for their children.

Four out of five people in Wales could not speak the language, but the majority of these considered themselves to be as 'Welsh' as those who did. It did not follow that because the language had found a firm foothold in schools a 'Welsh' education distinctive from that in England was being offered to the whole population. Despite Sir Owen M. Edwards's efforts fifty years earlier, little progress had been made in devising a Welsh scheme of education. Since 1870 the curriculum of primary and secondary schools had differed little in Wales from that in England, attempts to incorporate specific Welsh interests largely revolving around the teaching of Welsh.

The notion of a curriculum for Wales aroused only the most sporadic interest. Apart from *The Curriculum and the Community in Wales*, produced by the Welsh Department of the Ministry of Education in 1952, and a Schools Council for Wales discussion paper, there was little official guidance on what might be an appropriate curriculum which might, for instance, centre on cultural traditions, the significance of the geography and history of Wales and the experience of industrial development, so providing an intellectual foundation for the 'Welshness' of non-Welsh-speakers.

The success of pressure groups in promoting the Welsh language was not limited to schools, as dramatic changes in higher education focused attention on this sector. Although the student body increasingly comprised fewer numbers of native Welsh students, steps had been taken to promote Welsh interests. In 1974, a working party was set up to consider establishing a Welsh-medium college. The national financial crisis meant that prospects were unfavourable, but schemes for teaching some subjects through the medium of Welsh went ahead at Aberystwyth and Bangor. Four years later, Aberystwyth was keen to press ahead with a pilot scheme for an external degree. The time was auspicious, for the UGC was prepared to give additional funds to support specific initiatives reflecting the obligations of the university to the Welsh community in matters such as Welsh-medium teaching, external degrees and a 'Welsh for adults' scheme using the intensive 'Wlpan' model devised in Israel for teaching Hebrew to incomers (the word itself is derived from the Hebrew for 'studio'). Two years later Aberystwyth was able to go ahead with its external degree scheme, offering courses in Welsh, Welsh history, drama, music, Breton and religious instruction, modelled on Open University study patterns.

Essentially, the development of higher education in this period fell into two distinct parts. Unprecedented expansion continued until the financial crisis resulting from the Arab oil embargo in 1973. In the late 1960s there were two significant additions to the University of Wales. The oldest institution of its type in Wales, St David's College, Lampeter at last became a constituent college and Cardiff's College of Advanced Technology was incorporated in 1967 as the University of Wales Institute of Science and Technology (UWIST). Thus the Welsh School of Pharmacy and the Welsh School of Architecture, which had been part of the College of Technology, were now an integral part of the university. With the crisis came the suspension of the 1972–7 quinquennium plan for university funding midway through its period, and its replacement by a system of annual funding. Generous capital spending gave way to restricted recurrent grants. The extensive building programme of the 1960s came to an end and predicted expansion in student numbers was drastically revised downwards to a virtual standstill. But the legacy of expansion continued to provoke debate.

The enormous expansion in student numbers in the 1960s produced a welter of criticism and misgiving across the United Kingdom, many doubters being concerned about falling standards. Additionally in Wales, opposition had a dimension which culminated in a rancorous debate in the mid-1970s. As expansion proceeded in the 1960s the proportion of Welsh-born students in the University of Wales continued to fall from its level of 73 per cent in 1957–8 to below half (47 per cent) for the first time in 1964–5. There was sufficient concern for the university to set up a working party to consider the problem of expansion; at the same time, it commissioned Clive Williams of the Department of Education at Aberystwyth to investigate the difficulties of persuading Welsh students to enrol in Welsh colleges. He reported that although only 4,000 students living in Wales enrolled in the University of Wales there were 10,000 Welsh students in British universities. English universities were finding similar difficulty in recruiting students from their own regions. Part of the emancipation of the young in the 1960s was to seek to study further away from home and live in the numerous new halls of residence; for many students this appeared to represent a greater spirit of enterprise and adventure – in the case of many Welsh-born students it meant going to a large English city. Encouragingly, the report also showed that the proportion of students with 'A' grades in A Level examinations entering the University of Wales was comparable with that at most British universities, with the exception of London, Oxford and Cambridge. Furthermore, the proportion of students from 'blue-collar' homes in the Welsh colleges was higher than the average for British universities.

After considering Dr Williams's report the working party produced its own report in October 1973. It argued that there was no such thing as an 'ideal' size for a university and accepted as reasonable the plans for expansion presented by the various colleges. At the same time, it respected the idea of a quota system to ensure a minimum number of Welsh students at the colleges. The leading protagonist of those against expansion on the grounds of the diminishing 'Welshness' of the university was Alwyn D. Rees, director of Extra-Mural Studies at Aberystwyth. His arguments were enshrined in a paper, *The Alienation of the University of Wales*, which he submitted to the university in the summer of 1973. Rees pointed out that between 1954 and 1969 English universities had expanded by 108 per cent, whereas the University of Wales had expanded by 162 per cent. Was such expansion necessary for the Welsh nation? he asked. Each college, he claimed, had proceeded with its plans without any regard for Welsh needs. The future expansion plans of the colleges were based on greed, amounting to a 'plan for the permanent alienation of the University of Wales from the Welsh nation'. All expansion, he argued, should be 'stopped forthwith'.

Rees's report and that of the working party were considered by the Council of the University at Swansea in November 1973, to the accompaniment of a noisy demonstration outside orchestrated by Cymdeithas yr Iaith Gymraeg. A delegation invited inside argued that the University of Wales was already greater in size than was necessary to meet the needs of Wales; further expansion would merely drive the last nail in the coffin of the 'Welshness' of the university.

A month later the same reports were dealt with by the Court of the University, the situation being further confused by yet another submission, this time from the students of the university. During the 1960s Welsh students had demonstrated the same militant involvement as their peers throughout Europe and the USA. There were marches, demonstrations and sit-ins on issues such as the Campaign for Nuclear Disarmament (CND), apartheid, and the Vietnam War, as well as specifically Welsh issues such as the Welsh language. They clamoured to be allowed to participate in decision-making in the university, both administrative and academic. Initially, college authorities tried to neutralize protests by offering students places on college bodies; this was not enough, however, and by 1969 student representatives had been accepted on the Court and Council of the University. By 1979 the Central Students' Representative Council (CSRC) had firmly established itself in the governing processes of the university and students had to be consulted on all matters affecting them. In the main they were critical of expansion but against any nationalist moves to increase the Welshness of the university. After considering all the reports the court condemned 'with utmost disquiet the expansion projected for 1972–82'. This was a serious blow to the prospects for expansion, for the court membership was widely representative of educational institutions and local authorities in Wales.

Ironically, this pronouncement almost coincided with that of Chancellor of the Exchequer, Anthony Barber, on 17 December 1973 that the country was facing serious financial difficulties. A month later the UGC circulated a letter to all universities warning them of impending cuts in government funding. The predicted expansion to 27,530 students in the University of Wales by 1981–2 was cut back to between 20,000 and 24,000. In fact, by 1977–8 the number of students had fallen to 18,832. In the event, the standstill in numbers had been effected not from pressure within Wales, but as a consequence of events in the Middle East.

By the mid-1970s over four-fifths of the Welsh university colleges' income came from the Treasury. As the economy deteriorated the UGC attitude hardened from being one of polite guidance to one of issuing memoranda specifying what was and was not allowed. In this period of stalemate the University College at Cardiff went against the trend shown in the other colleges and most British universities; it actually expanded, principally through establishing an English Centre for Overseas Students. There were three large institutions of higher education in Cardiff, all reliant on largesse from the Treasury, the university college, University of Wales Institute of Science and Technology and the Welsh National School of Medicine. Since 1937 pharmacy had been taught jointly between the former technical college, precursor of UWIST, and the university college, and in 1967 a joint library for English and law, together with a joint department of law, was established. Otherwise, the two institutions were quite separate. In 1979 UWIST had looked unsuccessfully for a site at Llantarnam near Newport to relocate and expand. Five years later the UGC visited Cardiff to press the case for merger between UWIST and the university college, but it was 1988 before such a merger was effected, with the two institutions coming together as the University of Wales College of Cardiff after the effective bankruptcy of the university college.

The proposals put forward by the Robbins Committee in 1963 for a radical expansion of higher education based on a place for every qualified student, inevitably involved huge costs which soon led to an announcement in 1965 that there would be no further new universities during the following decade. Apart from cost, there was the question of control. Although the Treasury was supplying the greater part of the annual income of universities, the government had limited influence over universities in the face of the principle of university autonomy. One partial remedy would be to incorporate major colleges of technology in the system of higher education. This was the approach adopted by Anthony Crosland when Secretary of State for Education, in his binary system of higher education which developed in the late 1960s, when thirty colleges were designated polytechnics; they remained under local-authority control, the intention being that they would constitute a sector of higher education more responsive to the nation's industrial and commercial needs.

In Wales, the Glamorgan College of Technology, which had begun life as a School of Mines, founded and funded by a group of leading coal owners, now became a polytechnic, continuing its eventful history. During the Depression of the 1920s the coal owners decided that they were unable to continue to maintain the school, which was consequently taken over by the Glamorgan Education Authority. In the post-war years, with a broadened curriculum and a considerable building programme, it accommodated a growing number of students. In 1949 the school was renamed the Glamorgan Technical College and, in 1957, following a government White Paper, it was designated an area college with the new title of Glamorgan College of Technology and, in 1969, became Glamorgan Polytechnic. With new teaching blocks, halls of residence and student facilities appearing on campus, academic work was greatly expanded.

The reorganization of teacher training in the 1970s saw the Glamorgan College of Education at Barry merge with the Glamorgan Polytechnic to form the Polytechnic of Wales in 1975, although three years later initial teacher training was discontinued and the site at Barry given up. The merger had brought an infusion of arts and social-studies students. By then the college had grown to comprise eleven academic departments, that of mining and mine surveying which had been part of the School of Mines at its inception now being the smallest, reflecting the sharp decline in the south Wales mining industry. Civil engineering, business studies, estate management, industrial design and computer engineering attracted degree, Higher National Diploma and Certificate (HND and HNC) students, as did courses for health visitors and careers advisers. The policy of serving industry and commerce was reflected in the continuing strength of engineering, building construction, business studies and other technologies, while the college remained firmly embedded in the local community, with 40 per cent of its students living at home.

Equally radical change affected further education. During the mid-1960s one in three school-leavers in England and Wales became an apprentice at fifteen years of age, but a decline in manufacturing industry led to a massive drop in apprenticeship and to youth unemployment, a situation further exacerbated by the oil crisis in 1973. Youth unemployment, rapidly accelerating from 10,000 in 1974 to 240,000 in 1977, became a major problem, successive governments introducing a series of stopgap measures which failed to solve the problem. In 1973 the Employment and Training Act established the Manpower Services Commission (MSC) which began work in January 1974. It devised special training schemes for school-leavers and took over the Training Services Agency which had been formed in 1972. Job-creation schemes followed in 1975 and two years later a committee chaired by Geoffrey Holland producing a report, *Young People at Work*, which recommended an expansion of the MSC with an increase in its powers. In the following year, a Youth Opportunities Scheme (YOPS) was introduced, designed to provide work experience for school-leavers. Critics claimed that this merely generated a pool of cheap labour with the majority of the several thousand young people on YOPS courses ending up on college courses anyway.

The government, through the agency of the MSC, was increasingly influencing the way further education was developing, and its grip was to tighten further in the 1980s. However, it could be argued that the MSC, through its various schemes, was providing a pool of students for the further-education colleges which partly compensated for the loss of day-release students resulting from the decline of manufacturing industry and the consequent demise of apprenticeships. At the same time, the colleges were entrepreneurial in providing a range of O and A Level courses, some of which were not available in schools. The colleges were quick, too, to take advantage of the new interest in a 'return to learning' of adults who had failed to prosper during school life by providing 'access' courses for beginners, while continuing to provide technical and commercial courses leading to RSA, City and Guilds and BTEC awards. The sector grew rapidly. In Wales, by 1979, some 80,000 students enrolled, and the colleges employed about 4,000 full-time staff. There were 21,362 students on full-time courses, 2,999 sandwich students, 32,131 part-time day students and 22,938 evening students in maintained, assisted and grant-aided establishments. In addition, 127,411 students attended adult-education centres of various kinds.

During the 1960s it became increasingly recognized that education was not a process which simply stopped at the ages of sixteen or eighteen or twenty-two. In particular, with the rapid increase in technological development and the exponential expansion of knowledge, it was impossible to educate a person for a lifetime in the first cycle of life, even if that lasted twenty years from nursery school to doctorate. As one vice-chancellor put it, education should not be likened to 'an act of salvation which, once experienced, enables us to remain pure for life'. As a result, higher-education institutions faced extra pressures, for, in addition to providing a plethora of taught postgraduate courses, they were expected to give greater emphasis than hitherto to the promotion of what were termed 'post-experience' courses, in-service courses for professional groups such as teachers, social workers, nurses and engineers, and also to meet local and community needs generally.

Wales shared with England the analyses and attempted remedies for other educational shortcomings highlighted in this period. In the 1960s attention focused on the impact of social deprivation on the educational development of children, with 'community education' schemes and educational 'priority areas' as possible remedies. Research evidence revealed that adult illiteracy was widespread, in spite of a century of compulsory schooling. In response, the Adult Literacy Resources Agency (later, the Adult Literacy and Basic Skills Unit) was established with government money to combat adult innumeracy as well as illiteracy, a focus due to take on new sharpness in the education system by the end of the century. Compared with European countries and North America, fewer were proceeding with education beyond school. Participation by children from working-class backgrounds, in particular, had scarcely increased proportionately since the 1930s. Furthermore, as the Robbins Committee pointed out in 1963, males outnumbered females by a ratio of four to one at university. The committee noted that only 8 per cent of the relevant female age group entered higher education, compared with 22 per cent of males, despite the fact that as many girls as boys passed O Levels.

It was becoming ever more obvious that adverse social factors affected the educational prospects of children from working-class backgrounds; poverty, large families, inadequate housing, poor health and stunted environments all took their toll. But this was only a partial explanation of why females, working-class children and older adults were minority groups in the student population. Adverse personal factors such as unfavourable experience with a particular teacher, the death or illness of parents or personal illness at a critical stage of schooling were often as true for the middle-class child as for children from working-class backgrounds, while, for girls, lack of parental support, stereotype images of 'femininity', 'peer-group' pressure and the impact of advertising, especially with regard to clothes and cosmetics, were powerful influences.

Of course, for individuals who came to a realization in their post-school years of ability and ambition unfulfilled there had always been the possibility of a 'second chance' – Birkbeck College and Ruskin College, for example, for men and women in England, and in Wales, Coleg Harlech. There were, too, innumerable correspondence courses, while in 1963 the National Extension College was established to promote home-study courses for adults.

Opportunities were greatly extended with the inauguration in 1970 of the Open University (OU) – in itself a response to the concentration by the traditional universities on the most able eighteen-year-olds. The Open University in Wales constituted one of the Open University's regions in the United Kingdom. From its administrative centre in Cardiff it arranged an extensive programme of courses in study centres throughout Wales, using a team of senior counsellors, staff tutors and an array of part-time staff drawn mostly from existing higher-education establishments to provide teaching, counselling and support. At the heart of the courses was the correspondence material, supplemented by radio and television programmes, summer schools and optional residential weekend tuition at local-authority colleges such as The Hill, Abergavenny. Many students who apply have few formal qualifications, and the OU relies on the provision of short preparatory courses in LEA institutions, providing a booklet for the guidance of institutions interested in putting on such courses. In 1978 an agreement was concluded between the University of Wales and the Open University on the mutual recognition of credits, whereby students who have successfully completed part, but not all, of their first-degree studies at one university may be able to claim advanced standing on first-degree course at the other.

The success of the OU in Wales is indicated by the large number of applications it received each year – 1,864 in 1979, which comprised 4.1 per cent of all applications to the university in the United Kingdom. The geographical distribution, however, was not uniform; probably for practical reasons there were greater numbers of applications from urban areas – 12.7 per cent in South Glamorgan and 10.4 per cent in Gwent – compared with rural counties – 7.3 per cent in Gwynedd and 7 per cent in Powys. The largest number of applications in the early years came from teachers and lecturers anxious to top up their existing qualifications to degree level, closely followed by housewives, while technical and clerical staff were also prominent. In 1979 some 8 per cent of applications were from retired adults, a figure higher than that for the UK as a whole. Applications from women, however, were lower in Wales than in the UK. Surprisingly, the proportion of students following courses in sciences and technology was higher in Wales than in the UK generally, 29.3 per cent compared to 22.5 per cent.

In spite of the Open University's large numbers, only a small minority of university students in England and Wales in the early 1970s were over twenty-one, fewer still over twenty-five. However, there was an increasing readiness to accept mature students without A Levels, and some research surveys indicated that mature students were more successful than eighteen-year-old entrants in some subjects. There were few opportunities for part-time study but strong support in its favour came from *Adult Education*, a report published in 1974 by a joint committee of vice-chancellors and principals and the Universities Council for Adult Education. Subsequently the UGC proposed a new principle to replace that put forward by the Robbins Committee in 1963 which had placed all its emphasis for expansion on eighteen-year-olds. The committee stated that 'courses of higher education should be available for all those who are able to benefit from them and who wish to do so'. The more favourable attitude towards adult students coincided in 1978 with dire DES predictions that the potential cohort of eighteen-year-old students would decrease drastically by the 1990s owing to demographic change.

In this changed climate of the 1970s the WEA, university extra-mural departments, colleges of further education and adult-education centres embarked enthusiastically – often in alliance with universities, polytechnics and institutes of higher education – on promoting an array of appropriate 'access' courses under such titles as 'Return to Study' and 'Fresh Start', women being a particular target group by means of New Opportunities for Women (NOW) courses. Many access courses were short, but others took one or two years' part-time study, sometimes validated by the local university or polytechnic and leading to the award of certificates and diplomas which could exempt students from part of a degree programme.

The greater readiness of universities and polytechnics to accept older students, through either A Levels, special procedures or success in an 'access' course, was reflected in the fact that by the early 1980s some 10–15 per cent of first-degree students at most universities were over twenty-one, while between a fifth and a half at polytechnics were over that age.

The University of Wales had long made provision for the admission of mature students over twenty-three years of age who had been recommended by a constituent college of the university as having attained a satisfactory standard of general education. In the early 1980s it introduced external degrees of BA, B.Sc., LLB and BD and an external Diploma in Theology; it also made provision for suitable mature students whose lack of formal qualifications was compensated for by relevant experience to study for a master's degree. At Aberystwyth, where all mature students were assigned a personal tutor, normal entry requirements for candidates over twenty-three years of age could be waived, provided selectors were satisfied that the applicant had a reasonable chance of completing the course successfully. By 1980 10–20 per cent of students on first-degree courses in the Welsh university colleges were over the age of twenty-one, and all colleges welcomed applications from suitable and committed students. The Polytechnic of Wales, where over a quarter of students were over twenty-one, followed the CNAA's policy on the admission of mature students, applicants over twenty-one years of age without the normal entry requirements being admitted if they could produce evidence that they were likely to benefit from study on a degree course. With the exception of the South Glamorgan Institute of Higher Education the Welsh institutes and colleges of higher education had even higher proportions of mature students, up to 60 per cent in the case of the North East Wales Institute of Higher Education. The age of the 'mature' student had truly arrived.

In the 1970s the grip of teachers, educationalists and, increasingly, local authorities on the education system had loosened as central government started to claw back control. Under Mrs Thatcher's administrations its control tightened further, the power of local authorities diminishing, with accountability, standards and parental choice becoming mantras. No essential distinction was made between Wales and England in essentials. Nevertheless, the Welsh-language lobby had achieved much in strengthening the position of Welsh-language teaching generally and fostering Welsh-medium schools particularly. Welsh-language education helped to preserve the language among the young. Its products also made an incalculable contribution to their culture and society.

CHAPTER EIGHT

⋈

An Education for Wales, 1979–2003

Rejection of devolution in 1979 seemed to leave Wales politically bereft of direction, or, more correctly, with even less moral authority to withstand direction from outside. Shortly after its people rejected the opportunity for limited self-government they found themselves governed by a party which had always been in a minority in Wales. The new government followed a radically new approach to the relationship between the state and its inhabitants which fundamentally affected both the Welsh economy and the public services, among which education was so significant.

In terms of state education across England and Wales this revolution meshed with longer-term fundamental trends. To take one example, much of the education expansion of the 1960s and very early 1970s had been consequent on the steep population increase of the post-war period, the birth rate peaking in the mid-1960s. Gradual decline thereafter began to feed through first to the primary schools and then, from 1979, into the secondary schools.

If the 1979 referendum revealed confusion of political direction in Wales, this was complemented by the undermining of one of its icons of effectiveness, its secondary-school system. The scene was set by concerns emanating from the 1978 Welsh Office-sponsored conference at Mold which concentrated minds on the strengths and weaknesses of the Welsh comprehensive-school system. The Loosmore Report, initiated at this conference, was published in 1981 and demonstrated that 25 per cent of pupils in Wales were leaving school without an O Level pass. The conclusion drawn was that, while Welsh comprehensive schools seemed to be serving more able pupils well, they were not as effective with lower-ability pupils and were less successful in the examination stakes than their English counterparts, having yielded an advantage associated with the former grammar schools. Subsequent studies pointed accusing fingers at old-fashioned teaching based on grammar-school models, and lack of attention to low achievers. This prompted research into disaffection, underachievement, management structures in schools and school-effectiveness policies that only later came to dominate debate in England.

While these studies established Wales at the forefront of school-effectiveness research, which was to become ubiquitous, it was a dubious distinction to have done so on the basis of such worrying data. It was only in the 1990s that further research into social deprivation and school achievement indicated that Welsh comprehensive schools were not guilty as charged, performed at least as well as their English counterparts and were (and continue to be) successful institutions. By that time the 'myth' of Welsh school underachievement, as it is now labelled, had been sufficiently embedded in political consciousness to allow Welsh parallels to school-effectiveness philosophies and practices in England to take effect less controversially than might otherwise have been the case.

While the main trends in the Welsh economy had been apparent previously, the years of Thatcherism highlighted and accelerated them. The Welsh rural economy, based on farming and concomitant industries, has always been relatively poor, conditioned by so much land being suitable only for sheep farming. Areas of lowland Wales – Dyfed, the Vale of Glamorgan, the border counties – are exceptions, but generally it has only been European Union subsidies which have helped to preserve the fabric of farming in recent years. The fragility of this economy was frighteningly exposed in the 1990s as subsidies tailed off and, later, animal diseases deeply damaged stock breeding and sale.

Heavy industry – coal and particularly steel – which characterized the Welsh economy after the Second World War and had already been drastically thinned in the 1970s, came under renewed onslaught in the 1980s. Because Wales was still disproportionately reliant on these industries, the disappearance of about a third of the manufacturing base in Great Britain in the 1970s and 1980s hit particularly hard. New light industries were established, but only in the late 1990s did investment in the hardware and software of computing in schools and further education begin to provide a ubiquitous educational infrastructure. The Welsh share of research and development has remained disproportionately small.

Wales did share in the phenomenal growth in the service sector of the economy – over three million jobs being created in Great Britain in the 1970s and 1980s – which became, with the financial sector, the major sources of employment at the start of the new millennium. Tourism, in particular, grew rapidly as Wales capitalized on its historic past and the beauty of its landscape and seascape. Here again, relevant vocational courses in schools and further education were slow to develop, though in some areas there is now healthy provision. Such observations, of course, raise questions fundamental to the future of Wales, involving the relationship between vocational education and training, and the way in which higher-education support interacts with regional and national economies. There is certainly no straightforward relationship between them.

Without the economic capital, the research base and managerial expertise locally available are minimized in their practical implications; at the same time, without a skilled workforce the economic impact of investment and research is negated.

From the 1970s to the very recent past, the British economy continued to grow, but more slowly than those of its developed rivals, and there remain dramatic regional variations. Wales has lower per-capita income than any region on the British mainland other than the North-East of England. Social deprivation, measured by housing, job opportunities and unemployment, is more evident than in England. The extent of current European Union Objective One funding, taking in whole swathes of rural and industrial Wales, is sufficient indication of relative poverty. In this context, there has been dramatic change in the nature of employment – the growth of part-time and seasonal work, a major increase in jobs for women. So it is easy to understand that, in the absence of any watertight theory of the relationship between the economy and formal education, compounded by lack of decision-making powers, Welsh education was able to adapt only slowly to new situations, and only within the context of government initiatives often driven by wider priorities. The traditional haven of academic courses leading to examination success, with higher education providing the route to the professions, not surprisingly remained the safest port as the storms raged.

This route seemed firmly entrenched as governments struggled to find alternatives to the apprenticeship system, which had attracted over 30 per cent of boys leaving school in the 1960s, though only 5 per cent of girls. Changes in the nature of the economy both demolished the old system and led to the search for a new. As we have seen, a whole raft of palliatives was devised by central government. Industrial training boards, the Manpower Services Commission, established in 1974, job-creation programmes, youth-opportunities programmes and even the ambitious Technical and Vocational Education initiative of 1982 failed, as such initiatives always had, to transform school cultures. Vocational programmes continued to be regarded as the preserve of less able pupils. Nevertheless, an attempt was made to provide a qualifications structure with the establishment of the National Council for Vocational Qualifications in 1986, though its work, again, was dogged by perceptions among pupils, parents, staff and many politicians that its awards were second-class substitutes for existing examinations.

All these initiatives carried into Wales, with no different effect. Attempts to mould the higher-education sector to reflect government preoccupation with the shortage of science and technology graduates were again only marginally successful and impinged hardly at all on Wales. This country has shared in the dramatic extension of the formal-qualifications culture, part of which at least has been driven by the demands of the new economy in which numbers of manual jobs decreased rapidly while the service and professional sectors increased. Nevertheless, Wales lags behind in numbers of post-sixteen-year-olds who take up further education, a situation compounded by the scarcity of better-quality jobs.

For those who were successful in the education system, in Wales and England alike, the rewards since the 1980s have been more obvious than ever as the gap between rich and poor has widened and salaries for those on average wages have increased ten times as fast as the incomes of the poorest 10 per cent of the population. The significance for Wales is that there is a disproportionately low number of high earners. The enormous growth in female employment has thrown into high relief the concentration of women in lower-paid jobs, or receiving smaller wages for the same jobs as their male counterparts. Overall, gross domestic product in Wales per head is one-fifth less than the United Kingdom average, and nearly 20 per cent of the population have no educational qualifications. Unemployment in Wales is 4 per cent above the United Kingdom average. Reforming the skills and qualifications base of the education system in this economic context will indeed be a litmus test of the effectiveness of a separate Welsh government.

The National Assembly's 2001 paving document, *The Learning Country*, has made an impressive contribution both in acknowledging the problem and proposing solutions – a modern skills diploma, an extension of modern apprenticeships, individual learning accounts (dropped in England) and a commitment to further review in 2003 – but it is perhaps the tone of genuine concern with getting to grips with the practical problems of lifelong learning for personal and economic reasons that provides most encouragement. It remains that higher education in Wales produces more highly qualified personnel than the relatively low-skilled and restricted economic base can accommodate.

Although the economic transformation of the last thirty years has left Wales poor compared with almost all regions of England, it still shares in disparities between pockets of wealth and swathes of poverty. Areas of burgeoning bureaucracy such as Cardiff, its dormitory in the Vale of Glamorgan and the more affluent suburbs in other Welsh conurbations produce schools with records of high achievement and high proportions of pupils proceeding to post-school education. But there are also areas of great poverty in cities and towns, and, however qualified, the link between economic resource (as measured for example by free school meals) and educational achievement remains significant. It is not a watertight correlation. The relative poverty of parts of rural Wales by no means coincides exactly with underachievement – just the opposite. Nevertheless, the coexistence in individual authorities of schools with widely disparate examination results is a constant reminder of the continuing limitations of school-effectiveness research in providing practical solutions.

As a result of the iron determination of the Prime Minister, Mrs Thatcher, to bring the coal miners to heel, the deep-mining industry in Wales virtually disappeared in the 1980s. The steel industry, especially the flagship works at Port Talbot and Llanwern, seemed vulnerable to world trends and lost staff steadily, but it was only in 2001 that closure in Ebbw Vale and the cessation of manufacturing in Llanwern signalled the end of steel-making as a focal point of the Welsh economy. There has been compensating growth in, for example, engineering of components for car and aircraft industries, light industry on proliferating industrial estates and the ubiquitous tourism, now more significant for the rural Welsh economy than farming. Nevertheless, the south Wales Valleys, whose population depended on heavy industry, have been deprived of an economic rationale, and face unemployment and social deprivation in isolated housing estates. The education sector, like the provision of health services, faces enormous difficulties as a result. It is not only adequate provision of schools and colleges which is essential but the motivation and the parental and social support which encourage achievement in these environments. In some of these areas, and some parts of the conurbations, there are particular problems of underachievement, especially among boys, higher rates of absenteeism, low take-up of post-compulsory education, and illiteracy among adults. Just as the condition of housing in these areas is poor, measured by the amenities taken for granted in modern properties, so is the condition of school buildings which, after years of neglect across Wales, requires massive investment to provide the right kind of positive environment. This problem is only now being addressed by the Welsh Assembly with an investment of £300 million over three years.

The economic and social changes of the 1980s were driven by a London-based government motivated by doctrine rather than pragmatism, and little inclined to countenance Welsh priorities or demands. Although the revolution which began in the 1980s had not been unheralded, it was given a particular twist by the Prime Minister's own strongly held beliefs. Despite the creeping devolution of the 1970s in education, the people of Wales were in the weakest of positions to withstand any aspect of policy with which they might disagree. We have seen that James Callaghan, in his 1976 Ruskin College speech, had laid out an agenda for action. Crucial to it was a reassertion of central control over education and training, in response to perceived economic and personal needs, at the expense of local authorities and teachers. Grafted on to this by Tory governments of the 1980s was a belief in the supremacy of the market. One of the fascinating features of educational history in this period is the attempted reconciliation of consequent innate contradictions.

It is in this context that we must assess the lasting impact of this realigned politics of education on the situation in Wales. We have seen that once the battles between some Welsh local authorities and the Ministry of Education had been resolved largely in the latter's favour by the end of the 1950s, there was a period of relative consensus in education, with the pattern authorized by central government and gladly endorsed by local authorities and teachers. With the acceleration of comprehensivization and progressive teaching methods in primary schools in the 1960s, officially bolstered, as we have seen, by Plowden and Gittins in both England and Wales, simmering right-wing discontent with 'liberal' education policies surfaced.

The economic context made it inevitable that there would be reappraisal across the political spectrum. The last monument to affluence and expansion in the system came with the publication of a White Paper, *Education: A Framework for Expansion*, which heralded an era of contraction. Even before the publication of the White Paper, the Heath government had clamped down on public expenditure but, in 1973, following the oil crisis, Chancellor of the Exchequer Anthony Barber imposed draconian cuts. With the emollient of educational expansion having disappeared, and the notion of value for money now being inscribed on the hearts of both parties, right-wing disillusionment seemed to be a natural concomitant of economic disillusionment, fortified by the social disillusionment which came to a head in the winter of discontent in 1978/9.

Against this background, the publicity given to the William Tyndale scandal of 1975, complemented by television fly-on-the-wall images of a comprehensive-school shambles in Faraday School, etched itself into the chattering classes' consciousness. The literature of right-wing reaction, sometimes highly incisive and intelligent, sometimes scurrilous and occasionally downright daft, in a series of Black Papers starting only a year after the student sit-ins in the universities in 1968, added an element of intellectual weight and responsibility (liberally mixed with prejudice) to media frenzy.

Although, of course, Wales was an integral part of the suffering economy, the rest was so much froth as far as her practice of education was concerned. We have noted that none of the contributors to the Black Papers was from Wales. If HMI criticized Welsh primary schools for anything it was their conservatism in implementing progressive teaching methods such as integrated days or project work or new approaches to reading. The inspectorate's summary of 1984 is unequivocal:

> in most primary schools considerable prominence is given to certain aspects of language and mathematics and much less prominence to most other areas of the curriculum . . . within individual classes the general

pattern of organisation is for the mornings to be devoted to language and mathematics and for the afternoons to be devoted to the remaining curriculum areas.

It is a pattern which teachers in the 1950s would have recognized and it is certainly a template for what is happening in 2002. The fact that literacy and numeracy hours are not statutory in Wales as in England need not be a matter of concern for Welsh parents – and never need have been.

Nor was Wales involved in the creation of influential think-tanks in the 1970s, such as the Centre for Policy Studies created by Keith Joseph and Margaret Thatcher in 1974, which were to prove so influential in the 1980s. Nevertheless, because Wales was tied to educational legislation for 'England and Wales' these developments were of profound significance. Whatever answers the Tories came up with in government would affect Wales as radically as England. We have seen that the major issues of accountability, value for money, links with industry, problems with the curriculum, standards of learning and teaching, and illiteracy were spelled out by James Callaghan in 1976, reflecting an element of consensus within the two major parties. Nevertheless, the answers to the questions raised in his Ruskin College speech were dealt with very differently by his government and that of Margaret Thatcher after 1979. The influence of right-wing think-tanks was ominous.

It took some years before the Tories could mould the practicalities of educational reform to the often mutually contradictory theories which underpinned their approach. The neo-Liberals, as they have been called, believed in leaving everything to market forces, a modern version of some nineteenth-century theories of government. On the other hand, the neo-Conservatives believed that the government, certainly a Conservative government, knew best and must assume control. In the midst of this ideological contradiction, much of the 1980s, particularly under Sir Keith Joseph, were taken up with dithering. Again, Welsh educational priorities received no attention and there was minimal involvement in the battle of wills. However, if government were to endorse the centralist approach then the significance of devolutionary measures, particularly since 1964, would be of great consequence when the practicalities had to be worked out.

It is therefore hardly surprising that, in the immediate aftermath of the 1979 election, change was slow. Labour's directive to local authorities to convert to a comprehensive system was withdrawn, but this was of little relevance to Wales which, by 1980, was in essence a country of comprehensive secondary schools. The Welsh local authorities resented transfer of some of their functions to school governing bodies, but the assisted-places scheme, although opposed, affected Wales only marginally.

More worrying for pupils in Wales were substantial cuts in services. Free school milk had long been axed and LEAs were not even required any longer to provide transport to school, although all those in Wales continued to do so. Cuts in capital expenditure accentuated that decline in the fabric of buildings which continues to plague the system to this day.

In 1981 the Department of Education and Science was handed over to Sir Keith Joseph. Wales shared in the immediate macro-political decision by the Manpower Services Commission to introduce the Technical and Vocational Education Initiative which at least brought some much-needed money to schools, although many sections of the teaching profession, particularly on the arts side, were apprehensive about encroachment on their teaching time. Here was yet another attempt to bolster the status of these aspects of the curriculum, rather more successfully than usual. One of Joseph's stranger decisions, of some benefit to Wales, was the amalgamation in 1985 of the General Certificate of Education and the Certificate of Secondary Education in a common sixteen-plus qualification, the General Certificate of Secondary Education (GCSE). It is true that some writers have seen this, too, as part of a sinister centralization, an attempt at increased social engineering, but it did cause consternation in Tory ranks which, from then on, only had Advanced Level to endorse as the examination gold standard. They objected to the scaling-down of 'one-off' written examinations and a far greater element of assignment work. Constant carping by the press and in Parliament ensued. However, a major survey of 1989/90, the most comprehensive of its kind in England or Wales, which assessed the impact of GCSE in Wales, revealed that, at least in history, geography and Welsh, teachers and pupils endorsed the new system enthusiastically. Wales also still maintained its pioneering Certificate of Education.

Keith Joseph, soulmate of the Prime Minister, wanted far more radical measures than this. He was an advocate of the voucher system which, given the nature of educational provision, was the ultimate talisman of privatization. His department dissuaded him, but the idea did not die. A Labour government of 1997 immediately rescinded a system which, by that time, the Tories had put in place in primary schools. Higher education was set on a yet more radical course in the 1980s. The Prime Minister and many in her think-tanks believed that trainers of teachers in the 1960s and 1970s were the inaugurators of the ills of progressivism which, in their view, undermined the education system. The process of controlling the curriculum of teacher-training courses, subjecting them to detailed inspection and allowing schools a far greater say in the training process had begun. So too had attempts to bring the universities to heel, by subjecting them to a far greater degree of state regulation, particularly financially, and destroying the right of academics to tenure.

It was, therefore, a process of state intervention rather than market-based initiatives which were setting this government's tone. When the Schools Council had been established in 1964 it had appointed a Schools Council Committee for Wales which produced some fascinating documents but, nevertheless, reflected its parent body's limited powers. Far too teacher-centred for Joseph, it was killed off in 1982. Along with its demolition came the destruction of the Advisory Councils for both England and Wales, and the Advisory Council on the Supply and Training of Teachers.

By 1987, the government had taken on the teaching profession. In the short term, teacher strike action against the government's proposals on pay and conditions had a deleterious effect on extra-curricular activities and, particularly, school sport. While teachers were pilloried in the media, this signalled an onslaught on their independence as it related to the curriculum and their formal hours of work. This process has continued inexorably, since 1997 under a Labour government. With advisory bodies and local authorities emasculated (less painfully in Wales than England), threshold agreements and performance-related pay coming on stream from 2001 in Wales constitute another stage in this process. It is significant that the infant National Assembly for Wales opposed the latest approach to pay agreements, but the limits of its power were starkly delineated when the Department for Education refused to allow any Welsh divergence.

The 1980s, then, saw a sea change in the administration of education in Wales, prompted by political priorities in England. In the early part of the decade there was much agonizing that policies for schools lacked direction, but what followed were crucial changes at the micro-level as political dogma changed the direction of school government. Ever since 1944 managers of primary schools and governors of secondary schools had tended to be decorative rather than influential, wheeled out at speech days to rubber-stamp policies of head teachers or the local authority. They did so willingly because the vast majority were appointed by the local authority. The 1980s Conservative government gave radically new direction to ideas which had long been in circulation – in 1967 the Plowden Report had called for a thorough review of primary-school management. The pace quickened in the 1970s, forming part of the increasing bureaucratization of the education system on which a management culture has now been superimposed. There were calls for increasing participation by parents, and in 1977 the Taylor Report, revealing the paucity of parental representation and the extent of head-teacher authority, made change inevitable. The report recommended that each school should have its own governing body composed of representatives of the local authority, the staff of the school, parents and the local community, and should also have a greater say in deciding on school aims and monitoring progress towards achieving them. At this stage, only a minority report looked forward to greater financial control by governing bodies.

The legislation which emanated from the report in 1980 was half-hearted, leaving governing bodies under the control of local education authorities and only making recommendations as to their make-up. As with all aspects of policy, the government implemented increasingly radical policies in due course. An Education Act of 1986 required local education authorities to devise instruments of government for schools that included balanced representation of their own nominees and parents. More significant, the Act made clear that the responsibility for the direction of the school lay with the governors, who were required to provide policy documents relating to the curriculum. Here, then, was the radical transformation that has left its lasting legacy on the way in which schools are now run in Wales as in England. This Act saw the origin of the annual parents' meeting and the involvement of governors in the appointment of senior staff, together with a power of suspension over existing staff. Only at the start of the new millennium were questions being raised both by governors and by government about the wisdom of loading volunteers and generalists with such a plethora of powers, including issues of law.

Government initiatives in 1987 and the Education Reform Act of 1988 superimposed on these extended powers the notion of local management of schools. Governors now had the responsibility of ensuring that the new National Curriculum was being taught and, for the first time, took over full responsibility for determining schools' spending within the sum allocated by the local authority. That in essence, although there has been some further delegation, is the situation today. For the first time, parental power had been institutionalized. Even more significant, that target of Thatcher wrath, the local education authorities, had been stripped of the central role which had been theirs since their inception in 1902. The thrust of the 1988 Act was to undermine local education authorities even further by allowing governors of secondary schools and large primary schools to apply for grant-maintained status, so creating a sector entirely independent of the local authorities. The policy was even less acceptable in Wales than it was in England, although there were acrimonious debates in some governing bodies which translated into confrontation with the local authority. Only twelve of the 228 secondary schools in Wales were grant-maintained when legislation under the new Labour government of 1997 did away with the concept. The local-authority hold on school education in Wales had not been undermined by this potentially revolutionary policy.

The pace of change was frenetic under Kenneth Baker, who replaced Sir Keith Joseph in 1986. Some of this change was irrelevant, such as the 1986 proposal to set up City Technology Colleges, none of which has been opened in Wales. But two other strands of government thinking were dovetailed and had a profound impact on Welsh education. As we have seen, schools in Wales, as in England, were put in charge of their own financial affairs in 1987, and this was consolidated in the 1988 Education Act. The other central component of the 1988 Education Reform Act was provision for a National Curriculum and, in this instance, the inexorable centralization of control was crucial because Wales had to be allowed an input, however tiresome to the DES this might be.

The 1988 Act, then, combined local management of schools with a centralized curriculum. Central government had devolved local control while at the same time dramatically extending its own grip on the curriculum and overall structure of the system. It had introduced the concept of grant-maintained schools whose funding bypassed the local authorities altogether, though they did not catch on in Wales. Nevertheless, in the philosophy of the educational market encapsulated in the 1988 Education Reform Act, Welsh school education was turned upside down. In Lowe's telling phrase, 'social democracy had given way to social Darwinism'. Schools now had to compete with each other for pupils and therefore for money. They had to produce glossy brochures to attract students. The philosophy of cooperation and social justice which had often, though of course not invariably, characterized the approach of local education authorities was now irretrievably undermined. Since this philosophy, after long years of social deprivation, and numerous manifestations of the egalitarian principle, was considerably more entrenched in Wales than in England the revolution was the greater.

This was not only a historical, even philosophical, divide over the implementation of a 'free-market' system in education, with its inbuilt illogic. In practical terms, over much of Wales parents had no choice either of primary or secondary school. Indeed, such is the extent of small primary schools in Wales that the far more politically significant issue is keeping open local schools for the linguistic and community cohesion of the areas they serve. In rural Wales, the size of primary schools dictates that the prevailing philosophy ought to be cooperation over, for example, school governance and in-service training, not competition based on key-stage results. Getting their offspring to the nearest secondary school in Wales is sufficient of a logistical problem for many Welsh parents without any consideration of getting to one even further away, however outstanding its results might be.

Centralization of curricular control in government hands had much more significant effects. There existed a sufficient political and bureaucratic infrastructure for Wales to insist on an element of separate consideration. The school curriculum was something of a poisoned chalice for the Tories. Prime Minister Thatcher, along with many from the radical wing of her party and think-tanks, wanted to solve the problem of low-achieving schools by subjecting them to market forces. This would require an objective benchmark of performance, an idea which meshed perfectly with her notion that education should revert to the three Rs. The foundation stone was laid by the Task Group for Assessment and Testing (TGAT) which, in 1987, produced a complex, sophisticated combination of teacher and external assessment nationally – which in this instance meant England and Wales, since there were no effective demands for a distinctively Welsh system of testing. Mrs Thatcher had envisaged a far simpler, indeed simplistic, assessment, probably similar to the eleven-plus tests. However, for the moment, the TGAT held sway. She had also envisaged that only core subjects would form part of this assessment and of any statutory curriculum, since the rest could be left to market forces to determine. If this had been implemented, there would have been no National Curriculum distinctive to Wales other than in Welsh-language or bilingual schools. However, Kenneth Baker had different ideas, and the ten- or eleven-subject National Curriculum was born. Once the foundation subjects were included in the scheme some kind of separate treatment for Wales was inevitable. The realities of the situation were underpinned institutionally. The 1988 Education Act had created a Curriculum Council for Wales, but there was no separate assessment body. Wales was subject to the School Examinations and Assessment Council. It was not until 1994 that a Welsh quango assumed responsibility for assessment.

Instituting a National Curriculum of this kind was the oddest of initiatives from a Conservative government. In the first place, it was the ultimate comprehensive measure, prescribing for pupils of all ages from five to sixteen in all state schools – the private sector was exempt – what should be taught, and it was the same for everybody from Northumberland to Cornwall, though not quite the same across Offa's Dyke. Second, it was the first time ever that the state had endorsed the notion of an entitlement curriculum, that all pupils across the ability range wherever they were should be entitled to be taught a specific range of subjects to predetermined levels. In the context of all that had gone before in the history of state education, but particularly since the Second World War, this was a dramatic change. Strangely, it was an unsung revolution because attention centred on the issue of state control, and the internal conflict in the Conservative Party as to the nature of that control. Teacher attention, of course, was diverted to the implications for their own professional autonomy.

While politicians in Westminster were anxious to ride the wave of radicalism and leave their indelible imprint on the education system, devolution meant that there were ambitious Secretaries of State in Wales wanting to follow suit. Of course, Welsh politics remained the art of the possible. Any notion of diverting the London government from its market principles for the sake of Wales was pie-in-the-sky. On the other hand, involvement in the detail of the curriculum was a possibility, and an alliance of a sympathetic Minister of State, Wyn Roberts, with a talented inspectorate working along with gifted civil-service allies in the Welsh Office, was a powerful combination. The DES published *The National Curriculum 5–16* in July 1987; almost immediately the Welsh Office produced a version for Wales, a process which caused some fluttering in the DES dovecot. Educational professionals in Wales were deeply involved in the curriculum-construction process. The administrative channel for this existed in the Welsh version of the National Curriculum Council (NCC), the Curriculum Council for Wales (CCW), a body which, at this crucial time, had a profoundly significant influence on both the National Curriculum and, a little later, the implementation of the Curriculum Cymreig.

The National Curriculum gave rise to some substantially different subject orders in Wales, for example in history and geography, and in effect to a distinctively Welsh National Curriculum. This was not planned. With the obvious exception of the Welsh-language curriculum the pattern was that the working groups selected to devise a curriculum for individual subjects should each contain one member from Wales who, presumably, would safeguard any Welsh interest. In the case of history, this strategy was modified, partly at least because of the influence of the Association of History Teachers in Wales, whose case for a separate working group meshed with the wishes of HMI and civil servants in the Welsh Office. Things worked out less well in the Working Group for English, where no Anglo-Welsh literature found its way into the proposed syllabus. This group's report turned out to be merely the prehistory of the battle for the curriculum in English. Right-wing opinion was strongly opposed to any watering down of standard English, encouragement of creativity at the expense of accuracy and the freedom of approach allowed by the absence of set texts. Opponents of such ideas had sufficient political clout to bring about a review of the curriculum in English by the National Curriculum Council in 1992. The Council required more emphasis on standard English and set texts reflecting the pinnacles of the English literary heritage. The Curriculum Council for Wales demurred but was forced to conduct a review. Nevertheless, it demonstrated its maturity by sticking closely to the original working-party proposals, eschewing set texts and endorsing a less rigid approach to standard English. A further small but significant indication of independence came in 1993 when the government required the NCC to review standards of religious education. The Welsh Office did not require the CCW to participate.

The National Curriculum in Wales was inevitably structured along the same lines as that in England. It was divided into core and foundation subjects. In Welsh-speaking schools Welsh is a core subject; in all other schools in Wales it is a foundation subject but is compulsory to the age of sixteen. All other subjects, other than religious education which is treated separately, are foundation subjects. This has since been augmented by a statutory Curriculum Cymreig. These elements combine with the education responsibilities of the National Assembly to make it possible now to speak of a Welsh educational system. But distinctiveness in an education structure is no virtue of itself; it is worth fighting for only if it enriches the educational experience of pupils. Even in our materialist era there is still a widespread belief that the object of education is to cultivate knowledge of, and pass on an understanding of, a people's culture. There is no question that, in terms of language, music, history, literature, even sport there is much which is distinctive about the Welsh past, so inherently valuable that it would be an abnegation of what is worthwhile about education were it not to constitute part of schools' programmes.

The creation of a statutory curriculum unique to Wales is an educational achievement to compare with the political achievement of devolution. It could not have come about were it not for the centralizing tendencies of the Department of Education and Science in the 1980s. But that merely provided an opportunity which might easily have been let slip. It was certainly not in the interests of the DES to allow a separate route for Wales – just the opposite – and after 1979 there was certainly no political imperative to do so.

Once the National Curriculum had taken shape the proactive stance and enlightened leadership of the Curriculum Council for Wales were crucial. There were two strands to its policy. First, individual subject orders in music and art were modified for the Welsh situation. Second, the Curriculum Council for Wales established a working group to advise on how the curriculum might be given a distinctively Welsh aspect. The product in 1993 was CCW Working Paper 18, *Developing a Curriculum Cymreig*, which provided suggestions as to how the curriculum, indeed the whole ethos of schools, might reflect the distinctive language, culture and heritage of Wales. The basis of the document is that all pupils in Wales are entitled to develop a sense of place, heritage, belonging, knowledge of the contribution which the Welsh language and literature have made, and an understanding of the importance of creative arts and religious beliefs and practices in Welsh life. It argues that the Welshness of the curriculum should permeate the school by means of National Curriculum subjects, cross-curricular themes and a Welsh ethos.

There was a sympathetic reception among school staff when the report was launched in 1993, and the Curriculum Cymreig became statutory. That position has been endorsed in the revised curriculum from 2000. There is no necessity for it to be obtrusive, and it can be adapted to meet the needs of schools from Anglesey to Monmouthshire, but it is an element in any statutory external assessment of a school's performance and it should form part of any internal survey.

Modifications of the National Curriculum resulting from the Dearing Report of 1993, complemented by an equivalent Curriculum Council for Wales investigation, and the revamped National Curriculum of 2000, have institutionalized the separateness of the curriculum in Wales. What, in 1988, seemed unthinkable now appears entrenched and even traditional. At the same time, the modifications set in train in 1993 did water down the full-blown National Curriculum in ways which were not to Welsh advantage. The general response of teachers in Wales, certainly those in primary schools, had been broadly sympathetic to a national curriculum, with its emphasis on structure and planned progression. However, in response to teachers' accusations of overload and mechanistic assessment schedules, and a cottage industry in tick boxes, it was inevitable that Kenneth Baker's plan for national statutory assessment in foundation as well as core subjects would be modified. As a result of the Dearing proposals, effective from 1995, and subjected to further modification in 2000, the National Curriculum now essentially ends at age fourteen, with only core subjects and Welsh to be mandatory from fourteen to sixteen. Statutory testing of non-core subjects was also jettisoned and the scope of non-foundation subjects curtailed.

Although the scaffolding of a National Curriculum along Baker lines remains, its essential structure is now, inadvertently, a Thatcherian core of subjects to be nationally tested. Along with the increasing emphasis on literacy and numeracy, stressed by successive governments in a 1990s consensus, and culminating in England, though not in Wales, with literacy and numeracy teaching structures at key stages 1 and 2, a traditional curriculum pattern has emerged, particularly in primary schools. The emphasis on English, or Welsh, and number work has been reasserted with a vengeance, with foundation-subject work relegated to its traditional afternoon slots. In that the Welshness of the curriculum resides substantially in the foundation subjects this undermines the Curriculum Cymreig to some extent.

The notion of Welshness being reflected in school curricula will, however, be extended if the pilot Welsh Baccalaureate proves successful and is extended. Both the original ill-fated Institute of Welsh Affairs-sponsored scheme and the pilot being undertaken by the Welsh Joint Education Committee involve a compulsory element of Welsh studies within the structure.

In 1994 the Curriculum Council for Wales was replaced by the Curriculum and Assessment Authority for Wales (ACAC, later ACCAC). Its significance lay in the fact that it was now responsible for assessment as well as curriculum matters. This body, too, pursued an independent line in pre-Assembly days so that, for example, individual primary-school results are not published in Wales as they are in England. However, in terms of assessment, it could do little about the situation which it inherited. School success is substantially judged by children's performance in national tests in the core subjects. Foundation subjects are assessed only internally. The rigorous, if over-prescriptive, statements of attainment within the various attainment targets, which provided detailed ladders of progression, were replaced in 1996 by general 'best-fit' level descriptors incorporating as best they could all the elements of the original attainment targets. They are less valid.

It is often taken as axiomatic that the post-war education consensus between the political parties, neatly christened 'Butskellism' after the two moderate wings of the Conservative and Labour Parties, was rudely disrupted by the advent of the Conservative government in 1979. In fact, practicalities of policy in education since James Callaghan's Ruskin College speech of 1976 have converged. However different the emphases, similarities in such fundamentals as assessment and curriculum in schools, or the refinement of accountability in higher education, even the emphasis on private initiatives, have characterized Labour Party as well as Conservative Party policy.

Nevertheless, the election of a Labour government in 1997 did herald some changes which were significant for emphasizing the special position of Wales in the period before the establishment of the National Assembly. For example, the Welsh Office minister responsible for education, Peter Hain, immediately announced the death of the voucher system in Wales, a scheme representing the ultimate in market forces at work in primary schools and anathema to public opinion in Wales. On the other hand, the proposed feasibility study of a distinctive new Welsh 16–19 qualification, the Welsh baccalaureate, was shelved and had to wait on the greater degree of independence exercised by the Assembly.

Similar Janus-like tendencies emerged over the reforming White Papers, the Welsh version of which was entitled *Building Excellent Schools Together*. It is significant that there was a Welsh version; it is also notable that the White Papers resulted in the School Standards and Framework Act of 1998, common to both England and Wales, even if it specified different targets for literacy and numeracy to be achieved by children in Wales by 2002. Even before the advent of the Assembly, the notion of education action zones found no favour, providing a platform for the Assembly to reject the notion of specialist schools, due to proliferate now under a second Labour administration. More central, because of its implications for pedagogy across Wales, the Welsh Office was not prepared to accept literacy and numeracy strategies which laid down minimum times and a blueprint for teaching. Not surprisingly, the general thrust of practice in England in these areas has penetrated to Wales. Nevertheless, ACCAC has relied on independent investigation to determine the most effective literacy policies specifically for Wales.

If the overall structure of the present education system remains similar in Wales and England, reflecting a common legislative core since the advent of state education, there is increasing divergence. To get some sense of the scale of this system in Wales, and its centrality in both input and output to the economy, it is necessary to review the statistics. In 2001, in the maintained sector, there were 41 nursery schools, with 92 full-time equivalent teachers; 1,631 primary schools, with 12,756 teachers; 229 secondary schools with a total of 12,692 teachers, and 45 special schools with 555 teachers. All maintained schools are now subsumed under new labels – community, foundation voluntary-aided and voluntary-controlled schools. There were 779 nursery pupils, 262,751 primary school pupils, 210,396 secondary pupils and 3,727 pupils in special schools (all full-time). In addition there were nearly 25,000 part-time pupils distributed across the age range. Fifty-four independent schools accommodated 9,257 full-time pupils being taught by 972 full-time equivalent teachers. The total number of teachers in all schools had risen by the end of 2001 to 28,700. While there is no overall teacher shortage in Wales there are pronounced shortfalls in some subject areas.

This represents a broad similarity of school provision in Wales compared with England. As a result of the Welsh Intermediate Education Act of 1889 most of the endowed schools in Wales were brought within the purview of the county schemes, so that both the private sector and schools of Roman Catholic and Anglican provision account for only a small proportion of pupils – about 8 per cent in the voluntary-aided secondary sector and only some 2 per cent in private schools (compared with 8 per cent in England). Indeed, of the old endowed schools only Christ College in Brecon, Llandovery College, the Howell's Schools in Denbigh and Llandaff, Ruthin School and the Monmouth Schools for boys and girls survive in the independent sector.

The traditional foundations continue to be of high status, with boarding facilities, and purpose-built buildings, adopting a similar approach to the well-known English public schools. The rest of the private sector in Wales has been characterized by Gorard as privately owned, profit-making, held in converted accommodation, co-educational, urban and catering for fewer, often many fewer, than a hundred pupils in each unit. The curriculum on offer is likely to be restricted, particularly on the sporting and practical sides, reflected in the cheapness of the fees.

Of the estimated 112,300 persons aged sixteen to eighteen in 1999, 57 per cent were continuing their education, either full-time in school (25,959), in higher education (10,388) or in further education (27,782).

There were twenty-nine further-education institutions, with 42,367 full-time and sandwich students and 161,777 students originally enrolled on part-time courses, with 19,457 signed up for 'Welsh for adults' courses at further- and higher-education institutions.

In the same year there were thirteen higher-education establishments, of which eight, including the University of Wales College of Medicine, were constituent institutions of the University of Wales, the largest federal university in the United Kingdom after the University of London. In 1999–2000, 62,131 full-time and 30,067 part-time students enrolled for courses (a small number of these taking higher-education courses in further-education colleges), over 50 per cent of full-time students in higher education coming from outside Wales. The University of Glamorgan is independent of the University of Wales, while the Open University in Wales is part of the Open University in the United Kingdom. Nearly a quarter of the 19–24 age group in Wales proceeded to higher education, a figure which has since risen. Some 23,000 jobs in the Welsh economy are provided by the higher-education sector alone and, in 2000/1, total income was £641 million, 45 per cent of which came from the Higher Education Funding Council for Wales. Per-capita student funding has just climbed above that in England, though it remains well below the Scottish figure.

Gross current expenditure on education by local authorities has grown steadily and makes a massive contribution to the Welsh economy. In 1996/7 it was £1,372,589,000. This had grown by 2000/1 to £1.49 billion, now deriving from the National Assembly and from the local-authority rate. The bulk of it goes to schools according to formulae devised by individual authorities, though the resulting discrepancies cause protests among teachers, their unions and governors. Local authorities employ advisers who liaise closely with schools. The inspection function is controlled by Her Majesty's Inspectors who corporately comprise 'Estyn', and cyclical school inspections are undertaken, after individual tender, by private independent inspection teams under a registered inspector.

Wales is a country with two main languages. In 2001, 27 per cent of maintained primary schools had classes where Welsh was the sole or main medium of instruction. In primary schools 49.9 per cent of primary school pupils spoke some Welsh, 15.1 per cent fluently. There were 440 Welsh-speaking primary schools and fifty-two Welsh-speaking secondary schools – in general terms a Welsh-speaking secondary school being one in which more than half the subjects are taught through the medium of Welsh. Of maintained secondary schools, 22.3 per cent taught Welsh both as a first and second language, 9.2 per cent as a first language only. In terms of pupil numbers, 14 per cent of pupils were taught Welsh as a first language, 84.5 per cent as a second language (Welsh is compulsory for all pupils to age sixteen).

The success of the Welsh-language schools, from pre-school playgroups, through the increasing number of pupils using Welsh as their first language in primary schools, to the increased number of Welsh-language and bilingual secondary schools, has been a feature of recent decades. The movement was slowest in the secondary sector. Nevertheless growth has been steady after the highly significant establishment of Ysgol Glan Clwyd, Flintshire, in 1956 as the first designated bilingual school. Early in the 1960s, four more such schools, including Rhydfelen and Strade, had been set up; by 1990 there were twenty-two across Wales. These schools, together with the naturally bilingual secondary schools, totalled fifty-two in 2000, eight more than a decade before. Eighteen per cent of secondary-school pupils attend these schools. So the growth has accelerated after quiet beginnings.

Formal education must always be part of far wider linguistic influences. Particularly, non-state education through Urdd Gobaith Cymru, the Welsh League of Youth, has been crucial since the movement was established in 1922 by Sir Ifan ab Owen Edwards. Its youth camps at Llangrannog and Glanllyn have been particularly influential in providing a more informal atmosphere in which Welsh can be the language of communication, while the Urdd eisteddfod, with its infrastructure of county competition, provides a televised showpiece every year for a vibrant and talented youth culture.

Also particularly influential outside the state sector has been the pre-school Mudiad Ysgolion Meithrin (Welsh-medium nursery schools movement), established in 1971, a voluntary movement, though subsidized by the Welsh Office from 1973. By 1984 there were 420 neighbourhood groups, with a further 160 'mother-and-child' groups. By consolidating Welsh among pre-school-age pupils these groups provide an invaluable base for Welsh-medium primary education.

This revolution in the place of the Welsh language in compulsory education has been achieved with relatively little controversy. In Anglicized areas some parents and pupils at key stage 4 express reservations on utilitarian grounds. However, the most significant controversy arose in reaction to the language policies of the two western counties as they were before 1996 – Gwynedd and Dyfed. The latter's policy of dividing schools into categories, the Welsh category involving the whole work of the school being conducted in Welsh, caused protests among some English-speaking parents. Generally, however, parents now seem to be convinced by the arguments advanced by experts like Colin Baker that learning the Welsh language has such beneficial effects as closer integration into Welsh-speaking communities, wider opportunities for assimilating another culture and its literature, stimulating cognitive development in all areas, assisting in the learning of other foreign languages and making pupils aware of their local and national identity. Almost certainly the most significant factor is that job opportunities which require knowledge of the Welsh language have increased.

This revolution in attitude towards the teaching of Welsh in schools has come not a moment too soon for those who have the interests of the language at heart. According to the 1991 census fewer than 20 per cent of the Welsh population now speak Welsh and the areas of Wales in which Welsh is the community language shrink by the decade. In this context the census figures in 1991 indicating that Welsh-speaking was increasing in the school-age population assume the greatest significance. Nevertheless, school Welsh on its own is anything but an instant – or even long-term – palliative. It is true that there is now virtually blanket teaching of Welsh in maintained schools, though its extent and effect are variable. More significant is the steadily declining proportion of pupils pursuing their education through the medium of Welsh as they proceed through the system. While 20 per cent of pupils receive a Welsh-language education in the primary schools, 12 per cent use it as a first language in secondary schools. Only 6 per cent of all A Level papers were taken in Welsh in 2000. Teaching in the Welsh language in further and higher education is very restricted – 2 per cent in 2000 – a matter of concern not only to the Assembly government.

In essence, the limitations of education's effectiveness in social engineering are all too evident in the example of the preservation of the Welsh language. It is now accepted internationally that bilingual education is central to the health and continuance of minority languages and is effective in countering extraneous influences. However, the pervasiveness of such a powerful international language as English just cannot be ignored. Allied to the scale of in-migration to Welsh-speaking communities, its permeation cannot be counteracted only by formal-education policies even if, in this period, there have been dramatic changes in the social position of the Welsh language which have had a crucial impact on informal education. Radio Cymru has broadcast since 1979 and, more significant, S4C, the Welsh-language TV channel, has transmitted about thirty-five hours a week of Welsh-language programmes since 1983. Publishing in the Welsh language has increased substantially, with about 400 book titles a year appearing in the early 1990s. Bilingual road signs and communications from, for example, the DVLC, indicate a much-changed status for the language. Expert research into first- and second-language learning all indicates that formal schooling must interact with the outside world, especially in the cultivation of those social networks in which the language may be used naturally, if it is to fulfil the high hopes which some Welsh opinion places in it.

It has to be accepted, then, that formal education, of itself, can only be of limited influence in moulding society, whether in language, religion, or even economics. There are far more fundamental forces at work and, arguably, the history of education demonstrates that it is these which determine education systems, rather than education which changes society. This principle is again borne out when we look at attitudes towards the way in which boys and girls, men and women have been educated in the state system. Provision of formal state education in Wales has been far more egalitarian between the sexes than in England. The board schools educated boys and girls alike, though with some differences of curriculum. Secondary education, through the Welsh intermediate schools, provided for the education of boys and girls, sometimes in separate school buildings, and always with devices for keeping them apart socially, but secondary co-education was common in Wales, far more so than in England, so that the transition in the 1970s to co-educational comprehensive schools was less significant in gender terms. Although there was differentiation in the curriculum in such subjects as woodwork, needlework and cookery, the core academic subjects, especially those which provided the all-important matriculation qualification, were open equally to both sexes. Social attitudes certainly decreed that in times of poverty it had been boys who took precedence in scholarship take-up or university place, but this was a reflection of wider social attitudes rather than prejudices in the education system.

Nevertheless, career profiles within both the elementary and secondary sector discriminated against women. Until after the Second World War women teachers had to relinquish their posts on marriage, as did women civil servants, and their opportunities for promotion were restricted compared with those of their male colleagues. For many decades, salary differentials favoured men. Far more stark was the wider difference in career destination. During the first half of the twentieth century, in particular, professional work for women products of the secondary system tended to be in teaching and in nursing, with high proportions of women not taking up paid employment at all. More generally, the greatest proportion of girls leaving the elementary schools were destined for employment in household service.

The impact of both world wars was of significance for women in that they were drafted into employment previously reserved for men, though historians disagree about the long-term impact. After both wars, domestic and family stereotypes reasserted themselves, with the media constantly reinforcing the crucial domestic role of wife and mother but, from the 1960s especially, the employment of women increased dramatically until, by the late 1980s, they comprised nearly half the working population. Perhaps the most significant feature, however, was that nearly as many women were in part-time jobs as in full-time. Certainly since the Second World War in Wales there has been substantial equality of opportunity within the school system, and increasingly in the further- and higher-education system, for both sexes. This has not been reflected in post-school equality of opportunities of employment, promotion or pay. Nor has it dramatically transformed the patterns of employment for women which characterized the twentieth century – the most popular job for women being clerical, with strong representation in the teaching and caring professions. In terms of part-time work most women are employed in personal service industries.

The Welsh grammar schools remained conservative in differentiating between subjects appropriate for boys and girls. The coming of comprehensive education, while enhancing the co-educational structure of Welsh schooling, continued to make some subjects, such as catering, exclusive to girls. Despite the education system and despite a raft of legislation and government initiatives such as the Department of Education and Science 1980 report, *Girls and Science*, gender stereotyping continued in school and more obviously in employment. It continues into the present, ironically overlaid in recent years by agitation over the higher achievement of girls compared with boys in the school system.

In the last two decades the participation of women in further and higher education has increased significantly. Nevertheless, universities in Wales, like other universities, still have almost wholly male-dominated departments of engineering, with women orientated far more towards the arts and biological sciences, while women professors remain a rarity. Differentiation is even more marked among school staffs. While secondary-teacher training courses in most subjects contain a substantial representation of both men and women, those in primary education contain few men.

In 1999 there was a revolution in the government of Wales with the creation of the National Assembly for Wales, even if it has no powers of primary legislation. Its impact on education, particularly schooling, has been crucial. Originally, education was the responsibility of two Assembly ministers and two corresponding education committees, with a divide at age sixteen. The present situation (2002) is that there is one Minister for Education and Lifelong Learning who is a member of the National Assembly Cabinet. The Assembly also has a committee system of which that for education and lifelong learning is one of the most important committees. This committee carries out crucial reviews, for example on the organization of higher education and the supply of school places.

From April 2001 there was substantial change in the administration of further and higher education and training in Wales. The Higher Education Funding Council for Wales remains responsible for the disbursement of funds to that sector. The National Council for Education and Training for Wales, with community consortia, will take over the functions, including funding, of Training and Enterprise Councils, the Further Education

Funding Council for Wales, funding of adult continuing education and, from April 2002, the funding of school sixth-forms. This body has a budget of over £360 million per annum and works in tandem with the Higher Education Funding Council for Wales. The two bodies together are known as Education and Learning Wales (Elwa).

The National Assembly interacts with the twenty-two unitary local authorities which have increasingly embraced cabinet-style government, with a cabinet member responsible for education, sometimes combined with another remit. Elected local-authority government is supported by a director of education and support staff. Each authority receives a block grant from the Assembly. In 2001 it was decided that National Assembly earmarking of councils' education budget within block grants would cease, to the disquiet of some in the education sector.

The relationship between the Assembly and local authorities in Wales is markedly closer than that in England. This has resulted, for example, in the administration of the contentious threshold payments for teachers being the responsibility of local authorities in Wales, rather than of a private company as in England. Nevertheless, possibilities for confrontation remain: for example, over policy for the closure of rural schools, substantially different in different authorities, but a matter of national as well as local concern.

Local-authority control over individual schools has been further reduced over the last decade, although there are local-authority representatives on all boards of governors. Although local authorities continue to be the legal employers of teachers, individual governing bodies exercise the crucial right of appointing and, if necessary, disciplining teachers, including head teachers. From 2000, teachers in Wales have their own General Teaching Council which endows them with a degree of professional independence and some control over members – the kind of professionalism which has long been taken for granted in the medical and legal spheres. From June 2001 the General Teaching Council for Wales has been empowered to register teachers and discipline those guilty of unacceptable professional conduct or serious professional incompetence, as well as any convicted of a criminal offence that raises questions about their suitability for the profession.

The evolution in Wales of a system created for England and Wales, but increasingly developing features unique to Wales, has implications far beyond the Welsh border. Not the least will be the comparisons which may be drawn between the effectiveness of policies in the two countries. In terms of nursery-school places, it has been a case of England catching up with Wales, with free places offered to all four-year-olds in 1998 when Wales had already virtually achieved this target. In England the target is now free places for all three-year-olds by 2004, from a baseline far behind that of Wales in 1997. Infant-school class sizes, with very few exceptions, have been cut to thirty or under in both countries, though the situation is less satisfactory in junior schools. Although the targets vary in Wales, the emphasis on improving test scores at key stage 2 will continue, at least for the moment. Wales shares in this element of target setting for primary schools, which the government claims has helped to raise core-subject standards. The key stage 3 problem is as intractable in Wales as in England, among boys in particular, of whom fewer than 60 per cent reached level 5 in the core subjects in 2000. The government target is 70 to 80 per cent achieving this level by 2002.

The concomitant problems will have to be addressed – an examination culture which makes children in England and Wales the most regularly assessed in the western world. Much informed opinion in the profession is wary of the strait-jacket which this imposes on the curriculum and of the stresses on pupils. At least the pressures are fewer in Wales in that external testing no longer takes place at age seven, test results are not published for each individual primary school, and, from 2001, publication of secondary-school examination results has also stopped. If such differences in emphasis prove to have no effect on relative standards of attainment, then the league-table mentality underpinning the approach in England will have been shown to be unnecessary.

Teacher training has been reformed in Wales as in England, with its national curriculum enforced in 1998 varying hardly at all between the two countries. Nevertheless, significant differences have emerged. Courses in Welsh institutions have been approved by 'Estyn' with none of the controversy over failure generated in some English institutions. The highly contentious testing of trainees in maths and science, now being done by computer, and mandatory before the award of qualified-teacher status, has been confined to England. An illogical situation exists whereby students from Wales or Scotland who are not required to take the tests are nevertheless free to assume qualified status in English schools.

Similar patterns of dependence and independence are revealed across the board. From June 2001 the regulation of the teaching profession will be the responsibility of separate General Teaching Councils in England and Wales. Comprehensive-school patterns are set to diverge dramatically. In June 2001, there were 500 specialist comprehensive schools in England, the number trebling since 1997. They have been ruled out in Wales. We may be grateful to be spared the enormous expenditure of attention and emotion on the effective break-up of the comprehensive-school system in England if the Labour Party pursues its policy of making half of English state secondary schools into specialist schools. This appears neither practically nor ideologically acceptable in Wales. Education Minister Jane Davidson's response was that 'the focus of the National Assembly is that all local schools offer the widest opportunities for their children. We could not contemplate a situation where specialisms are concentrated too narrowly.'

Further divergence is likely in school external examinations. The Westminster government, like so many of its predecessors, has attempted some broadening of the Advanced Level base and some reconciliation between academic and vocational paths. In 2001, students took AS Level examinations for the first time, in up to five subjects. These form the first year of A-Level courses and, according to complex formulae, have currency at this level, so ending a long-established pattern. Vocational A Levels are now available (ostensibly with parity of esteem with academic A Levels), which have replaced advanced general national vocational qualifications (GNVQs). In England and Wales there is general agreement in the schools that the new system is causing undue pressure, both academic and bureaucratic, and proposals for reform are already emerging from teachers. It is particularly interesting that both the Scottish system of Highers and the proposed Welsh pilot of the baccalaureate are being referred to enviously in England. If the baccalaureate pilot is pursued with integrity in Wales it could provide a more coherent and constructive answer to sixteen-plus study. It certainly provides a striking opportunity for progressive divergence from the English system.

Divergence has less quantifiable manifestations. Wales benefits from its small size in that education professionals tend to know many in their own field, whether subject specialists, directors of education or the inspectorate. Interaction between these groups is therefore facilitated. This goes some way to explain why the inspectorate in Wales has developed a much more sympathetic tone in administering the new regime of testing. Since 1970, the inspectorate in Wales has, in practice, been independent both administratively and in its mode of operation. In 1992 this independence was cemented in the creation of the office of Her Majesty's Chief Inspector in Wales which, in 1999, evolved into Her Majesty's Inspectorate for Education and Training in Wales (Estyn). These government departments remain entirely separate from the Office for Standards in Education in England. Estyn enjoys a far higher reputation than Ofsted as a result of its more encouraging and sympathetic approach towards teachers and an absence of the abrasiveness associated with the regime of Chris Woodhead in the 1990s. Again, while the threshold system of teacher pay and appraisal applies in Wales as in England, its link with performance indicators has been viewed much more suspiciously by the Assembly.

Devolution may provide opportunities to tackle more intractable problems. While average and above-average pupils have benefited measurably from government initiatives since 1997, there is still unacceptable underachievement, associated, as it always has been, with economic underprivilege and low teacher expectation. In 1996 a quarter of Welsh adults of working age had no qualifications. Major dysfunctions within the assessment system remain. For example, the time-honoured problem of technical and vocational assessment and status is only marginally nearer a solution. Converting GNVQs into GCSEs from 2002 will not of itself solve the problem of status, because insisting on parity of status with academic subjects will make the courses less attractive for those, often disaffected, youngsters for whom the solution is being devised. The ambition that all eighteen-year-olds should have five GCSEs or equivalent seems difficult to attain, although it will doubtless be common to both countries. In 2000, 92 per cent of sixteen-year-olds passed one GCSE at grade A to G, while 84 per cent had five such GCSEs or their equivalent at GNVQ or national vocational qualification (NVQ) level.

Many would argue that it is now the post-school, post-eighteen section of the population whose education warrants the most attention. It is taken as axiomatic that a high level of technical and computer skills is essential to any improvement in the Welsh economy, the gross domestic product of which is considerably below that of England and the progress of which will have to be in competition with the rest of the United Kingdom, let alone other world economies. This is an extremely tall order. Nevertheless, the Assembly and Elwa can hardly be criticized for lack of initiatives – the Wales Management Council, a £500,000 skills development fund, individual-learning accounts, modern apprenticeships, Careers Wales, Future Skills, work-based learning for adults, credit frameworks, a modern skills diploma for adults, initiatives in Welsh-medium education – the list is close to endless. The Assembly even has its own e-Minister (at the time of writing, Andrew Davies, like the Education Minister, a trained teacher).

It will require careful monitoring and research to evaluate the success of such initiatives and, in the longer term, the impact they make on the lives of individuals and the economic health of the nation. Those who have devised this plethora of programmes will also need to counter criticism that the level of adult education may even have declined in recent decades, and to face the more pertinent problem, that the cornucopia of qualifications and certificates has taken the fun out of learning.

The recent history of education in Wales as in England, as we have seen, has been that of a degree of centralization inconceivable only thirty years ago, accompanied by a measure of political devolution which, at the time of the referendum of 1979, appeared impossible. These developments remind us that there is a lively debate as to where change at individual and local community level is best initiated. Expert opinion would indicate that, within reason, the nearer both policy formulation and implementation are to the immediate locality the more creative, lively and relevant they are likely to be. Logic and, increasingly, experience would seem to indicate that the existence of the Assembly, with its specific responsibility for three million people rather than sixty million, is proving that policies can be devised which address needs common to both England and Wales overlaid with those of particular relevance to Wales.

The implications have not always been welcome. The main bone of contention in individual schools in Wales is funding. Here the difference of approach between the Assembly government and the Department for Education has been more controversial. Policy in Wales is to channel increased Treasury funding for schools, along with the rest of the education grant, through the local education authorities rather than, as is the case in England, to allocate lump sums directly to schools according to size. For example in 2001, secondary schools in England each received a lump sum of £70,000. The money for Wales was allocated to the National Assembly, thence to the local education authorities, and the largest secondary schools received a sum of £25,000. This money, having the express purpose of improving facilities and encouraging curriculum development was used, so many head teachers claim, to stave off redundancies and maintain the status quo. The reaction among teachers, governing bodies and unions was not favourable. The Assembly and LEAs point out that funding per pupil is actually higher in Wales than in all but two regions of England. Governors and unions retort that, in the absence of a standard spending assessment and ring-fencing of money, as happens in England, local authorities can divert money to other services.

Local authorities certainly tend to keep more money in the central pot in Wales – in 1999/2000 only four of the Welsh authorities passed on 80 per cent of their education budget to schools – but claim that they alone can take the wider perspective necessary to deal with, for example, special-needs services. It is not the principle of divergence of policy from England which is the bone of contention but that the English system seems to be more effectively distributing money to schools. Nevertheless, it is an inevitable result of the Assembly's principle of allowing local authorities to administer their own funds. Arguably, education lobbies should be able to operate more effectively at this micro-level to secure their interests.

The decision to depart from policy in England over the disbursement of funds to schools was incorporated in a 'paving document', *The Learning Country*, published by the Minister for Education and Lifelong Learning (ELL) in September 2001. This was a landmark document for those who hoped that the Welsh Assembly would not just nibble at the edges of educational policy-making but would also conjure up a wider vision of an education system to serve the Welsh nation. The document amounted to a major strategic policy statement, the first on education from the Assembly government, equivalent to the English White Paper, *Schools Achieving Success*, published at the same time. It signalled a radical departure from the English vision. It started off with an acknowledgement of the scale of the problem which, over the years, has not been tackled successfully by 'England/ Wales' approaches, an educational problem underpinned by economic disadvantage. This in itself was a historic statement.

The decision to propose having no more tests for seven-year-olds in primary schools, along with the minister's statement that they had no purpose which could not be served equally well by internal assessment, breached that edifice of Standard Assessment Tests deemed so crucial in England to the educational health of that nation. Some of its other commitments, such as the provision of nursery education from the age of three for all who want it, cuts in junior class sizes to thirty or fewer by 2003, a new foundation stage for three- to seven-year-olds, with due attention given to learning through play, further concentration on the transition from primary to secondary education, and the eschewing of a literacy and numeracy strategy for eleven- to fourteen-year-olds, are equally laudable details of policy. The development of the Welsh bacca-laureate goes further, in that it signals a peculiarly Welsh policy in the crucial stage of 14–19 education currently baffling the policy-makers in England.

There is yet another level of ambition in the document, that of pro-viding Wales with an education system based on different social principles, which amounts to a statement about the nature of Welsh society. The minister's decisions to endorse without cavil the principle of the compre-hensive school, to refuse private involvement in the running of schools, to determine that neither specialist schools nor city academies have any place in the Welsh system, amount to an unprecedented government vision of Welsh education and society. It has been made possible by the better performance of Welsh comprehensive schools than their English counter-parts. It also amounts to a vindication, if such were needed, of the value of a National Assembly.

The role of education lobbies and pressure groups is more central in a devolved Wales. In 2001, the Education Minister for Wales listed among her priorities spending more money to improve run-down school build-ings and addressing the needs of small rural schools – a problem not only apparent in Wales, but certainly unique in its social and linguistic implica-tions. The village school provides a focus for community activities as well as formal education. Its continued existence may also play a crucial role in the preservation of the Welsh language in that community. With 14 per cent of schools in Wales having fewer than fifty pupils, and one-third fewer than 100 pupils, direction from the Welsh Assembly Government is essential because local-authority policies diverge substantially. For example, Pembrokeshire reviews the future of all schools with fewer than fifty-four pupils; Carmarthenshire has traditionally considered schools of under sixteen pupils to be at risk but, at the time of writing has, controversially, decided to close a number of village schools. Given the rural similarities between the two counties, and the fact that, in both, so many of the small schools are Welsh-speaking, this is obviously a matter on which it is crucial for the Assembly to adjudicate, even considering financial adjustments for schools which are more expensive to run. It is a matter on which local communities will need to take a stance.

The Welsh Assembly Government is committed to taking action on such contentious issues. Least problematic, indeed gratifyingly ambitious, is the National Council–Elwa's £1.5 billion expenditure over ten years to increase the numbers of working adults with at least one level-3 NVQ or its equivalent from 18 per cent to 60 per cent by 2010, and those with level 4 from 10 per cent to 30 per cent. While this development of the skills base is crucial for the economy as well as individual prospects, the most heart-warming target is that of boosting the level of functional literacy from 72 per cent to 90 per cent. If the target is met, many lives will be transformed.

Targets in the higher-education sector, by contrast, are interwoven with the most contentious planning issues. The Education and Lifelong Learning Committee's review into higher education, appeared early in 2002, to be followed in March 2002 by *Reaching Higher*, an Assembly government strategy for the higher-education sector in Wales. It is an attempt to programme a rationalization of the revolution in higher education in Wales. The committee and the minister will have been aware of turbulent times in the past. Almost against the odds, the University of Wales has been preserved as a federal university, despite regular pressures, particularly from its college in Cardiff, to split the university into its constituent parts. In 1960, Cardiff initiated another attempt to defederalize, generating acrimonious debate. It took until 1964 before a commission produced majority and minority reports, the former advocating four separate universities, only for the Court of the University of Wales to reject this.

Already the massive growth in student numbers was under way, changing the physical configuration of each of the colleges. That growth accelerated. We have seen that, in 1967, the Welsh College of Advanced Technology, then in 1971, St David's College, Lampeter, became con-stituent institutions. In 1977 Llandaff College of Education (Home Economics) was taken over by Cardiff University College. With expansion came higher proportions of students from England and pressures within the University of Wales to extend Welsh-language teaching. A Welsh-medium university college was rejected in the early 1970s, but worries about the frenetic expansion of student numbers and their effect on both the language and the federal structure of the university continued.

If expansion based on affluence brought some strains, the end of affluence, from 1974, turned out to be instrumental in revolutionizing the University of Wales. Its historian, Prys Morgan, has divided the period into three. For the remainder of the 1970s the colleges cut back on plans for expansion. During the 1980s there was a fight for survival. At the instigation of the University Grants Committee, the University College in Cardiff and the University of Wales Institute of Science and Technology were already locked in talks about a merger which both institutions opposed. The Jarratt Report of 1985 set the universities on the road to far greater institutional independence, paralleling businesses, but the financial chaos in University College, Cardiff eventually resulted in the University Grants Committee's intervening in unprecedented fashion. With bankruptcy imminent, Cardiff had to accept take-over by UWIST in 1988 as the University of Wales College of Cardiff. Cardiff's recklessness not only served to undermine dramatically the authority of the University of Wales as an institution, making radical reform both more inevitable and more easily accepted, but also was instrumental in the government replacing the University Grants Committee with the Universities Funding Council and its far tighter financial controls. At least it was to have a Welsh Committee.

There had already been one attempt at a radical reorganization of teacher training in Wales in 1977. The closure of Swansea College of Education was announced, only to be rescinded. The Polytechnic of Wales, now incorporating Barry College of Education, saw its teacher-training function cease. In 1987, the Secretary of State for Wales restructured teacher training once more, without any reference to the University of Wales or its Faculty of Education. The reforms were dramatic. Training of primary and secondary teachers at University College, Cardiff was transferred to Swansea. The university education department in Bangor was cut back and Aberystwyth numbers expanded.

Between 1988 and 1993, with Thatcher government cutbacks, stress on accountability and the measurement of performance, came major efforts to restructure the university. The Daniel Report attempted to rationalize teaching and research on an all-Wales basis. By the time of its publication in 1989 the University of Wales had been transformed. In addition to the Cardiff merger, St David's, Lampeter and the School of Medicine had, since 1988, become full member colleges. Already, there had been reorganization within the colleges – for example music was to be taught only in Cardiff and Bangor – causing upheaval and heartache. Now, the Daniel Committee proposed a joint development board, and a deputy chancellor with unprecedented central powers.

The university accepted the proposals, and the day of enhanced federal powers with strong central steer seemed to have arrived. From the beginning, however, this was accepted with ill grace by the principals of

Cardiff and Swansea. As the upheavals in higher education continued in the 1990s the new system came under immediate and sustained attack from the anti-federalists. Nevertheless, the warning of the deputy pro-chancellor in 1992 was prescient. If the institutions clamouring for university status all developed separately this would prove disastrous. Sufficient have done so to make the present talk of radical change inevitable. The anti-federalists, in the event, had blinkered vision.

The disappearance of the binary line in 1992 sought to bring full-blooded market forces to the further- and higher-education section of the system, with further-education colleges and some higher-education colleges becoming private companies. As with schools under the 1988 Education Act, what actually transpired was uneasy compromise between market principles and nationalization of the sector by means of account-ability to the Funding Council and quality-control mechanisms. In the face of competition it is accepted that there has been a deterioration in staff conditions and morale in Wales as in England. Nevertheless, new, uniquely Welsh, bodies like Fforwm, the Association of College Principals in Wales, came into existence as a result, as did a rationalized curriculum by means of a credit and transfer scheme between the colleges.

In the higher-education sector came unprecedented expansion in Wales. *Ad hoc* reorganization saw the University of Wales being augmented by the University of Wales Institute Cardiff and the University College of Newport. The Further and Higher Education Act of 1992 brought into being separate funding councils for further and higher education in Wales. The Act made it inevitable that there would be yet another reappraisal of the relevant Welsh institutions, and a committee under the chairmanship of Sir Melvyn Rosser was required to report in 1993. It did so in a completely changed context. The University of Glamorgan had emerged in 1992 and the Higher Education Funding Council for Wales materialized in 1993, disbursing at that time £248 million annually to the University of Wales. Its potential in directing the fortunes of higher education was considerably enhanced by the creation of the National Assembly in 1999, and the Assembly is advocating, in 2002, providing the council with planning powers. The Rosser Report was in tune with the times and with the realities of academic politics. The centralizing experiment was over. The report advocated restricting the federal university to the role of granting degrees, safeguarding standards and being responsible for university institutions like Gregynog (the University of Wales conference centre) and the University of Wales Press. Symbolically, the constituent institutions of the university were renamed in 1993, taking on their present designations in which, nevertheless, the University of Wales remains the dominant part.

Reaching Higher presages yet more modification, this time with the Higher Education Funding Council for Wales (HEFCW) using its financial muscle (though with its powers circumscribed by university charters). It seems to be taken as axiomatic (the mantra being that 'the status quo is not an option') that the present thirteen higher-education institutions will have to be significantly reduced in number by process of 'clustering' and collaboration. Given the existing mix, constituent institutions of the University of Wales, the University of Glamorgan and free-standing colleges (not to mention the Open University, Coleg Harlech and theological colleges), funding based on student numbers and research, the weight of history associated with the University of Wales and traditional notions of university independence reinforced by the market model of recent years, this is set to be the most fraught of all the issues on which the Assembly may have to arbitrate. Its proposed financial incentives will help, but precedents indicate that the debate may well generate more heat than light. It may also be very difficult to prod the more well-funded institutions into action, particularly generous action. Market forces, including the removal of capping student numbers, sit uneasily with the give-and-take of collaboration. Already knives are drawn over the fate of the federal university which, despite Assembly government neutrality, is in some danger of disintegration. Sir David Williams's inquiry into the University of Wales has resulted in 2002 in a recommendation to offer constituent membership of the university to all higher-education institutions in Wales and may head off this fate. It remains the case that the only relatively uncomplicated major rationalization will be the merger of the University of Wales Cardiff with the University's Medical School.

An underlying problem is that higher education in Wales is under-funded compared with the rest of the UK. Revenue per student (the unit of resource) has just (2001–2) virtually caught up with that for England but is 22 per cent below that for Scotland. Recent experience has been of constant crisis management, especially in those institutions where there have been cuts in real terms. The National Assembly aims to increase research income dramatically, but given the existing strengths and weaknesses of individual departments within the traditional university institutions, and the inevitable use of the research assessment exercise of 2001 to determine the distribution of the majority of research income, it is not clear how this is to be achieved. One initiative that may herald future patterns is prompting the linking of research far more closely to business activities through a knowledge-exploitation fund which has, as one of its aims, the provision of higher-education-research help for small businesses.

Discussions proceed in tandem with experiments with courses, such as the new foundation degree, providing an alternative route to graduation from the traditional three-year honours course. The significance of life-long learning is not being taken lightly. There have been radical initiatives since the 1980s, with far more emphasis on access for mature students, whereas in the 1970s the major route towards a degree qualification for these students was through the Open University in Wales, with its sophisticated support structure of part-time tutors and counsellors. Originally this proved an ideal avenue for certificated teachers to top up their qualifications to degree level, though the OU provided a second chance across a whole spectrum of ages and occupations. Graduates in their eighties were by no means unheard of.

In the 1980s the traditional university outreach through extra-mural classes was much modified by two developments. First, initiatives across Wales allowed students to pursue part-time degrees. Second, the trend towards modular structures of degrees and postgraduate courses, together with a proliferation of qualifications, allowed for a much less traditional clientele and increasing opportunities for lifelong learning. A radical initiative was that of the Department for Adult Continuing Education in Swansea to establish the Community University of the Valleys at Banwen, which attracted sections of the community normally excluded from traditional residential university routes. Such initiatives brought substantial European funding and provided a precedent for lifelong-learning projects under the Objective One programme to run in Wales from 2001 to 2006. The Community University of North Wales provides a remarkable example of cooperation between ten further- and higher-education establishments. In a context in which the driving force for educational development is competition, these are attempts to break down the age, sex and qualifications barriers and to surmount the communications problems of sparsely populated rural areas by developing the potential of internet-based learning.

This potential is just beginning to be imaginatively exploited. Starting in October 2001, funded by the European Union, Enterprise College, Wales, the University of Glamorgan, seven colleges and the BBC are combining to provide modular courses to degree level via the internet and a teaching and support structure involving telephone and face-to-face tuition. While each module is self-standing, six modules amount to a BA Enterprise degree. In essence, this is taking the kind of techniques developed by the Open University one stage further, with the object of encouraging entrepreneurship in Wales.

The extension of opportunity in higher education has exacted its price from students. Means-tested maintenance grants were replaced by a student loan scheme under a Conservative government, then a Labour government in the late 1990s made students pay means-tested tuition fees (tuition had been free since 1944). The reason for such fundamental changes in policy was that the state decided that it could not afford traditional levels of subsidy for higher education against a background of dramatically rising student numbers. In the late 1950s fewer than a 4 per cent elite of the school-leaving age group went on to higher education; the figure is now over 35 per cent, with the government aiming towards 50 per cent. The implications in Wales were that numbers of undergraduates starting a degree course in Wales increased from 87,000 in 1995 to 102,000 in 1998, with the greatest impact on the 18–20 age group.

It is of particular concern to the National Assembly, as well as to the British government, that the expansion in student numbers should encompass as many as possible of those from social groups who have traditionally been under-represented in higher education. In this the Welsh institutions have a good record. Six per cent more Welsh undergraduates come from state schools compared with England. Thirteen per cent more students in Wales are from non-professional backgrounds – although the total figure is still only 26 per cent. This achievement is coupled with a relatively low drop-out rate compared with England. All Welsh institutions of higher education cultivate contacts with schools; some, like the University of Glamorgan, do so by a sophisticated mechanism of student tutors who visit schools regularly on a 'compact' basis.

In this context the issue of student loans and fees has been particularly fraught. The imposition of those charges deemed necessary by government in Westminster to finance the increase in student numbers might appear itself to act as a deterrent to expansion. The latest government proposals (2003) envisage top-up fees and potential individual student debts of up to £21,000. Whether Wales will be bound by these policies is not clear at present. There has been particular concern in Wales that those students from the most disadvantaged backgrounds would experience the greatest level of deterrence.

The Assembly government has unilaterally investigated the issue through the Rees Committee, which reported in 2001. Teresa Rees's report addressed one of the most contentious of Labour government policies because there was no reference to tuition fees in the 1997 election manifesto. Nevertheless, charges for tuition were introduced. The Scottish Parliament has since dispensed with them but, along with student loans for maintenance, they have been administered in Wales in the same way as in England. The report was radical indeed, although, as a result, the Welsh Assembly's capacity to implement all its provisions is limited. The report called for statutory maintenance allowances for students in higher and further education, subject to means-testing and need assessment. It recommended that tuition fees in higher education be abolished, to be replaced by a graduate endowment contribution dependent on the individual graduate's income in employment. It also contained crucial recommendations for modifying the present system so that, for example, student loans should not become payable until employment income has reached £17,000 per annum. If this did not happen within fifteen years, the debt should be written off. As an interim measure, within the purview of the National Assembly, the report recommended an immediate substantial increase in student support through access courses and help for mature students. The Assembly government responded quickly and uni-laterally by instituting its £44 million per annum (2002–3) learning grant allowing students up to £1,500 a year, dependent on a means test. As with the unique Scottish arrangements, there is an element of complication in this enlightened measure, in principle if not in practice, in that more than half the students who study in Wales are from outside the country, while more than half the higher-education students living in Wales go to a university outside Wales. Not only does this have a bearing on any separate initiatives on student funding but it also raises fundamental questions about the Welshness of higher education.

So it is that the office of Minister for Education and Lifelong Learning in the National Assembly for Wales government is proving no sinecure. Both office and title provide some measure of the extent to which the democratic deficit has been remedied at the beginning of the new millennium. Current potential for independent action in Wales over the whole spectrum of education provision would have been inconceivable to Forster or Morant or Butler. Neither O. M. Edwards nor successive secretaries of state for Wales since the 1960s enjoyed the freedom of manoeuvre in policy-making and implementation now vested in the Assembly government. The identity of Wales has, over the centuries, been associated with, for example, its language and religion, even sport. Not since the thirteenth century has the distinctiveness of Wales stemmed from its institutions of government and associated independence of action on behalf of its people. Now, once again, in the most different of contexts, the ability of the people of Wales to control their own destiny, however circumscribed, is a touchstone of nationhood.

Education, particularly formal education, moulds a nation to a greater extent than this. We have described the dramatic increases in investment in schooling, further and higher education since the state took over responsibility for the education of its citizens. Gradually, the years of compulsory schooling and the opportunity for education beyond these years have been extended for all sections of society. Most dramatic, perhaps, of developments since the Second World War has been the expansion of higher-education opportunities beyond 30 per cent, with an ambition to see 50 per cent of the age range involved. We have also seen that the numbers of young people with no, or few, formal qualifications remain stubbornly high, whatever the ambitions of politicians. Functional illiteracy is still a blight on the lives of the individuals affected, as well as having a wider social and economic cost.

These issues are matters of concern for the Welsh Assembly government, as they are for all governments. Our chapters dealing with the recent past chart progress. But it is underlaid by constants. Level of achievement in formal education remains the most significant determinant of an individual's employment prospects, income and lifestyle. The most important determinant of that level of achievement remains, overall, wealth and social class, whether in America, the European mainland or the countries of the United Kingdom. The democratic deficit in Wales has, to an extent, been remedied, not least in its ability to determine its educational priorities. We have seen that the history of Welsh education is punctuated with examples of attempts to compensate for its people's social and economic deficit. Such attempts have been more serious in Wales than in England and have brought inestimable benefits to the lives of countless individuals and Welsh society as a whole. But they stem, at least in part, from relative poverty. The Welsh Assembly government has, by its recent actions, shown the will to see practical pursuit of the principle of a more egalitarian, all-embracing system of education continue. Its task is enormous because of the limitations of formal education in changing the infrastructure of society. Nevertheless, education policy, more than any other, is a crucial determinant, with the highest potential to bring about a society in which equality of opportunity, meshing with national prosperity, becomes a reality.

The implications for education and for Wales are immeasurable.

Bibliographical Note

Even a highly selective bibliography for a book of this chronological span would occupy a disproportionate amount of space. The process of accumulating book and article references in these days of on-line library catalogues is, in any case, relatively straightforward. This note will therefore be confined to a few examples of the kinds of material which are available and which the authors have consulted.

In recent decades, sufficient histories of Wales have been published to provide a variety of interpretative frameworks. So, for example, Gwyn A. Williams's *When was Wales?* (Penguin, 1985) emphasizes the fractures in Welsh history, while John Davies's *A History of Wales* (Allen Lane, 1993) stresses the continuities. The standard general history of Wales, published by Oxford and Wales University Presses, is a multi-volume series covering the period from 1066 to 1980, though the volume on the nineteenth century has not yet appeared. The series contributors, R. R. Davies (*Conquest, Coexistence and Change: Wales 1063–1415*, 1987), Glanmor Williams (*Recovery, Reorientation and Reformation: Wales c.1415–1642*, 1987), Geraint H. Jenkins (*The Foundations of Modern Wales, 1642–1780*, 1987) and Kenneth O. Morgan (*Rebirth of a Nation: Wales 1880–1980*, 1981), are among the most distinguished, and their material on education authoritative. Each volume has a comprehensive bibliography.

The most accessible general printed documentary material is contained in the seven-volume *Welsh History and its Sources* series, edited by Trevor Herbert and Gareth Elwyn Jones, published by the University of Wales Press between 1988 and 1995 and ranging from the reign of Edward I to post-Second-World-War Wales, but attention to education is normally more tangential than specific.

It seems to have been accepted until relatively recently that general histories of education applied to England and Wales, or even to Great Britain. Curtis's *History of Education in Great Britain* (University Tutorial Press), having been published first in 1948, went to a seventh edition in 1967 and is an excellent example of a chronological, now old-fashioned, common approach which paid due attention to separate developments in Scotland but distinguished not at all between England and Wales. Some later authors have been more cautious. The newer approach to general educational texts is reflected early by J. Lawson and H. Silver in *A Social History of Education in England* (Methuen, 1973), intentionally, rather than inadvertently, restricting its geographical scope. On a more limited time scale, one of the most recent short surveys, by W. B. Stephens, *Education in Britain, 1750–1914* (Macmillan, 1998), reverts to a traditional title. However, the influence of new concepts of British history is in evidence here in that there is some attempt to note major developments in Wales and provide comparative statistics. No respectable account of recent trends would now omit Wales – for example, Liam Gearon's *Education in the United Kingdom* (David Fulton, 2002) puts Wales on a par with the other countries by means of a separate chapter. Other approaches, for example, R. A. Lowe's *Schooling and Social Change 1964–1990* (Routledge, 1997) provide valuable background material for any study of education in Wales because primary educational legislation was common to both countries in that period.

This fact, and an outdated view of the nation's history, help explain why general histories of Welsh education are very few and far between, while the history of Scottish education, for example, has prospered. The medieval period has had little coverage, despite Evan John Jones's taking *Education in Wales during the Middle Ages* as the subject of his published inaugural lecture in Swansea in 1947, after having produced a *History of Education in Wales* (Hughes and Son) in 1931 which did not go beyond the tenth century and was intended to be only the first volume of a lengthier history. There is no published general history of Welsh education in the early modern period, though L. S. Knight's short *Welsh Independent Grammar Schools to 1600* (Welsh Outlook Press), published as long ago as 1926, deals specifically with that important topic. The most significant recent work on schooling in this period has been Malcolm Seaborne's excellent *Schools in Wales 1500–1900* (Gee and Son, 1992). Among much else, his is the crucial source for school architecture in Wales. His approach can be supplemented by the occasional individual study, the best example being Gerallt Nash's *Victorian School-days in Wales* (University of Wales Press, 1991).

Most remarkable, the era of state education has not produced a general history. Jac L. Williams and G. R. Hughes projected a series of essays, *History of Education in Wales* (Christopher Davies), providing blanket coverage from post-Roman times but it was cut short with the publication of volume 1 (in 1978) which went up to the 1840s. Some of the contributions to it, such as that by Glanmor Williams on the medieval period, remain definitive. Books of research essays have occasionally appeared, the most recent being *Education Policy-making in Wales: Explorations in Devolved Governance*, edited by Richard Daugherty, Robert Phillips and Gareth Rees (University of Wales Press, 2000).

High-quality monographs are more in evidence. Here, the Board of Celtic Studies has made an immense contribution through its Studies in Welsh History series, three of which, by Richard Lewis, *Leaders and Teachers: Adult Education and the Challenge of Labour in South Wales, 1906–1940* (1993), W. P. Griffith, *Learning, Law and Religion: Higher Education and Welsh Society 1540–1640* (1996) and Robert Smith, *Schools, Politics and Society: Elementary Education in Wales 1870–1902* (1999), all published by the University of Wales Press, have taken education as their theme. That Press has also published monographs for the University of Wales Faculty of Education, important examples being Gerwyn Lewis, *The University and the Colleges of Education in Wales, 1925–1978* (1980), Wynford Davies, *The Curriculum and Organization of the County Inter-mediate Schools, 1880–1926* (1989) and Gareth Elwyn Jones, *Controls and Conflicts in Welsh Secondary Education, 1889–1944* (1982). A first-class monograph by W. Gareth Evans, *Education and Female Emancipation: The Welsh Experience, 1847–1914* (University of Wales Press, 1990) has begun to plug the gender gap and can be supplemented by more general recent work on children by, for example, Sandra Betts (ed.), *Our Daughters' Land: Past and Present* (University of Wales Press, 1996) and Deirdre Beddoe's *Out of the Shadows: A History of Women in Twentieth-Century Wales* (University of Wales Press, 2000). Work on another major gap in our knowledge, the education of ethnic-minority children in Wales, is sparse.

Recently published biographies of educationalists have been rare, even of educationists of the stature of O. M. Edwards, although Hazel Davies's relatively recent *O. M. Edwards* (University of Wales Press, 1988) has partially filled this gap and she has also edited his personal correspond-ence. Edwards, along with Griffith Jones, Thomas Charles and Hugh Owen, was also the subject of an essay in a Swansea Faculty of Education publication, *Pioneers of Welsh Education*, (n.d., *c*.1970). Griffith Jones has been the most popular subject, at least five biographies having been devoted to him. An excellent Welsh-language example is Geraint H. Jenkins, *Hen Filwr dros Grist: Griffith Jones Llanddowror* (Gwasg Gomer, 1983). Of higher-education scholars Viriamu Jones has probably com-manded most attention. One of the most fascinating recent approaches to biography is W. E. Marsden's *An Anglo-Welsh Teaching Dynasty: The Adams Family from the 1840s to the 1930s* (Woburn Press, 1997). Auto-biographies contain much incidental information relating to school and university days, though almost invariably they concern the successful and, of course, the literate. A fine example, and the most recent, is *Glanmor Williams: A Life* (University of Wales Press, 2002). Published reminiscences, even diaries, kept by individuals from the working class are few indeed, though oral history has helped to fill the twentieth-century void.

There is a whole range of publications on individual institutions, varying in quality from high scholarship to collections of schooldays and college days recalled. They all contribute to our understanding. The older colleges of the University of Wales all have their historians, and the university itself celebrated its centenary with the publication of excellent volumes by J. Gwynn Williams, *The University of Wales 1893–1939* (University of Wales Press, 1997) and Prys Morgan, *The University of Wales 1939–1993* (University of Wales Press, 1997). Most other colleges, including Coleg Harlech and the theological colleges, also have their historians, the most recent example being the *History of Trinity College Carmarthen 1848–1998* by Russell Grigg (University of Wales Press, 1998). School histories abound, the lengthiest being Wilfred Harrison's *Greenhill School Tenby, 1896–1964* (University of Wales Press, 1979), and probably the most recent, R. Brinley Jones (ed.), *Floreat Landubriense: Celebrating a Century and a Half of Education at Llandovery College* (Llandovery College Trustees, 1998). More generally, the Welsh nursery school movement has its historian in Catrin Stevens, *Hanes Mudiad Ysgolion Meithrin, 1971–1996* (Gwasg Gomer, 1996), while Gwennant Davies published *The Story of the Urdd (the Welsh League of Youth), 1922–1972* (Urdd Gobaith Cymru, 1993). A major gap has recently been filled with the publication of a history of the Welsh-language-schools movement, *Gorau Arf: Hanes Sefydlu Ysgolion Cymraeg 1939–2000*, edited by Iolo Wyn Williams (Y Lolfa, 2002).

All such material is grist to the mill of writers of general histories and monographs, which will have been based also on learned articles, official papers, higher-degree theses, newspapers and original documents. Articles with educational themes feature in such journals as the *Welsh History Review* (from R. W. Hays's 'Welsh students at Oxford and Cambridge Universities in the Middle Ages', 4 (1968–9), to H. G. Williams's pioneering work 'A study of the Kynnersley educational returns for Caernarfonshire', 13 (1986–7), the *National Library of Wales Journal*, the *Transactions of the Honourable Society of Cymmrodorion* and the *Bulletin of the Board of Celtic Studies*, as well as in all the county historical journals. There have been numerous articles on historical subjects in *The Welsh Journal of Education*, originally known as *Education for Development*, one special number (10, 1 (1985)) being devoted entirely to the history of education in Wales. Some articles explore completely new ground, such as Stephen Gorard's investigation of private education, 'Uncharted territory: the missing schools', 6, 2 (1997). Publishing on Welsh education is not confined to Welsh journals. *History of Education*, in particular, is a rich source of material, and one special number (19, 3 (1990)) was devoted to Wales.

Printed primary sources abound, particularly but by no means exclusively, in the form of official publications in the era of state education. Invaluable statistical data are provided in L. J. Williams, *Digest of Welsh Historical Statistics* (2 vols., University of Wales Press, 1985). Instances of data from the early modern period, for example, are the invaluable *Alumni Oxonienses*, ed. J Foster (Oxford, 1891–2) and *Alumni Cantabrigiensis*, ed. J. and J. A. Venn (Cambridge, 1922), containing information on students attending those universities. For the eighteenth century, Griffith Jones's *Welch Piety* records all aspects of the work of the circulating schools, with *Selections* edited by W. Moses Williams (University of Wales Press, 1938), while Mary Clement provided 'A calendar of Welsh letters to the SPCK 1745–1783' in *The National Library of Wales Journal*, 10 (1957).

With increasing state intervention, printed records proliferate, with British Parliamentary Papers a crucial source. The report which has reverberated most in Welsh history is the Report of the Commissioners of Inquiry into the State of Education in Wales, published in 1847. State papers also include annual reports and statistics of central government, from the Board of Education (with its Welsh Department from 1907) to the present Welsh Assembly and the Department for Education and Skills. Policy documents of crucial importance in Welsh education have now begun to emerge from the Welsh Assembly government, including, recently, *The Learning Country* (2001) and *Reaching Higher* (2002).

Particularly from the 1960s to the 1980s higher-degree theses on the history of education proliferated. Master's degree dissertations tend to concentrate on secondary or primary education in a small area, or even on individual schools. While all merit consultation some are of the highest calibre – like E. J. Davies's 'The origin and development of secondary education in the Rhondda Valleys (1878–1923)' (MA Wales, 1965). Doctoral theses range more widely and are sometimes indispensable, like J. R. Webster's 'The place of secondary education in Welsh society 1800–1918' (Ph.D. Wales, 1959). Some, such as Anita Jordan's 'History and development of the education of the delinquent, mentally and physically handicapped and pauper children in Wales from 1833 to 1933 (Ph.D. Wales, 1977), or Peter Harries's 'Colleges for miners: a history of the provision of technical education to the south Wales mining industry, 1882–1939' (Ph.D. Wales, 2000) map uncharted territory. Others help fill the biographical gap – an excellent example being that of B. L. Davies which led to a short published biography, *Hugh Owen, 1804–1881* (University of Wales Press, 1977).

It is impossible to list all the types of documentary sources available. Thousands of files of government papers relating to education are housed in the Public Record Office (PRO) in London, and those over thirty years old are available to researchers. For example, the Ed 35 category contains files on all the Welsh Intermediate/County schools, while the Ed 53 category has information on central-government dealings with all local authorities. More recent papers are kept in the Welsh Office/Welsh Assembly but a selection of them is destined, eventually, for the PRO. They cover everything from material on individual schools to negotiations relating to major legislation. At the other end of the spectrum, housed usually in county record offices, are school log-books, recording day-to-day events, particularly since the 1870s, in elementary schools. As well as providing insights into the routine life of the school and, equally significant, the events which were deemed important by the head teacher, in aggregate they yield important information about, for example, causes of truancy and the incidence of contagious diseases among the young.

Spanning a similar spectrum of events to documents, but with a different perspective and provenance, are newspaper accounts, again proliferating with state education. However, earlier newspapers inadvertently provide crucial material for historians with their advertisements for various kinds of schooling. The later journals and newspapers, ranging from *The Times Educational Supplement* to local papers, are invaluable sources of news and opinion, though the *Supplement* has paid Wales scant attention until relatively recently. For historians concerned with the history of their local school, local newspapers might provide accounts of such matters as school openings, speech days and examination successes, material which would otherwise be forgotten except, perhaps, in school magazines. Newspapers also tend to give full accounts of local controversies as, for example, with the attempts by the Swansea County Borough Council to implement a comprehensive system of secondary schools in the 1940s and early 1950s. The Swansea *Evening Post* covers this in detail.

Since the 1960s the richness of oral history has been appreciated in the history of education as in social history generally. The best example of a systematic and catalogued resource is that in the South Wales Miners' Library in the University of Wales, Swansea, which is particularly rich in material on adult education. Moreover, the library itself is a historical source of particular importance in that it has preserved the kind of reading material available in the miners' institutes in the twentieth century. The media have also contributed significantly, the best example being the BBC television series, *All our Lives*, available on cassette (1994–6), and *Second Chances: The History of Adult Education in Wales* (BBC tape, 1992).

Index